Ground Plan

"Small Egyptian Scraps"
1874.

Tih:
A Priest & Noble af Memphis.
IVᵗʰ Dynasty.

EGYPTOLOGISTS' NOTEBOOKS

TEMPLE INSCRIPTIONS 1931-2.
SERIAL NUMBERS & PROVENANCE.

EGYPT EXPLORATION SOCIETY'S CAMP

WITH BLOTTING
PAPER

PLEASE RETURN THIS TO HOUSE EVERY EVENING.

EGYPTOLOGISTS' NOTEBOOKS

The Golden Age of Nile Exploration in Words, Pictures, Plans, and Letters

CHRIS NAUNTON

Getty Publications
Los Angeles

→ 'TOPOGRAPHICAL SKETCH OF HELIOPOLIS
AND SURROUNDING LANDS', from the journal
of Joseph Hekekyan. He surrounded his map
with further drawings: the 'old Bridge of Heliopolis';
the 'Temenos of Heliopolis from the Western end of
the Avenue of Sphynxes, close to the fragments of the
colossal Sphynx ... taken on the 20th of October 1855';
and a detailed cross-section drawing of the alluvial
deposits in the area, and so this single sheet of paper
contains a staggering amount of useful information.

H OF HELIOPOLIS AND SURROUNDINGLANDS

sent and at the Epoch of the hidrymatisation of the Obelisk.

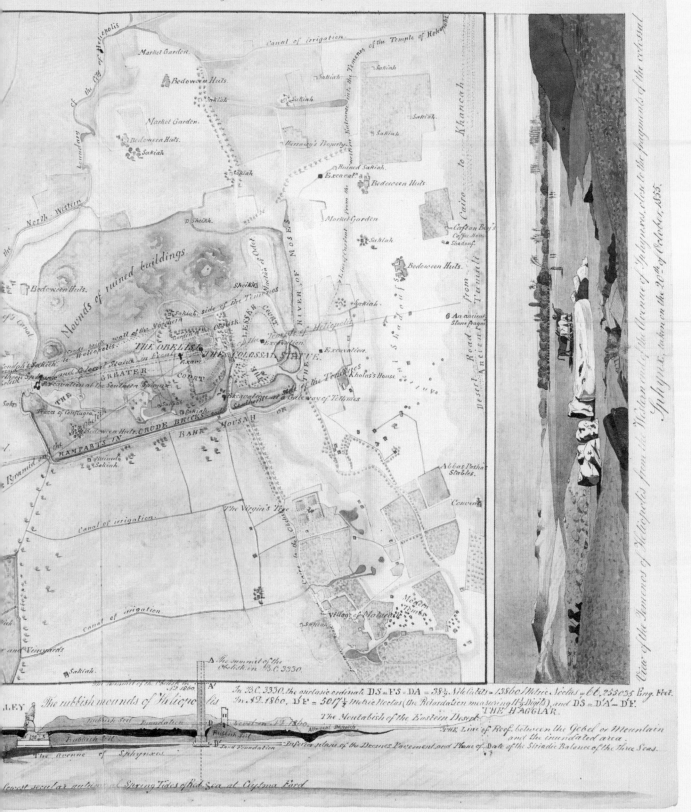

In B.C. 3330, the curtasic ordinate DS = VS - DA = 38½ Metabits = 13860 Metric Nectas = 66,255035 Eng. Feet.
In A.D. 1860, DF = 5017½ Metric Nectas (the Retardation measuring 11½ Digits), and DS = D'A' - DF.

CONTENTS

THESE ROUGH NOTES
INTRODUCTION

> '**These were the graves of the ancient Aegyptians .... Under every one ... descents are discovered like the narrow mouthes of wells ... some wel-nigh ten fathoms deepe; leading into long vaults ... hewne out of the rocke, with pillars of the same. Betweene every arch the corpses lie ranckt one by another, shrouded in a number of folds of linnen,... the brests ... being stained with Hieroglyphicall characters.**'

GEORGE SANDYS

Vast agricultural plains and canals criss-cross the Delta; rocky wadis rule the high desert. Silent boats drift gently down the Nile, while travellers make their way across pristine desert sands on foot or on a camel's back. Ubiquitous sunshine and baking heat give way only at the rapid and spectacular setting of the sun to the crisp cool and crystal clarity of the night skies. Hear the distant chanting of the holy man; the braying of a mule; the lapping of the water at the river's edge; the crunch of the loose limestone scree as the adventurer ascends into the mountains where the dead are buried.

This is Egypt, as it has been for thousands of years. And nowhere are its natural beauty and man-made wonders captured better than in the private scribblings and sketches of the travellers who first set out to explore it.

There was a time when Egypt was so little known to the West that ancient Greek and Roman accounts were the best available guides to what the modern visitor was likely to encounter. Imagine landing on the shores of Alexandria, where Strabo promised 'most beautiful public precincts and also the royal palaces ... building upon building', only to find it shrunk to a fraction of its former glory, its fabled monuments lying in ruin, though still visible in every direction. A short journey through the canals and marshes of the Delta to the far side of the crumbling splendour of Cairo – a relative newcomer on the landscape, but nonetheless centuries old itself – would grant the thrill of glimpsing the pyramids for the first time. First spied from a distance, their massive presence and the immensity of the ancients' achievement in building them must have become ever more apparent with every step forward on the long approach to meet them. Think of the dawning realization: you are standing on the ground of the ancient capital city of Memphis, seat of the biblical kings of Egypt, or among the 'hundred gates' of Homer's city of Thebes. And yet the locals are entirely unmoved by the historic wonders lying all around them – indeed, they seem utterly bewildered by the strange foreigners' delight in these monuments, and still more so by their desire to capture them in notes and sketches.

This was the earliest travellers' experience of Egypt. All were entranced by the beauty and majesty of the country's natural landscape, and its harmonious relationship with the remains of tombs cut into the natural rock of hillsides and remote wadis. They saw ancient temples and cities gently consumed by drifting sand, as well as the buildings and trappings of modern occupants living in and around them, and were gripped by the urge to document the magnificent things they had discovered. Without recourse to photographic equipment they wrote descriptions, often lyrical and full of nostalgia for a lost world of which only traces remained, but above all, even obsessively, they drew and they painted, copying the strange symbols and architectural feats they encountered. As more and more intrepid adventurers began to make the journey up the Nile, each sought to improve on the records of those who had gone before, their surveys more comprehensive, ever more accurate. As the records began to accumulate, scholars were encouraged in their desire to understand this great but mysterious civilization, and in particular to read the inscrutable inscriptions they found on the walls of temples and tombs and on all manner of curious and beautiful objects (many of which had begun to travel home with

← The British archaeologist James Quibell taking notes while surrounded by wooden coffins during his excavations at Saqqara. Quibell trained with Flinders Petrie and was appointed Inspector of Antiquities at Saqqara in 1905.

de Droite . de 3 Milieu

1.72

76

76

94

94

94

Kom-Ombos

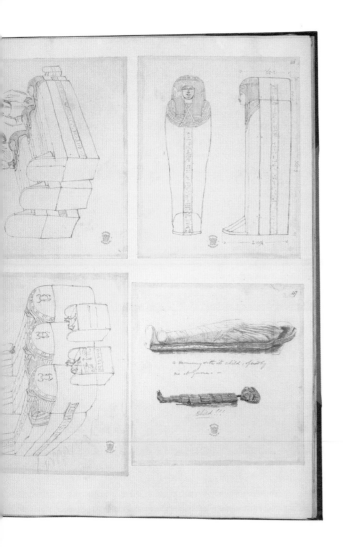

our adventurers, and could be seen in Europe's greatest museums). Thus, Egyptology was born.

The notes and sketches that the adventurers brought home with them recorded Egypt at a particular moment: to us, another Egypt of the past, albeit a more recent one. In their journals we discover Egypt at a time when it was changing rapidly. Again and again, in their observations we are confronted with an awareness that the ancient sites and monuments they sought to record for posterity were not just changing, but disappearing before their eyes. By faithfully recording the monuments in the condition in which they found them, collectively our travellers paint a picture of a landscape in rapid transition. Many of the monuments they saw have now disappeared – a near-intact temple of the New Kingdom pharaoh Amenhotep III on Elephantine island; the portico of a temple of the Ptolemaic king Philip Arrhidaeus at Hermopolis; the fine Corinthian gate of the Roman emperor Hadrian's city of Antinoopolis – along with dozens of tombs and thousands of inscriptions now defaced, unceremoniously removed for sale, or crumbled away under the influence of the elements. All now lost.

Beyond what they tell us about ancient Egypt, these notebooks also reveal to us the personalities of the early Egyptologists. How much more of a sense of the man or woman of the hour does one get when what they were seeing and doing is recorded in their own handwriting or drawings? Sketches made on notepaper pilfered from Cairo hotels or the back of cigarette packets and daybooks bundled up and packaged inside Fortnum & Mason's crates conjure up the journeys these adventurers chartered for themselves at a time when they were often travelling into the unknown.

So much knowledge has been gained thanks to the records of our adventurers, but something has also been lost – the *not* knowing. No longer can we truly feel the sense of mystery and wonder or the awe that must have been experienced by those for whom Egypt arrived only at the end of a long and arduous journey, and for whom staying to get to know it meant all manner of discomforts and adjustments – to dry and dusty landscapes, baking heat, unfamiliar languages both ancient and modern, unexpected customs, and novel ways of getting around, whether serenely floating, carried by the currents of a glassy Nile, enduring the lolloping ups and downs of a camel ride or worse, being shaken about on the back of a harried and hurrying donkey. *Yalla!* No longer can we experience such adventures, except vicariously, through these early Egyptologists. Their notebooks, their maps, plans, drawings, paintings, sketches, doodles, letters and telegrams, open for us a window onto the world of these early pioneers, allowing us to reach back to that golden age, when there was little to know and everything to discover, and to retrace the path they trod that led us to understand an Egypt of the far distant past.

↑ Sketches by Robert Hay of anthropoid wooden coffins and two shabti boxes from tombs in the Theban cemetery of Sheikh Abd el-Gurna. The fourth sketch shows a mummy case for the body of a child, 'opened by me at Gourna'.

← An unfinished sketch of two brightly painted column capitals of the Ptolemaic or Roman period by Nestor l'Hôte.

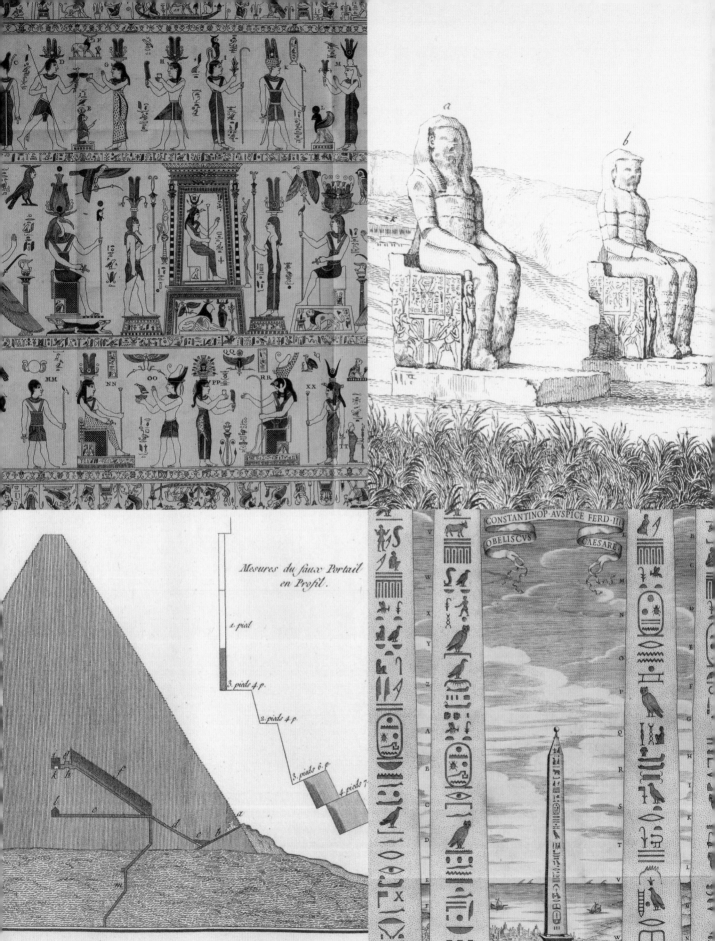

CONSTANTINOP·AVSPICE·FERD·IIII

OBELISCVS   CAESARE

Mesures du faux Portail en Profil.

1. pied

3. pieds 4. p.

2. pieds 4. p.

3. pieds 6. p.

4. pieds 7.

...his, avec les Canaux et Chambres Sépulcrales

...anal. c, Troisième Canal. f, Quatrième Canal, ou Corridor. g, Entresole. h, Cinq...
...épulcrale d'en bas. m, Puits.

OBELISCVM HVNC CONSTANTINOPOLITANVM
olim á Theodosio Augusto in Bizantino Circo Erectum.

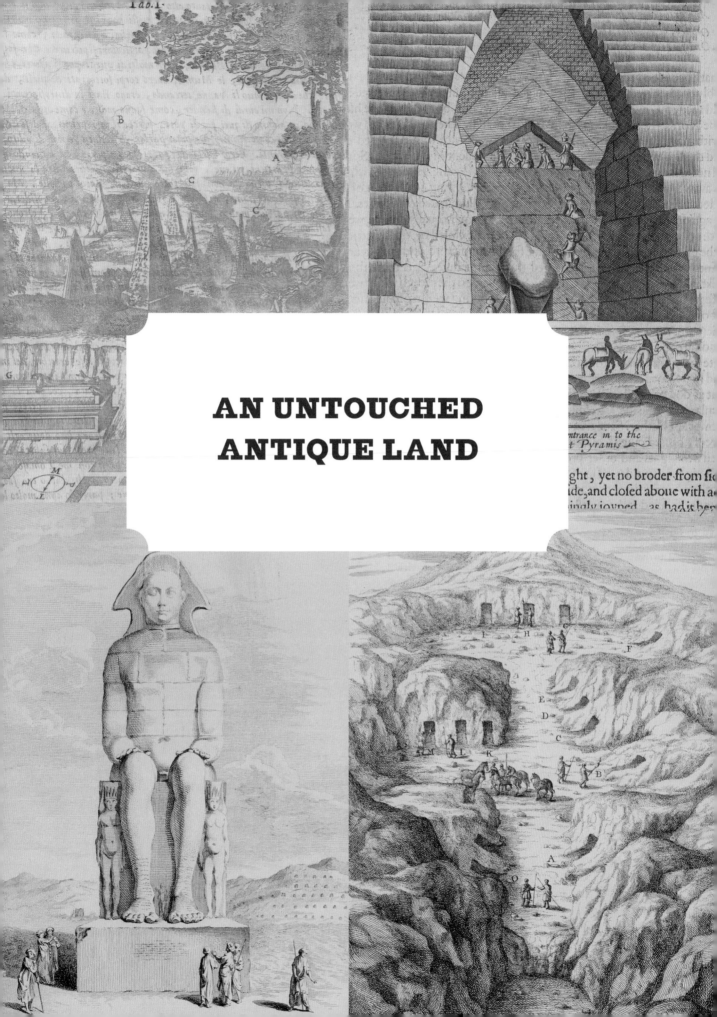

AN UNTOUCHED ANTIQUE LAND

'With delighted eyes we beheld that souveraigne of streames, and most excellent of countries. Southward and neare hand the Mummes afar off diverse huge Pyramides; each of which, were this away, might supply the repute of a wonder'

GEORGE SANDYS

Ancient Egypt seems so familiar to us now, its place as one of the earliest and greatest civilizations in human history beyond doubt. For thousands of years pharaonic dynasties and kingdoms rose and fell; at its peak, the Egyptian empire dominated peoples hundreds of miles to the north and south of its own borders. It left a powerful impression on the Hellenistic and Roman empires that would succeed it, and that laid the foundations of much of Western culture. And yet almost everything we know of the ancient people of Egypt has been learned relatively recently. Up until a little over two centuries ago, ancient Egypt was visible only through the lens of the better understood historic cultures.

The *Histories* of Herodotus, an account of the Greek's travels in the 5th century BCE, would perhaps have been foremost in the minds of the earliest Egyptologists. From him they learned that Min was the first king of Egypt and founded a city called Memphis, followed by three hundred and thirty rulers, eighteen of whom were Ethiopian, one a queen, and the others all Egyptian men. His immediate successor, Cheops (Khufu), brought utter misery to his people over his fifty-year reign, compelling them to construct a great pyramid, 240 metres (800 feet) tall. Gangs of a hundred thousand men laboured for twenty years on the enormous monument; no block was fewer than 9 metres (30 feet) in length, and each was polished and most exactly fitted. While many of Herodotus' claims must have seemed dubious to European scholars – and indeed many more than even they suspected have been proven wrong – there was at least a grain of truth in much that he wrote. His description of mummification, which intrigues children and adults alike to this day, remains one of our best sources of information on the process.

There was much in the classical works to inspire European scholars to travel to Egypt to see the ancient monuments for themselves. Diodorus Siculus, a Greek historian writing four centuries after Herodotus, wrote of the Giza pyramids that 'by the immensity of their structures and the skill shown in their execution they fill the beholder with wonder and astonishment.' Strabo, a Greek who travelled to Egypt and further south to Kush (Nubia) in the early years of Roman rule, shed light on the country's geography: 'Memphis itself, the royal residence of the Aegyptians, is also near Babylon; for the distance to it from the Delta is only three *schoeni*. It contains temples, one of which is that of Apis, who is the same as Osiris; it is here that the bull Apis is kept in a kind of sanctuary, being regarded, as I have said, as god.' Travellers such as George Sandys seem to have had the writings of the classicists constantly at hand; when, for example, he visited the Great Sphinx, he reflected: 'This but from the shoulders upwards surmounteth the ground, though Pliny give it a belly which I know not how to reconcile unto the truth, unlesse the land do cover the remainder.'

Egypt was also familiar to Europeans prior to the 19th century as the stage for many of the Bible's best-known stories: a prosperous but despotic land, where Abraham found brief respite from famine and Joseph thrived as pharaoh's right-hand man, and from which Moses eventually led the Israelites out of slavery. In the Book of Chronicles, the pharaoh Shishak brought a mighty army of Egyptian and Kushite charioteers against Rehoboam, king of Judah, son of Solomon and grandson of David. Joseph and Mary's 'flight into Egypt' with their newborn son, Jesus, whom they feared would be killed by King Herod, was a common theme in European art.

Yet travellers to Egypt at this time were few and far between. Leo Africanus (*c*. 1494–*c*. 1554), born al-Hasan ibn Muhammad al-Wazzan al-Fasi, visited Egypt as a diplomat; his *Descrittione dell'Africa* (Description of Africa) became a landmark resource upon which later geographers relied in tackling the Nile Valley. The accounts written by the first Europeans to make the journey, such as the diaries of George Sandys (pp. 22–27), are fascinating, revealing the awe inspired by the first glimpses of a new and unchartered territory – or at least one new to Westerners. Histories of Egyptology have generally been written from this perspective, ignoring the scholarship of the medieval Arabian world, whose writers had drawn on different sources and traditions and were more aware that aspects of the ancient culture of Egypt – certain religious practices and elements of the administration, language and scripts – had survived into more modern times. The writings of 9th- and 10th-century scholars such as Ayub Ibn Maslama, Ibn Abd Al-Hakam and Ibn Umail concerned the hieroglyphic script and attempts to decipher it, ancient Egyptian religion and burial practices, mummification, kingship and administration. Despite their scholarly value, their contribution to Egyptology remains underappreciated. They were simply unknown to the first Europeans who visited Egypt, schooled in Western traditions and gathering knowledge for the edification principally of other Westerners.

These travellers were also gathering artefacts to take home, and would further arouse the curiosity of those interested in this most foreign and ancient culture. Athanasius Kircher (pp. 16–21), one of the first to study ancient Egypt seriously, devoted much of his career to his (misguided) attempts to translate the hieroglyphic script without ever setting foot in Egypt itself. As interest in ancient Egypt grew, more and more adventurers were compelled to explore the country for themselves, leading eventually to the first of the great expeditions: that of Napoleon Bonaparte, which ushered in a new era of Egyptology.

Athanasius Kircher

1602–1680 German priest and antiquarian

Kircher was one of the first modern scholars to devote serious attention to the decipherment of hieroglyphs, identifying the link between the spoken Coptic and ancient Egyptian languages that would be crucial to Champollion's success almost two centuries later. But his belief that hieroglyphs were used only to record esoteric wisdoms related to Hermeticism was flawed and led him to many false conclusions.

→ The Great Pyramid of Giza, shown with two double-entrances at its base on the northern and western sides, inaccurately – the pyramid is entered some way up the northern face. The drawing also shows Memphis on the same bank as the pyramid; if Kircher realized that Giza and Memphis were both on the west bank, then Heliopolis, which appears on the opposite side of the river, lies to the south in the drawing, when in reality it is to the north.

Athanasius Kircher was born in Geisa, a small town in the Rhön Mountains of Germany, but his academic career would take him all across Europe in pursuit of historic material for his ground-breaking studies of ancient Egyptian hieroglyphs. He never travelled to Egypt – few did at this time. Instead he relied on material already in European collections, and in particular on the obelisks that had been brought to Rome in the classical era.

By the time he was sixteen he had mastered Latin, Greek and Hebrew at the Jesuit gymnasium in Fulda, and he continued his philosophical and theological studies in Paderborn, taking his first monastic vows in 1620. But his training was interrupted by the Thirty Years' War, during which life, for someone so openly showing his denominational colours as a Jesuit monk, was not easy. He was compelled to flee to Cologne in 1622, where he was able to complete his education in scholastic philosophy before taking up a succession of teaching posts further afield. It was probably not long after his ordination in 1628 in Gau um Speyer that Kircher saw Egyptian hieroglyphs for the first time, in Herwart von Hohenburg's *Thesaurus Hieroglyphicorum*, a veritable 'paper museum' containing illustrations of all the objects the author could find that were relevant to his interest in Egyptian antiquities. Kircher's own interests and expertise were extremely wide-ranging; he was a polymath in the truest sense, and has been called 'the last man who knew everything', but the ancient symbols evidently sparked a fascination in him, and he would return to them again and again over the course of his long and varied career.

It was not long before Kircher moved to France, there being little future for a promising young Jesuit scholar in Germany. There he met Pierre Gassendi, a leading French scholar who asked him to decipher his collection of Ethiopian, Coptic and Arabic manuscripts. This led Kircher to publish his *Prodromus Coptus sive Aegyptiacus* (Introduction to Coptic), in which he argued – correctly – that the Coptic language, the language of Egypt's Christian Church, bore a relation to the ancient language of Egypt that was written in the hieroglyphs. At the end of this book he published the contents of what he intended to be his next: a much more ambitious, three-volume work entitled *Oedipus Aegyptiacus*.

But it would be nearly twenty years before Kircher published the first volume of that book. In 1634 he accepted a position at the Roman College in Rome, as professor of mathematics, with a special commission to study the Egyptian hieroglyphs. Here he had to be careful in conducting his scientific research: only the previous year, Galileo had been summoned before the Inquisition and forced to desist from teaching his theory that the Sun, and not Earth, was at the centre of the universe. Nonetheless, from 1641 Kircher published an encyclopaedia on a scientific subject every three or four years, beginning with *Ars Magnesia* (on magnetism). By 1643 he had turned

AN UNTOUCHED ANTIQUE LAND

Pyramides Omnium Superstitum Antiquitatum
vetustissimæ integræ et adhuc incorruptæ à
priscis Ægypti Regibus Chami poste-
ris exstructæ.

Barbara Pyramidum sileat mira-
cula Memphis. *Martialis. l.1.*

Heliopolis

Nilus fluv.

Nilus fluv.

Memphis

Cryptæ Subterraneæ

Cryptæ Subterr.

↑ A page from Kircher's *Oedipus Aegyptiacus* and his reproduction of the obelisk of Constantinople, which stood then, as it does today, in the Hippodrome. The reproduction of the hieroglyphs is legible in parts, but the signs are clearly not copied accurately.

his attention back to the Egyptian language, using material collected by the traveller Pietro della Valle – including two vocabularies in the Bohairic dialect of Coptic, the liturgical language of the Coptic Orthodox Church – to compile his *Lingua Aegyptiaca Restituta* (The Egyptian Language Restored). This landmark study, which contained a vocabulary of Coptic, Latin and Arabic arranged in three columns, would be used by Jean-François Champollion (pp. 98–103) in his decipherment of hieroglyphs almost two centuries later.

Thus, in spite of the fact he had never visited Egypt, Kircher gained a reputation as an expert in its ancient script. Pope Innocent X commissioned him to restore the inscription of a fallen obelisk that he had re-erected in the Piazza Navona. This resulted in Kircher's first publication on hieroglyphs, *Obeliscus Pamphilius*, in 1650. The three volumes of *Oedipus Aegyptiacus* followed in the years 1652

↘ Sketch by Giovanni Battista Balatri in *Oedipus Aegyptiacus* of a 'mummy crypt' based on an earlier illustration sent to Kircher by Tito Livio Burattini. Balatri's version adds a vision of the cemetery above ground, shown as a field of distinctly tall pyramids clustered together very closely, looking nothing like either Dahshur, where the crypt is thought to have been found by Burattini, or any other pyramid field in Egypt.

to 1654. In these he set out his belief that hieroglyphs were purely symbolic – underestimating the script's complexity and completely failing to understand it. Kircher had been schooled in the tradition of the Florentine Platonists of the 15th century, who had promoted the idea of an 'earliest theology' that was the common inheritance of all peoples. One of the sources of this theology was the Egyptian *Corpus Hermeticum*, and Kircher believed that hieroglyphs represented the same spiritual ideas.

Nowadays Kircher is known to Egyptologists for being wrong; in fact, spectacularly so. And his approach – one part observation of the evidence, a dozen parts guesswork – seems indefensible by modern

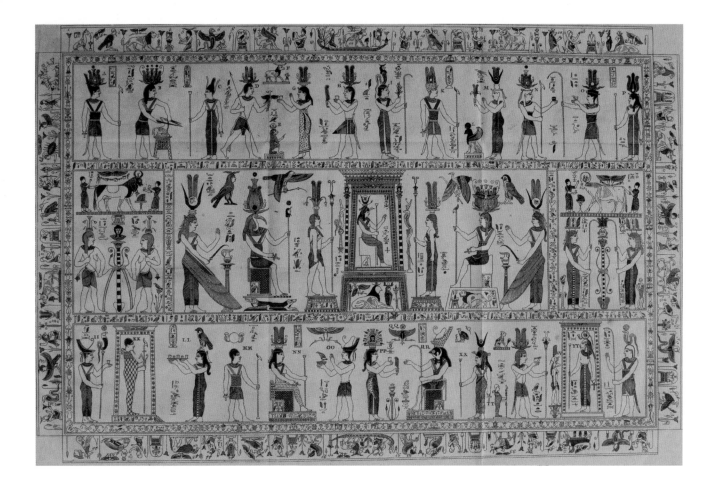

↑ The 'Bembine Table of Isis' or *Mensa Isiaca*. Kircher was fascinated by the elaborate designs and made extensive use of the object in trying to decipher the ancient Egyptian script and language, but the object was made in Rome and the inscriptions are meaningless.

standards of scholarship. Such concerns were even raised in 1633 by his French patron, Peiresc, who pointed out that his translations had been based in part on inaccurate copies of the signs on the Lateran Obelisk in Rome, which had been excavated and restored by Pope Sixtus V in 1588, and in part on the work of a Babylonian rabbi, Barachias, who had a similar desire to see Neoplatonic ideas in the ancient Egyptian script. Even so, Kircher was famed for his ability to decipher the glyphs. When Pope Alexander VII erected another broken obelisk found in Rome, this one near to the former temple of Isis, Kircher once again assisted, studying the hieroglyphs on the three visible sides of the obelisk while it still lay in the ground. He came to the conclusion, on the basis of his readings, that the fourth would also be inscribed. Unsurprising though this was, when the obelisk was lifted and Kircher's hypothesis proven correct, it convinced people that he was indeed able to read the signs.

In his analysis of the ancient glyphs Kircher made particular use of the *Mensa Isiaca* or 'Bembine Table', a bronze tablet reproduced several times in Von Hohenburg's *Thesaurus Hieroglyphicorum*. One detail in particular among the lavish decorations caught Kircher's attention: a scarab beetle with a human head accompanied by a winged sun disc. Kircher took this to be the key to understanding the entire hieroglyphic script, and set about dissecting its various elements as if he were an anatomist: the sun disc became the soul of the world, a series of concentric oval shapes at the beetle's shoulder the planetary orbits, the human head the sun, and the disc above the moon. A cross

AN UNTOUCHED ANTIQUE LAND

↑ Kircher's drawing and translation of the inscriptions of the south side of the obelisk erected by Pope Innocent X in the Piazza Navona. Although made of granite from Aswan and believed by Kircher to be Egyptian, it was in fact made in Rome in the Egyptian style. Its inscriptions include hymns to the emperors Domitian, Vespasian and Titus.

within the moon disc represented the four elements: earth, wind, fire and water. In this view, the script was reduced to a representation of ancient cosmology rather than – as we now know it to be – a true linguistic script.

One of the flaws in Kircher's study was that the inscriptions on the Bembine Table were Egyptianizing, but not authentically Egyptian: the object was made by Roman artists who had no understanding of the Egyptian script or symbols. The iconography of the figures, who are probably intended to be gods, is confused, and the hieroglyphs themselves convey nothing but gibberish. A square object grasped by the beetle's front legs contains four characters that Kircher read as Coptic signs spelling the word *philo* meaning 'love'. Kircher believed that this sign encapsulated the Egyptian universe and Neoplatonic thinking. It was actually not a true hieroglyph at all, but an ideogram composed of Egyptianizing motifs by uncomprehending Romans.

Kircher scoured Europe for Egyptian relics, in particular those with hieroglyphic inscriptions, to provide material for his books. He illustrated mummies, coffins, sarcophagi and canopic jars in intricate detail, as he had the obelisks of Rome. Although he did not grasp their meaning, the hieroglyphs are often copied accurately enough that they can be read. He also included descriptions and illustrations of sites and monuments in Egypt although, uniquely among our Egyptologists here, he was entirely dependent on the records made by others. One such sketch is remarkable for being the first to show the pyramid field of Dahshur; its instantly recognizable Red, Bent and Black pyramids are all shown, along with a series of openings in the ground, labelled 'the places by which one goes into the mummy caves'. One of these was presumably the 'mummy crypt' discovered in Egypt by Tito Livio Burattini in 1640, whose drawing, made from memory, was reproduced in Kircher's *Prodromo Apologetico alli studi Chircheriani* (Apologetic Forerunner to Kircherian Studies) in 1677. Though this vault has never since been definitively identified, it is thought to lie somewhere at Dahshur.

Kircher clearly would not have accepted that the strange and beautiful signs adorning Egyptian relics and monuments could be used to convey not only sacred religious concepts but also much more mundane ideas. His interests were in Neoplatonism and ancient wisdoms, and he wanted to read nothing else into the hieroglyphic script, little realizing that the Egyptians used it to write a language that captured all aspects of life, from the journey of the sun-god through the night to laundry lists and tax receipts. But in spite of the theological bias that coloured his interpretations, Kircher's writings established the link between Coptic and ancient Egyptian that would be key to the successful decipherment of the hieroglyphs, as well as igniting an interest in ancient Egypt among his readers, who were to carry forward his investigations, eventually with more enlightened results.

George Sandys

1578–1644 British traveller and antiquarian

The seventh and youngest son of Edwin Sandys, archbishop of York, George Sandys embarked on the Grand Tour then customary for high-born young men in 1610, visiting France, Italy, Turkey, Egypt and Palestine. He was one of the first Westerners to create a record of their travels in Egypt, which he published as A relation of a journey begun An. Dom. 1610 *in 1615.*

→ A page from Sandys's *A relation of a journey begun An. Dom. 1610* showing the kinds of objects, perhaps amulets, that he found wrapped in the bandages of mummified corpses: 'their Gods inclosed in little models of stone or mettall: some of the shape of men, in coate-armours, with the heads of sheepe, haukes, dogs, &c. others of cats, beetles, monkies, and such like.'

Egypt, George Sandys wrote, 'is said to extend from North to South five hundred and threescore miles, for a long tract contracted between barren mountaines, in many places scarce foure, in few above eight miles broad, untill not farre above Cairo it beginneth by degrees to enlarge, and so continueth to do, even to the sea .... Foure miles below Cairo, [the river Nile] devideth into two maine and navigable branches ... making of the richest portion of the land a triangular lland named Delta, in that it beareth the forme of that letter ... amongst the hidden mysteries of Nature, there is none more wonderfull, then is the overflowing of this River: making of a meere desert (for such is Egypt unwatered by Nilus) the most fruitfull part of the habitable world.'

Sandys was a poet trained in Latin, who would go on to publish translations of Ovid's *Metamorphoses* and Virgil's *Aeneid*. His expectations of Egypt were drawn largely from the classical sources he had encountered in his studies, but he would visit a much changed land. His account of his arrival reminds us that, while navigating Egypt itself might involve serene journeys along the river or on camelback, getting there was not quite so easy, nor even guaranteed: 'Now having lost the sight of Rhodes, we saw no land until the third night after: in the evening doubtfully discovering the coast of Egypt. Fearing the lee shore, all night we bore out to sea: the lightning ministring uncomfortable light, intermixed with thunder and tempests. The next day we entred the haven of Alexandria, newly defamed with a number of wracks which scattered here and there, did miserably testifie the unsafe protection of that harbour.'

Of Alexandria itself, Sandys expressed not a little disappointment at the present state of the city, at odds with the 'Queene of Cities and Metropolis of Africa' described in the classical texts: 'But Ah how much different is That Niobe from this! ... Of Antiquities there are few remainders: one an Hieroglyphicall Obelisk of Theban marble, as hard welnigh as Porphir, but of a deeper red, and speckled alike, called Pharos Needle, standing where once stood the pallace of Alexander: and another lying by, and like it, halfe buried in rubbidge.' Little could Sandys have known that almost three centuries later even these obelisks would disappear, the fallen one removed to London in 1877, and the standing one to New York's Central Park in 1881. They are now known as Cleopatra's Needles, and were in fact originally a pair, commissioned by Tuthmosis III and erected at Heliopolis, that had been brought to Alexandria on Roman orders in 12 BCE to stand at the entrance to the Caesareum a few decades after it had been built by Cleopatra.

From Alexandria, Sandys journeyed to Rosetta (the famous Stone would not be discovered for nearly 200 years) and then south towards Cairo, and from there to Giza, where he visited 'those three Pyramides (the barbarous monuments of prodigality and vain-glory) so universally celebrated'. He was not deceived by the tradition that the pyramids

AN UNTOUCHED ANTIQUE LAND

affirmed to haue ftood fiue miles North-weft of that city, ftanding directly Weft, and full twelue from this. But the moft pregnant proofe hereof are the *Mummes,* (lying in a place where many generations haue had their fepultures) not far aboue *Memphis,* neare the brow of the *Libyan* defert, and ftreightning of the mountaines, from *Cairo* wel-nigh twenty miles. Nor likely it is that they would fo far carry their dead, hauing as conuenient a place adioyning to the Citie.

These we had purpofed to haue feene; but the chargeable guard, and feare of the *Arabs* there then folemnizing their feftiuall, being befides to haue layne out all night, made vs content our felues with what we had heard; hauing before feene diuers of the embalmed bodies, and fome broken vp, to be bought for dollars apeece at the Citie. In that place are fome indifferent great, and a number of little Pyramides, with tombes of feuerall fafhions: many ruinated, as many violated by the *Moores* and *Arabians,* who make a profit of the dead, and infringe the priuiledge of Sepulchers. Thefe were the graues of the ancient *AEgyptians,* from the firft inhabiting of that country; coueting to be there interred, as the place fuppofed to containe the body of *Ofiris.* Vnder euery one, or wherefouer lie ftones not naturall to the place, by remouing the fame, defcents are difcouered like the narrow mouthes of wells (hauing holes in each fide of the walls to defcend by, yet fo troublefome, that many refufe to go downe, that come thither of purpofe) fome wel-nigh ten fathoms deepe: leading into long vaults (belonging, as fhould feeme, to particular families) hewne out of the rocke, with pillars of the fame. Betweene euery arch the corfes lie ranckt one by another, fhrouded in a number of folds of linnen, fwathled with bands of the fame: the brefts of diuers being ftained with Hieroglyphicall characters. Within their bellies are painted papers, and their Gods inclofed in little models of ftone or mettall: fome of the fhape of men, in coate-armours, with the heads of fheepe, haukes, dogs, &c. others of cats, beetles, monkies, and fuch like. Of thefe I brought away diuers with me, fuch in fimilitude.

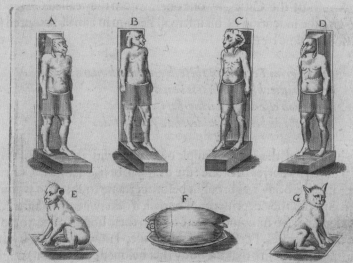

A. *This with the head of a Monkie or Baboon, fhould feeme by what is faid before, pag.* 103. *to haue bene worfhipped by thofe of Thebais.*
B. *Anubis, whereof Virgil,*

　　The monfter-Gods, Anubis barking, buckle
　　With Neptune, Venus, Pallas.

Omnigenúmq; deûm monftra, & latrator Anubis:
Contra Neptunum & Venerem, contráq; Mineruam,
Telatenent. AEn.l 8.
Some

→ Sandys's map of the lands through which he travelled, including Egypt. The locations of the more important sites he encountered are marked, including: Alexandria, Pharos, Matarea (site of ancient Heliopolis), Cairo, Babilon (Old Cairo), the pyramids of Giza, Memphis (marked as 'destroid'), Tentyra (Dendera), Coptos, Thebes and Syene (Aswan).

55   60   65   70   75   80   85

Sytlian
cheronesus   Bosphorus   Matriga   Tar:taria   50
             Scyth: Maura   Zichia

                           Col   Georgiani   CASPIAN
                           chis   SEA
BLACK SEA of PONTVS EVXINVS   Phasis flu   Derbent

                  Amisus   45
          Cappado: Euphrates flu
Anti: Scutari   Paphlagonia   cia
pole   Amasia   Trebezond
ria   Ancyra   Media
amon   Armenia
Bithinia   Prusa
hidos   Tigris flu
Phrigia   THE LESSER ASIA

                                                            ASSY:
Sardis   Iconium   Gensu flu   Mesopotamia   RIA   40
Ephesus   Smyrna   Pamphilia   Cilicia
Lydia   Tigris flu
   Lycia   Ibarus   Giulap flu:
                         Alexan: Aleppo
Rodus   Cerines   dretta
         CYPRVS   Olympus   Antiochia   Euphrates flu
Scarpanto   C S Pisano   Lapithos   anima grom   Orontes flu   Seleucia
C S Sidera   Papha   Nicosa   Famagusta   Syria
C S Salamon   Amath   Pedasium   Babilon   35
Scithe   usia   Phrom   Byblis   Libanus M.   Babilon
       Paphos   C delle Gatte   Tripoli   Antilibanus   Damascus
                      Baruti   BABILO
                 Sidon   Cesarea   Philippi   NIA
                 Tirus   Gallile
              C Bianco   Ar: Nazareth   Chaldea
              M Carmel   Samaria
              Castell Pelerine   Roma   Jordan
LAND SEA   Joppa   Jerusalem   Callirhoe
                     Akalon   Bethlehem
                         Iudea   Hebron
                   Gaza   Berseba
                         ARA BIA PETRÆA
P.le Colombi   Pharus   Rosetto   Idumaea
                Bochaeir   Damiata
          Alexandria   EGYPT   Thien   M Horeb   M Sinai   Arabia the desert   30
               Pyramides   Matarea
Caroberto   Mempou   Cairo
            destroied   Babilon   Sues   Tara
                   Pozi   Caiassa   Eltor
          M Troicus   Chifale   Beil
              Grondol   Bubutor
          Azirut   Genamam   Part of Arabia
             Zuguan   Sicaho
T OF THE KINGDOM   Daccatu
  OF NVBIA   Coptus   soridam   Jambut   Medina
              Nilus flu   Cossir   T'elnabi
       Tentyra   Tibith   monte   Farzi
                              marzoan   Almenuschi   the happie
         Thebe
RICA   Mecca
               Byge   Ziden
       Syene   Alachi   Muchi   Muchi
                                     Lysama

65   70   75   80

had been built as granaries by the biblical Joseph, recognizing them, correctly, as tombs: 'These, as the rest, were the regall sepulchers of the Aegyptians.' Despite his somewhat barbed comments, he could not have failed to have been impressed by the sheer size of these monuments, the Great Pyramid in particular: 'No stone so little throughout the whole, as to be drawne by our carriages …. A wonder how conveyed hither: how so mounted, a greater.' Indeed, he could not resist climbing to the summit, from which he caught a glimpse of further ancient wonders to come. At Giza Sandys also visited the Great Sphinx, which at this time was largely invisible, its body almost entirely concealed by the sand. Nonetheless, it left a striking impression: 'By a Sphinx the Aegyptians in their hieroglyphicks presented an harlot: having an amiable, and alluring face; but with all the tyrannie, and rapacity of a Lion: exercised over the poore heart-broken, and voluntarily perishing lover.'

Next, Sandys made the short journey to what he believed were the ruins of the ancient capital city of Memphis, based on descriptions of its location in classical accounts. He imagined that he would find 'the Fane of Venus, and that of Serapis, beset with sphinxes, adjoyning to the desert: a Citie great and populous, adorned with a world of antiquities'. Again, however, the scene he came upon was not quite what the classical texts had led him to expect: 'The very ruines now almost ruinated: yet some few impressions are left, and divers throwne downe, statues of monstrous resemblances: a scarce sufficient testimony to shew unto the curious seeker, that there it had bin.'

And yet Sandys did find something to capture his interest, and which further reinforced his certainty that he was standing on the ancient capital: 'The most pregnant proofe here of are the *Mummes*, (lying in a place where many generations have had their sepultures) not far above Memphis, neare the brow of the Libyan desert, and streightning of the mountaines, from Cairo wel nigh twenty miles. Nor likely it is that they would so far carry their dead, having as convenient a place adjoyning to the Citie.' Sandys had perhaps underestimated how many ancient towns and cities might have been accompanied by burial grounds containing the remnants of so many 'mummes', but it seems likely that he had come across one of the most substantial in the Memphite region, probably Saqqara. He gave a rich description of the remains of the cemetery: 'In that place are some indifferent great, and a number of little Pyramides, with tombes of severall fashions: many ruinated, as many violated by the Moores and Arabians, who make a profit of the dead, and infringe the priviledge of Sepulchers. These were the graves of the ancient Aegyptians … the corpses lie ranckt one by another, shrouded in a number of folds of linnen, swathled with bands of the same: the brests of divers being stained with Hieroglyphicall characters.'

↓ Sandys's illustration of the entrance to the Great Pyramid of Khufu at Giza: 'A most dreadfull passage, and no lesse cumbersome; not above a yard in breadth, and foure feet in height: each stone containing that measure. So that alwayes stooping, and sometimes creeping, by reason of the rubbidge, we descended'.

130   *The Pyramides.*   LIB. 2.

the bow of an arch, the way no larger then the former, about a hundred and twenty feete. Here we passed through a long entry which led directly forward: so low, that it tooke euen from vs that vneasie benefit of stooping. VVhich brought vs into a little roome with a compast rooffe, more long then broad, of polished marble, whose grauelike smell, halfe full of rubbidge forced our quicke returne. Climing also ouer this entrance, we ascended as before, about an hundred and twenty feete

This figure be-longeth to the former page but could not be there placed.

higher. This entry being of an exceeding height, yet no broder from side to side then a man may fathome, benched on each side, and closed aboue with admirable architecture, the marble so great, and so cunningly ioyned, as had it bene hewne through the liuing rocke. At the top we entred into a goodly chamber, twenty foote wide, and forty in length: the rooffe of a maruellous height; and the stones so great, that eight floores it, eight rooffes it, eight flagge the ends, and sixteene the sides, all of well wrought *Theban* marble. Atwhart the roome at the vpper end there standeth a tombe: vncouered, empty, and all of one stone: breast high, seuen feete in length, not foure in breadth, and founding like a bell. In this no doubt lay the body of the builder. They erecting such costly monuments, not onely out of a vaine ostentation: but being of opinion, that after the dissolution of the flesh

the

26   AN UNTOUCHED ANTIQUE LAND

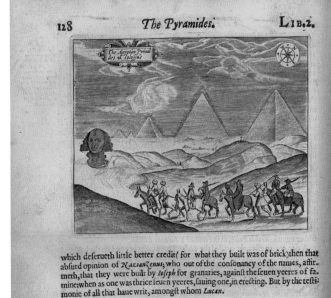

which deferueth little better credit(for what they built was of brick)then that abfurd opinion of *Nazianzenus*, who out of the confonancy of the names, affirmeth, that they were built by *Iofeph* for granaries, againft the feuen yeeres of famine;when as one was thrice feuen yeeres, fauing one, in erecting. But by the teftimonie of all that haue writ, amongft whom *Lucan*.

Cæum Ptol omæorum manes ferieni-
que podendam
Pyramides claudant.l.8.

          When high Pyramides do grace
          The Ghofts of Ptolomies lewd race:

and by what fhallbe faid hereafter, moft manifeft it is,that thefe,as the reft, were the regall fepulchers of the Ægyptians. The greateft of the three,and chiefe of the worlds feuen wonders, being fquare at the bottome, is fuppofed to take vp eight acres of ground. Euery fquare being 300. fingle paces in length, the fquare at the top,confifting of three ftones onely, yet large enough for threefcore to ftand vpon: afcended by two hundred fifty fiue fteps,each ftep about three feet high, of a breadth proportionable. No ftone fo little throughout the whole,as to bee drawne by our carriages: yet were thefe hewne out of the *Troian* mountaines,far off in *Arabia*; fo called of the captiue *Troians*, brought by *Menelaus* into Ægypt, and there afterward planted. A wonder how conueyed hither:how fo mounted,a greater. Twenty yeers it was in building; by three hundred threefcore and fixe thoufand men continually wrought vpon: who onely in radifhes, garlicke,and onions, are faid to haue confumed one thoufand and eight hundred talents. By thefe and the like inuentions exhaufted they their treafure, & imployed the people; for feare leaft fuch infinite wealth fhould corrupt their fucceffors, and dangerous

rous idleneffe beget in the Subiect a defire of innouation. Befides, they confidering the frailty of man,that in an inftant,buds,blowes,and withereth,did endeauor by fuch fumptuous and magnificent ftructures,in fpite of death to giue vnto their fames eternitie. But vainely:

    Not fumptuous Pyramis to skies vp-reard,
    Nor Elean Ioues proud Faine, which heauen compeerd,
    Nor the rich fortune of Maufoleus tombe,
    Are priuiledg'd from deaths extremeft dome,
    Or fire, or ftormes, their glories do abate,
    Or they,age-fhaken,fall with their owne waight.

Nam neque Pyramidum fumptus ad fydera ducti.
Nec Iouis Elei cœli imitata domus,
Nec Maufolei diues fortuna fepulchri,
Mortis ab extrema côditione vacant.
Aut illis flamma,aut imber fubduces honores
Annorum,aut ictu pondere victa ruent.Propert.l.3.Eleg.2.

Yet this hath bene too great a morfell for time to deuoure; hauing ftood,as may be probably coniectured,about three thoufand and two hundred yeeres: and now rather old then ruinous: yet the North fide is moft worne,by reafon of the humidity of the Northern wind,which here is ỹ moyfteft. The top at length we afcended with many panfes and much difficulty;from whence with delighted eyes we beheld that foueraigne of ftreames,and moft excellent of countries. Southward & neere-hand the *Mummes*: a far off diuers huge Pyramides; each of which, were this away, might fupply the repute of a wôder. During a great part of the day it cafteth no fhadow on the earth,but is at once illuminated on all fides. Defcending againe, on the Eaft fide, below, from each corner equally diftant, we approached the entrance, feeming heretofore to haue bin clozed vp,or fo intended, both by the place it felfe, as appeareth by the following picture, and conueyances within. Into this our *Ianizaries* difcharged their harquebufes, left fome fhould haue skulkt within to haue done vs a mifchiefe:and guarded the mouth whilft we entred, for feare of the wild *Arabs*. To take the better footing, we put off our fhooes, and moft of our apparell: foretold of the heat within, not inferiour to a Stoue. Our guide (a *Moore*) went foremoft:euery one of vs with our lights in our hands. A moft dreadfull paffage, and no leffe cumberfome; not aboue a yard in breadth, and foure feet in height: each ftone containing that meafure. So that alwaies ftooping, and fometimes creeping, by reafon of the rubbidge, we defcended(not by ftaires,but as downe the fteep of a hill) a hundred feet:where the place for a little circuite enlarged; & the fearful defcent continued, which they fay none euer durft attempt any farther. Saue that a *Baffa* of *Cairo*, curious to fearch into the fecrets thereof, caufed diuers condemned perfons to vndertake the performance well ftored with lights and other prouifion: & that fome of them afcended againe well-nigh thirty miles off in the Defarts. A fable deuifed only to beget wonder. But others haue written, that at the bottome there is a fpacious pit,eighty and fix cubits deepe,filled at the ouerflow by concealed conduits:in the midft a little Iland, and on that a tombe containing the body of *Cheops*, a King of Ægypt, and the builder of this *Pyramis*: which with the truth hath a greater affinity. For fince I haue bene told by one out of his owne experience,that in the vttermoft depth there is a large fquare place (though without water) into which he was led by another entrie opening to the South, knowne but vnto few(that now open, being fhut by fome order)& entred at this place where we feared to defced. A turning on the right hand leadeth into a little room: which by reafon of the noifome fauour, & vneafie paffage we refufed to enter. Clambering ouer the mouth of the aforefaid dungeô we afcended as vpô

          the

↑ Sandys's view of the Giza plateau, drawn from first-hand experience, is a considerable improvement on Kircher's (see p. 17). The pyramids are shown a little taller than in reality, but the positions and relative sizes of the pyramids of Khufu (far right), Khafra (second from right), Menkaura and two satellite pyramids are accurate and he seems to have made some attempt to capture the fine outer casing that survives at the top of the pyramid of Khafra. The Great Sphinx is drawn with a much greater degree of accuracy than in Kircher's attempt, shown buried up to its neck amongst undulating sand dunes that still concealed the mass of archaeological remains – mastaba tombs, temples, causeways – that we now know lay beneath.

Sandys was travelling at a time when scholarly knowledge of ancient Egyptian material culture was virtually non-existent, and so did not have the tools to capture what he saw in anything but the barest detail. But through his reference to the ruination of the site and its tombs, we can see that the destruction of ancient sites and monuments so often observed and lamented by later explorers and Egyptologists was already under way. Sandys made his journey in 1610; the destruction would only accelerate over the next three centuries before much of significance was done to arrest it. What else might Sandys have seen that has been lost since?

Sandys's account of his travels emphasizes just how little was known of Egypt from first-hand observations; in these earliest encounters, travellers were largely reliant on the centuries-old descriptions of the Greek and Roman pioneers who had gone before them to try to make sense of what they were seeing. Overwhelmingly, in seeing the ancient ruins through his eyes, the modern reader is filled with the sense of the traveller in a land unfamiliar not only to him, but to everyone back home. In the pages of his journal it seems as though the West comes upon Egypt almost for the very first time.

Frederik Ludwig Norden

1708–1742 Danish naval captain and explorer

Norden embarked on a journey to Egypt in 1737 to make a record of the country and its ancient monuments. His account was published only after his death but became one of the most important sources of information available in its day.

↗ Norden's illustration of the famous Colossi of Memnon, published in his *Drawings of some ruins and colossal statues at Thebes in Egypt*. The ruins of the Ramesseum appear in the distance, and the Theban hills, with the rock-cut pillars of the Middle Kingdom *saff*-tombs clearly visible, beyond.

→ Norden's drawing of the Great Sphinx with the pyramid of Khafra behind.

Frederik Ludwig Norden was born in Glückstadt, Holstein, then a part of Denmark (now Germany). He entered the Danish naval academy in 1722, and quickly impressed his superiors with his ability to draw maps. He was promoted to lieutenant and given the opportunity travel overseas, spending time in Holland, France and Italy.

In 1737 he was invited by King Christian VI of Denmark to accompany a mission to forge commercial relations between the Danish king, the emperor of Ethiopia and the lord of Madagascar that was to be led by the French count Pierre Joseph le Roux d'Esneval. The expedition was to journey through Egypt as far as Sudan to make a record of the country and its antiquities. This was fortuitous for Norden: at the time he was in Florence, where he had met Baron Phillip von Stosch, a Prussian antiquarian who had ignited in Norden a passion for Egyptian antiquities. As the unidentified author of the preface to Norden's *Voyage d'Égypte et de Nubie* recalled, 'The conversations that they had every day together, turned commonly on polite literature, and principally on history and antiquities. Mr de Stosch, full of admiration for those of Egypt, often regretted the uncertainty and defectiveness of the accounts of the country, as well ancient and modern. Our traveller [Norden] entered easily into the notions of his friend. Insensibly he let himself be carried away with a desire of seeing the borders of the Nile. The glory he found in informing the public of so many interesting singularities, made all the difficulties vanish from his sight, which he must surmount in order to arrive thither.'

In June 1737 the exploratory party landed in Alexandria, with its two ports and 'mixture of antique and modern monuments, which, on whatever side you turn yourself, offer themselves to the view....When you have passed the Little Pharillon, you discover a row of great towers, joined one to another by the ruins of a thick wall. One single obelisk standing, has sufficient height to make itself remarked in a place, where the wall is fallen down .... The new Alexandria makes a figure afterwards with its minarets; and above this town, but in a distant view, rises the column of Pompey, a most majestic monument.' Norden correctly guessed that the obelisks he saw were older than Alexandria and had been brought from somewhere else, but was wrong in his reasoning that 'it is known, that at the time of the foundation of Alexandria, they no longer made any of these monuments, covered with hieroglyphics, of which they had already long since lost both the knowledge and the use.'

After staying long enough for Norden to study the standing monuments, the expedition continued on to Cairo, arriving on 7 July, where they were delayed for several months owing to a revolt. Norden was confined to his bed for two of these long and fraught months, having contracted pneumonia. Nonetheless, over the course of their protracted visit he was able to make a survey of pyramids. His drawing of the interior of the Great Pyramid is particularly notable for its accuracy, even if his interpretations were not: 'I do not think

AN UNTOUCHED ANTIQUE LAND

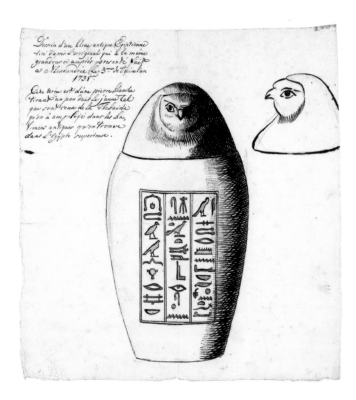

↑ Norden's drawing of a canopic jar, the only object he is known to have removed from Egypt, now kept in the Danish National Museum. Such jars were typically buried with deceased individuals in sets of four, containing the mummified lungs, liver, stomach and intestines. Each figure-head represented one of the Four Sons of Horus, in this case Imset, who is named in the inscriptions, although the falcon head more usually represents Qebehsenuef, suggesting the jars and lids from this set had become mixed up. The deceased, Tefnakht, is also named.

my supposition, that the Pyramids, even the last built, were long before the use of hieroglyphics, is without foundation. Thus I support it; is it to be believed, that the Egyptians would have left those superb monuments without the least hieroglyphical inscription, which they were so lavish of, on any considerable building? Not one is to be seen within, nor without the pyramids; not even in the ruins of the temples, of the second and third pyramids: is it not then probable, that the origin of pyramids preceded that of hieroglyphics.' In fact, the earliest known hieroglyphs precede the pyramids. His view of the Sphinx with the three pyramids in the background was nonetheless a considerable improvement on earlier attempts, such as those of Kircher and Sandys.

Finally, on 17 November the crew were able to begin their journey southward: 'We agreed with a barge-master to carry us to Essuaen [Aswan] for thirty Fendouclis, and a new coat'. In Cairo, they also engaged a janissary, a member of the elite corps of the Ottoman Empire, to serve as security, although this would not save them from repeated demands by locals throughout their journey for payment to access the ancient ruins and even the shore. Norden commented: 'Janissaries are to be had on very reasonable terms. They commonly speak what is called Lingue Franca. They accompany a traveller to every place it is lawful for him to approach. Nobody will dare to insult you while he is by. If they meet a person of distinction, they know how to give an account to him of those they escorte; and if the rabble offer to gather round you, they disperse them with menaces.'

On 9 December, the expedition was harassed by a mob who boarded the boat, to the bewilderment of the crew. The *reys* (skipper) explained that the locals believed any items of metal on the ship were made of either gold or silver: 'He then proposed our returning to Cairo, asserting at the same time, "They will kill you and me, in order to make themselves masters of those treasures they imagine you have. They will cause it to be reported over all the country; so that if you escape in one place, you will certainly perish in another."' Norden and his company tried to reassure the *reys* that they could defend themselves with their arms: 'Our intrepidity, and repeated assurances of defending his life, as well as our own, recovered him a little, and his answer of consent was, *Inschallach*, God grant it.'

The very next day, they faced a threat of an altogether different kind: 'THREE or four crocodiles, by chance, had chosen for their retreat those little islands we lay anchored off. We fired at them; two instantly plunged into the water; one seemed to remain without any motion. We imagined that we had killed, or at least wounded him severely, wherefore we ordered our bark to bear on him, and were armed with poles, and other instruments, with which we intended to dispatch him, in case he had not been already dead; but when we were within fifteen paces of him, awakened by our noise, he started away, and dived like the others. He was about thirty feet long. We saw that day twenty other crocodiles, stretched on sand banks, and of different extent, from fifteen to fifty feet.'

Successfully navigating these perils, on 11 December they reached Karnak and Luxor, but the *reys* told Norden it was impossible to go ashore owing to the sandbanks and islands. It seems that, in fact, he and his crew feared the villagers. From the boat, Norden observed the ruins, and deduced their location: 'It was four o' clock in the afternoon, when I began to perceive, on the east-side, an obelisk: a little after I discovered a great number of peristils, some portals, and antique structures, confusedly scattered up and down the plain. From these signs, I immediately concluded that I saw the ruins of ancient Thebes; but I could not prevail on our reys to put me ashore, by fair words, promises, or menaces. He did not here plead his fear of the Arabians; his only excuse was, the impossibility of landing, on account of the islands and sand-banks that obstructed. He swore, moreover, by his beard, that there was no going thither, without making a great round by land.'

Norden drew what he could from the boat, but lamented that accurately reproducing the hieroglyphs that covered the ruins would require 'more time than I could spare, and more conveniences that I was furnished with'. They eventually moored that evening on the west bank of the river, and in the morning Norden set out to visit the sites in the vicinity and to record as much as he could in the single day they would spend there. Among the ruins he recorded were the famous colossi believed to be images of Memnon, an Aethiopian king who was killed by Achilles during the Trojan War: 'I did not go far before I met two great colossuses, which at first I took to be those Strabo makes mention of; but I had good reason afterwards to think otherwise.' He came to believe that they represented a man and a woman; in fact they are both images of the 18th Dynasty pharaoh Amenhotep III, but this would not be recognized until almost a century later.

Upon resuming his voyage, Norden once again fell ill and confined himself to the boat, except when it reached the temple of Esna, which he could not resist the opportunity to draw. But as soon as the Europeans were discovered, they were bombarded with stones and fled to the ship – though the onslaught soon stopped once they had their weapons in hand.

When they reached Aswan, where they needed to swap to another boat – the First Cataract being impassable – Norden took advantage of the ongoing negotiations to visit the island of Elephantine. He was unprepared for the heat: 'During all this walk I suffered a great heat, I was ready to die with thirst; and tho' I was in the middle of the Nile, I could not get a single drop of water to quench my thirst. The swift flowing of the water made the rocks of granite so slippery, that I could not get to take up water in my hand. I made some useless attempts at it. Luckily, the native of

↓ Norden's careful drawing of the Great Sphinx was perhaps the first to show accurately the carved features of the king's face, including the cosmetic eyebrows, *nemes* headdress, and remains of a *uraeus* (cobra) at the brow. The weathering around the headdress and strata of the rock visible in the face are both drawn with striking care. Norden wrote: 'At the same time that travellers admire its enormous size, they cannot help expressing their indignation against the brutality of those who have so disfigured its nose.'

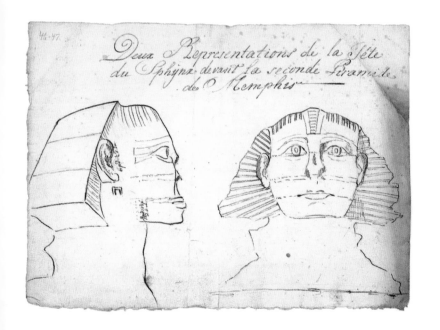

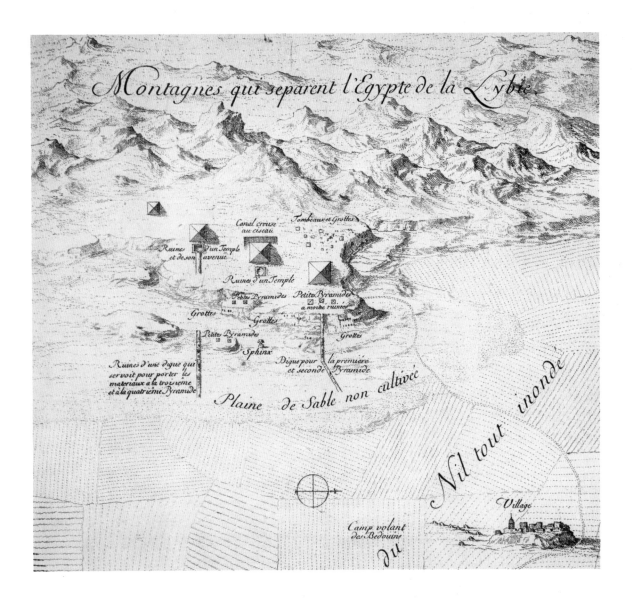

Montagnes qui separent l'Egypte de la Lybie

Canal creuse au ciseau

Tombeaux et Grottes

Ruines d'un Temple et de son avenue

Ruines d'un Temple

Petites Pyramides

Petite Pyramide a moitié ruinée

Grottes

Grottes

Petites Pyramides

Grottes

Sphinx

Petite Pyramide

Ruines d'une digue qui servoit pour porter les materiaux a la troisieme et a la quatrieme Pyramide

Digue pour la premiere et seconde Pyramide

Plaine de Sable non cultivée

Nil tout inondé

du

Village

Camp volant des Bedouins

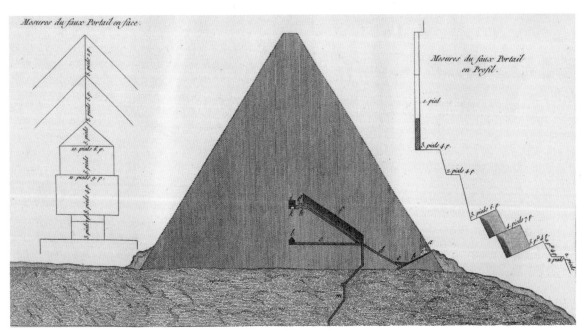

Mesures du faux Portail en face.

Mesures du faux Portail en Profil.

AN UNTOUCHED ANTIQUE LAND

← Norden's map of the Giza plateau. He seems to have considered there to have been four main pyramids, where we now consider there to be three, belonging to kings, accompanied by satellite pyramids belonging to female members of the royal family. The 'fourth' (far left) of Norden's map is one such, belonging to the pyramid of Menkaura (second from left).

← Like his plan of the Giza plateau, Norden's section drawing of the internal workings of the Great Pyramid, incorporating diagrams and measurements of the original entranceway, is striking for its accuracy. His description of entering the pyramid evokes a sense of adventure unavailable to today's tourists: 'At the opening of the first pyramid fire some pistols in order to dislodge the bats, then order the two Arabians to clear away the sand, that almost choaks up the farther entrance to it.'

Barbary was more dextrous than I. He made me stop, laid himself afterwards on his belly; and after he had washed his hands, he presented me some water, which I drank with a pleasure that I cannot express.'

The final southward leg of their journey was fractured and unsuccessful; d'Esneval was so eager to get to Ethiopia that, incredibly, he would not allow Norden to go ashore at Philae, and his notes and sketches were made from the boat. At the frontier between Egypt and Nubia the crew were ordered to go ashore to distribute their riches to the locals, but they refused and were shot at, returning fire themselves. They did not get much further.

On their return northwards, Norden explored the temple at Philae more thoroughly, but even then he was forced to stop by a crowd of natives. The crew stopped at Esna for repairs to the ship, and while there made enquiries about another European boat that had passed them that day. It turned out to be that of Richard Pococke (pp. 34–39). They arrived in Luxor on 3 February, Norden devoting a night to measuring the first pylon of Luxor temple. The following morning he devoted to the vast temple complex at Karnak. The captain of the boat was jubilant on their return, he himself never having dared to go ashore.

A little under three weeks later, Norden and his party arrived in Old Cairo. They would remain there, also spending a little more time in Alexandria, for a further four months before finally returning home. The king had commissioned Norden to publish his account upon his return to Denmark, but he was delayed when war broke out between England and Spain. The Danish king offered the services of some of his naval men to the English, including Norden, who consequently took up residence in London. While there he fell ill with tuberculosis and, much weakened, decided to go to southern France. He reached Paris but fell seriously ill and could not continue his journey. He died there in 1742, at the tragically early age of thirty-three, but had placed his papers in safe hands so that they might be published posthumously. In 1751 the work was released and subsequently translated into several different languages, including English as *Travels in Egypt and Nubia*.

One of the most striking aspects of Norden's commentary is his assiduous recording of the name of every village his party passed on their journey up and back down the Nile. His mindset was very much one of a geographer and cartographer – his maps of the Nile were extremely accurate and detailed, but just as importantly his account captured the difficulty of travelling through Egypt at this time and in particular the dangers posed by avaricious locals and hungry reptiles. These encounters serve to emphasize just what an achievement it was to make this journey, and to explain why it was made only by the most intrepid travellers, at least until such times as Europeans began to arrive in significant numbers and to be granted more protection by the Egyptian authorities. In Norden's day Egypt was a magical but also inhospitable place. The value of Norden's account thus lay as much in his writings as in his sketches; the quantity and quality of his visual record brought the strange sights he had seen to life for his audiences in Europe. No descriptions could do the splendour of the ancient monuments justice – just as today, some had to be seen to be believed – and while Egypt remained so distant and inaccessible, Norden's drawings were the closest most could ever get to seeing such wonders.

Richard Pococke

1704–1765 English clergyman and traveller

Pococke was the first English traveller to make a notable contribution to the study of Egypt. After earning his doctorate of civil law at Oxford University, he travelled to Egypt twice, first over the winter of 1737–38, and then from December 1738 to July 1739. His detailed survey of the country's monuments, A Description of the East and Some Other Countries, *was among the first of its kind, inspiring and informing future travellers.*

→ This extraordinary drawing of 'The Sepulchres of the Kings of Thebes' appeared in Pococke's *A Description of the East and Some Other Countries*: 'There are signs of about eighteen of them, as mark'd in the view in this plate ... the grottos are cut into the rock in a most beautiful manner in long rooms or galleries under the mountains ... and some of them painted, being as fresh as if they were but just finished, tho' they must be above two thousand years old.'

Richard Pococke was born into a family of high-ranking churchmen and himself made a successful career as a clergyman. In his late twenties he undertook a Grand Tour, visiting France and Italy in 1733 with a cousin, Jeremiah Milles. They returned when Milles was appointed to a position at Waterford Cathedral, but the cousins planned to return to their travels and departed in the summer of 1736 for some of the lesser-known countries of the Habsburg Empire. Milles was again recalled to Waterford, but this time Pococke continued his travels alone. Having acquired in Venice a passport that would allow him to travel to the Ottoman Empire, he set off for Alexandria. At this time very few Westerners would have considered visiting the country to look at ruined buildings, and he was clearly seen as something of an oddity. His account is full of remarks invoking the difficulties and discomforts of going about the business of making his study, and particularly of attracting the attention of the locals in spite of his efforts to work undisturbed: 'My observing so nicely, and so near the castle, was much taken notice of; and, as I was inform'd, several soldiers, who were that day on guard in the castle, were punish'd for permitting me to examine the port so exactly .... The first thing I did at Alexandria was to pace round the walls, and take the bearings; which I did with so much caution, that I thought I could only have been observed by the Janizary that attended me; not withstanding it was soon publicly reported about the town, that I had measured the city walls by palms.'

Pococke evidently had no recourse to any modern accounts of Egypt, instead relying on the works of Greek and Roman authors in seeking to recognize the cities and ruins he encountered. He used Strabo's *Geography* to correctly identify the ruins of the ancient capital city of Memphis at the village of Mit Rahineh: 'There are two distances mention'd by Strabo in order to fix the situation of Memphis; he says it was about eleven miles from Delta, and five from the height on which the pyramids were built, which appear to be the pyramids of Gize. Diodorus says that it was fifteen miles from the pyramids, which seems to be a mistake. Strabo speaks also of Memphis as near Babylon, so that probably it was situated on the Nile, about the middle, between the pyramids of Gize and Sacara, so that I conjecture this city was about Mocanan and Metrahenny [Mit Rahineh], which are in the road from Cairo to Faiume, on the west side of the Nile, and rather nearer to the pyramids of Sacara, than to those of Gize; for at Mocanan I saw some heaps of rubbish, but much greater about Metrahenny'.

He also produced the first modern account of the temple of Karnak at Luxor, ancient Thebes, again comparing it with the classical author's accounts: 'This is, without doubt, the temple mentioned by Diodorus Siculus, as of a most extraordinary size, though in no part incredible to any one, who has examined the great remains of this stupendous building, the ruins of which extend near half a mile in length, and he computes it to have been above a mile and a half in Circumference;

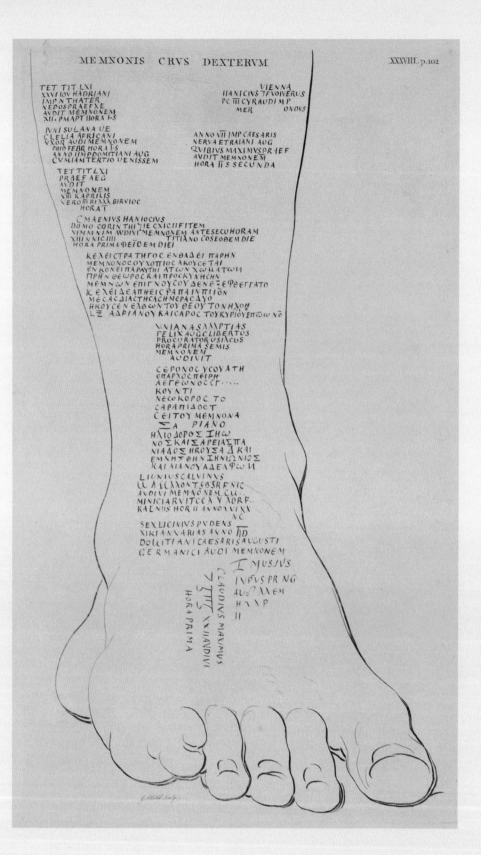

← One of the feet of the pair of colossal statues of Amenhotep III still known today as the Colossi of Memnon. The statues had been a tourist attraction for many centuries by the time Pococke visited them: 'on the insteps and legs, for about eight feet [2.5 metres] high, are several inscriptions in Greek and Latin, some being epigrams in honour of Memnon, others, the greater part, testimonies of those who heard his sound.' The northernmost of the statues, the upper part of which had collapsed when an earthquake struck in 27 BCE, was reputed to 'sing', perhaps in reality owing to water evaporating from cracks in the stone in the early hours of the morning, or to mischievous locals.

→ The northernmost of the two Colossi of Memnon. The statues are portrayed in a naturalistic style; Pococke was perhaps influenced by the classical art that was well known at the time, an indication of the extent to which the Egyptian canon was still completely unfamiliar.

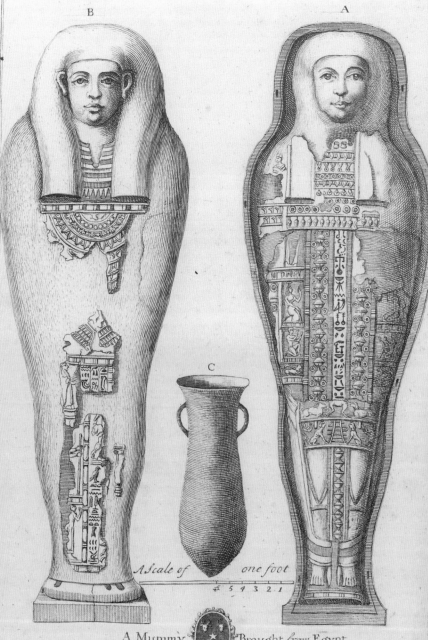

XX *p. 53.*

B   A

C

A Scale of   *one foot*

A Mummy   Brought *from* Egypt.
To the Right Honourable   *Lord* Charles Cavendish.

↑ A view looking west towards the Theban hills. The Colossi of Memnon in the foreground help to orient the viewer; the hills themselves, lying beyond a featureless plain, appear as two rows of almost comically steep-sided mounds. At the north (far right) end the hills are punctuated by openings in the rock, representing the entrances to tombs.

← Pococke's illustration of 'A Mummy Brought from Egypt' shows a painted wooden coffin of anthropoid form, the lid to the left, the box, containing a mummy covered with a mummy case, to the right. Both the lid and mummy case have strikingly realistic-looking faces, likely a reflection of Pococke's familiarity with such forms rather than an accurate reflection of the objects themselves, which probably had a more stylized, Egyptian appearance.

he says also that the height of the temple was forty-five cubits, and that the walls of it were twenty-four feet thick, in both which respects it will appear, that this temple, in some parts of it, exceeds the account Diodorus gave.'

At many of the sites Pococke visited he saw great standing monuments that have since disappeared. At Antinoopolis he reported seeing 'a very fine gate of the Corinthian order, of exquisite workmanship', and at Ashmunein (ancient Heliopolis, or 'as Pliny calls it, the city of Mercury') he found 'a grand portico of an antient temple ... consisting of twelve pillars, six in a row, nine feet diameter; there are hieroglyphics on every part both of the pillars and of the stones laid on them. I saw on the pillars some remains of paint, and the ceiling is adorn'd with stars; on several parts there are figures of pyramids, as with a door to them, which Kircher interprets to be ... the good principle; a person sitting, and one offering to him, is cut in several parts of the frieze. It appears that the pillars have been built up for about half way between, as in many Egyptian temples.'

It is, of course, a marvel that the ancients were able to build monuments of such scale, grandeur and solidity that they had survived into the 18th century, yet it is impossible not to regret what has been lost, the more so those that were seen recently enough for Western travellers to have recorded them. Though his journey was relatively brief in comparison with the grander expeditions of years to come, and his illustrations at times fanciful, Pococke's published survey of the country's ancient monuments offers a glimpse of a historic landscape that is now much changed, if not vanished entirely.

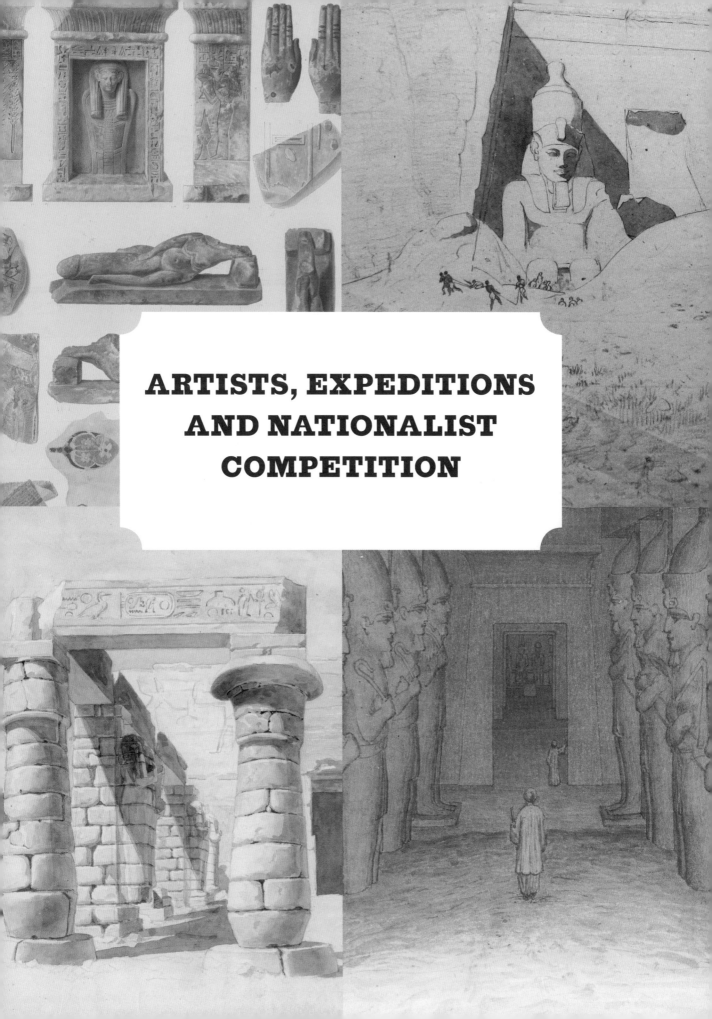

ARTISTS, EXPEDITIONS AND NATIONALIST COMPETITION

'The English have got the Rosetta Stone ... we must now be on the alert that they must not get this.'

BERNARDINO DROVETTI, ON A STONE
LIKE THAT OF ROSETTA BEARING
A TRILINGUAL INSCRIPTION

A watershed moment for Egyptology came in 1798, when Napoleon Bonaparte launched his great campaign to Egypt. While his mission ultimately failed, his decision to commission artists and scholars to accompany the expedition initiated a scientific programme on an unprecedented scale. Their great *Description de l'Égypte* (Description of Egypt), a comprehensive record of the country's ruins, was published between 1809 and 1829, eventually comprising twenty-six volumes of text, one of maps, and ten Elephant-folio-sized volumes containing 3,000 drawings. It is difficult to overstate the impact these mammoth publications must have had on the European public. Where previously Egypt was a faraway, almost mythical land, which could be experienced only through the wide-eyed accounts of the most daring travellers, here was a single scholarly resource with beautifully illustrated plates that made the country and its ancient past more visible than ever before.

Moreover, the Napoleonic expedition established a large settled presence of Europeans in the country, paving the way for the rapid acceleration of Egyptological activities. As travellers came to Egypt in greater numbers, so any stigma around visiting such a distant and difficult land began to disappear. Many of Napoleon's technological initiatives – the foundation of newspapers, a library and an Arabic–French dictionary – made visiting the country far easier. Scholars found a home at the Institut d'Égypte, and a consul-general assisted French visitors in Egypt. The first to hold this post was Bernardino Drovetti (1776–1852). The British maintained a military and diplomatic presence in the country, and appointed a consul-general of their own; from 1816 this post was occupied by Henry Salt, who would become a great rival to Drovetti. Both consuls recruited Europeans to act as agents in the acquisition of ancient artefacts, through purchase as well as excavation.

The Napoleonic expedition also brought fundamental political change to Egypt, seriously weakening the Mamluk ruling class. The Mamluks were a warrior caste, descended from slave soldiers, who in the Middle Ages came to rule a vast territory first as sultans and then as de facto rulers nominally under Ottoman rule. At the time of Napoleon's invasion, Egypt was ruled by two Mamluk chiefs, Murad Bey and Ibrahim Bey. They led the Egyptian troops against the French at the Battle of the Pyramids in 1798, but following a heavy defeat Ibrahim fled into Sinai, while Murad was chased into Upper Egypt. Britain acted swiftly to remove the French from the country, which they achieved in 1801. In the same year the Ottomans launched a campaign to reassert their power. Their forces included a unit headed by the Albanian Mohamed Ali; by 1805 he had assumed control of the country, and in 1811 he slaughtered the remaining Mamluk leaders and sent soldiers throughout Egypt to rout the last of their troops.

As Ottoman viceroy, Mohamed Ali Pasha embarked on an ambitious programme of modernization, building new infrastructure and factories, and equipping his armies with the latest military technology. His intention was to make Egypt wealthy and powerful enough that it could declare independence from the Ottoman Empire, establishing himself as the founder of a new ruling dynasty. He made use of European expertise to assist with his many projects, drawing more and more Westerners to the country. Pascal Coste (pp. 54–59) was invited to Egypt to consult on the construction of a saltpetre factory, James Burton (pp. 74–81) to find a source of coal in the Eastern Desert, and Frédéric Cailliaud (pp. 60–67) to locate the emerald mines there.

Rivalries between the European nations continued under Ali, particularly as the race to decipher hieroglyphs gathered pace. In England, Thomas Young made good progress, but a breakthrough by Jean-François Champollion (pp. 98–103) secured victory for the French. The need to discover and accurately copy new inscriptions gave direction to the efforts of many of the travellers of the era, including the Englishmen William Bankes (pp. 68–73), Robert Hay (pp. 88–97) and James Burton. It also led Champollion himself, with the assistance of the Italian Egyptologist Ippolito Rosellini, to launch the first great state-sponsored expedition to Egypt since that of Napoleon, in 1828. After Champollion's death in 1832 it was left to other scholars to improve upon his system of decipherment, and by the 1840s the Prussian scholar Karl Richard Lepsius (pp. 126–31) had become the world's leading authority on the subject. In 1842 he led an expedition that would expand enormously on the work of all previous missions. The resulting publication, the *Denkmäler* (Monuments), set new standards for the scholarly documentation and presentation of Egypt's ancient sites.

The great irony of the age is that the rapid increase in interest in ancient Egypt and efforts to uncover its material remains also brought about rapid and widespread destruction. The urge to free monuments from the sands resulted in unknowable archaeological losses – to the great frustration of modern Egyptologists. Even worse was the removal of paintings and artefacts to private and national collections.

Despite the failure of Napoleon's expedition and the departure of the British, Europe nonetheless came to conquer Egypt in some sense: visiting Europeans learned to negotiate with the Egyptian people, and navigate their customs and the landscape. The scholars that accompanied Napoleon and flocked in ever greater numbers to the country in the years that followed provided for the development of a powerful vision of Egypt's past and present. This vision – the essence of what has come to be known as 'Orientalism' – helped to create and reinforce the conceptualization of a disparity between cultures broadly understood as 'East' and 'West'. Europe was in the ascendant, contributing to a cultural dominance from which European powers would benefit in numerous ways. The scholarly investigation of Egypt's past was carried out for Western audiences and not for the Egyptian population. Recognition of the debt owed by the West in this has come very late, and attempts to redress the situation even later. The impact of the conduct of these early European visitors, and the context in which they operated, has been felt not only in Egyptology but also far beyond, shaping the modern Middle East and the modern world.

Dominique Vivant Denon

1747–1825 French antiquary, artist and scholar

Denon was a member of the commission of scientists and artists – 'savants' – who accompanied Napoleon's military expedition to Egypt in 1798 with the aim of making a comprehensive record of the country's natural and cultural features. He contributed to the vast resulting Description de l'Égypte, *but also published his own account, which appeared much more quickly after the expedition's end, capturing the public imagination and helping to spark great interest in ancient Egypt.*

→ A view of the temple of Luxor, still half-buried in centuries of accumulated debris. A mudbrick wall and gateway have been built into the pylon opening, and pigeon towers are visible beyond. The temple was cleared in the 1880s by the Antiquities Service, revealing the ancient monument in all its glory but erasing almost all trace of its later history.

Dominique Vivant Denon studied first law and then literature in Paris, where he became a favourite of King Louis XV of France through his erudition and conversational skills. He put these charms to use in his career in the diplomatic service, taking up posts in Russia, Sweden, Switzerland and Italy. When Revolution broke out in France in 1792 Denon was in Venice, and the following year he heard that his property had been confiscated and his name proscribed. Despite the danger he returned to Paris, finding favour at the salon of Joséphine de Beauharnais, who was to become Napoleon's first wife. This led to a meeting with Bonaparte, then an ambitious young general, and ultimately to an invitation to join the commission of scholars and artists who would accompany his great expedition to Egypt.

Napoleon's interests in Egypt were political and strategic: by invading and conquering the country he intended to defend French trade interests there, extend French territory and alliances, and to strike a blow against the British by weakening their access to India. In early 1798, 10,000 sailors and 40,000 soldiers were gathered at various Mediterranean ports, although their destination was kept secret from the troops in order to prevent the information from reaching the British. Denon accompanied the ranks as part of the 'Commission of Arts and Science', a group of 167 'savants' tasked with supporting the army by building a strategic canal, mapping out roads, growing grapes for wine and building mills to supply food, but also with recording the ancient monuments that they encountered. The fleet, headed by Napoleon himself, set sail on 19 May 1978.

Upon their arrival in Alexandria six weeks later, Napoleon issued a proclamation to the Egyptian people, explaining that the invasion was a punishment for the ill-treatment of French traders by the *beys* (Turkish rulers), and encouraging them to unite with his army and rise up against their Ottoman rulers. He also quickly established the Institut d'Égypte, to spread Enlightenment values (while promising that the French troops would respect the customs of the land) and to provide a base for the expedition's savants. Among the Institut's innovations were a table of standard weights and measures, an Arabic–French dictionary, an Egyptian/Coptic/European calendar and the modern printing press, which Napoleon introduced to Egypt for the purpose of issuing his proclamations, although the Arabic in which they were written was badly flawed and sometimes indecipherable.

Despite early victories against the ruling Mamluks, Napoleon found his military ambitions threatened by the British just one month after his arrival in Egypt. The French transport ships had returned to France, but the warships remained, moored in Abukir Bay. The British commander, Lord Horatio Nelson, discovered them there on 1 August, commencing the three-day-long 'Battle of the Nile'. By 3 August over half of the French ships had been destroyed or captured, and the remainder fled. Bonaparte was not deterred, however, issuing further

↑↑ This painting, now in the collections of the Victoria and Albert Museum and believed to have been made by Denon, is entitled 'Family of Egyptian Fellahin, at Tomb Entrance, about 1788–9'. The family are seated before a rock-cut tomb of the Old Kingdom style, upon which large images of the tomb owner holding a staff signify his seniority and status. The scene at right is shown as if facing outwards when in reality it was probably carved on the inner face of the entrance, and would have been invisible to the viewer from this angle. The sight of ancient ruins inhabited by the modern people of Egypt is one that Denon and other explorers would have encountered frequently. The location is unknown.

↑ Drawing of Denon himself sketching at Hierakonpolis, the ruins of the ancient site just visible in the background in the form of a ruined gateway.

proclamations claiming to have liberated the Egyptian people from their Ottoman and Mamluk overlords and praising the tenets of Islam, in keeping with his promise that the French troops would respect the customs of the land. He celebrated the birthday of the Prophet Muhammad and took measures to protect Egyptian pilgrims visiting Mecca. But he also imposed taxes to fund his army and remained unpopular with the Egyptians, who revolted against the 'infidels' on 21 October. Armed rebels fortified key locations around the capital and murdered Frenchmen in the streets. Napoleon ruthlessly suppressed the uprising, driving the rebels into the Great Mosque and then breaking down the gates and massacring those inside.

After a series of further clashes with the Ottomans, Napoleon withdrew from Egypt in August 1799, but tensions with the British remained. In early 1800 the Convention of El Arish was negotiated by

↓ Plan of the temple of Montu at Armant (Hermonthis). The temple was built by Tuthmosis III, and extended in the Ptolemaic era, when Cleopatra VII added a *mammisi* ('birth house') to commemorate the birth of her son by Julius Caesar, Caesarion. Tragically, the majority of the stone was removed between 1861 and 1863 for the construction of a sugar factory and only the lower course of stone now remains, tracing the plan of the ancient buildings but leaving the visitor with no sense of their former majesty.

↓↓ Sketch of the ruins of the Ptolemaic and Roman temple of Khnum at Esna (Latopolis). By Denon's time the modern town had grown up around the temple, the continual cycle of construction, decay, demolition and rebuilding causing the ground level to rise above the level of the ancient floor so that the temple appears to have sunk.

representatives from France and the Ottoman Empire in the presence of a British representative. It was intended to effectively end the French campaign, returning territory to the Ottomans on the condition that French troops were safely evacuated from the country. But the Convention crumbled when a communication that had been sent by the British government to their representative in Egypt arrived, proscribing any treaty that allowed the French repatriation. In March 1801, the British commenced a land offensive, defeating the French at Alexandria, then Fort Julien, and finally in Cairo. The French capitulated, and a second treaty was signed, providing for the French to be repatriated on British ships. It also gave the British possession of the hoard of antiquities collected by the French, which included the Rosetta Stone.

While Napoleon ultimately failed in his military mission, his scientific and scholarly programmes proved a great success. Denon

was among the first of the savants to see the full splendour of Egypt, accompanying one of Napoleon's generals in their pursuit of Murad Bey into Upper Egypt for nine months from December 1798. Though Denon was impressed by the 'huge masses of the ruins' of the portico of Hermopolis, which gave him 'the earliest idea of the splendour of the colossal architecture of the Egyptians', travelling with the military was not ideal: 'There are some unlucky moments, when every thing one does is followed by danger or accident. As I returned from this journey back to Benesuef, the General charged me with carrying an order to the head of the column; I gallop on to execute it, when a soldier, who was marching out of his rank, turning suddenly to the left as I was passing to the right, presents his bayonet against me, and before I could avoid it, I was unhorsed by the blow, whilst he at the same time was thrown down. "There is one savant less," said he while falling (for with them every one who was not a soldier was a *savant*); but some piastres which I had in my pocket received the point of the bayonet, and I escaped with only a torn coat.'

↓ Denon's drawing of the ruined portico of the temple of Thoth at Hermopolis (so-named by the Greeks owing to the connection they saw between their god, Hermes, and the local deity). It was built *c.* 370 BCE and inscribed for the short-lived successor to Alexander the Great as pharaoh, Philip Arrhidaeus, but had been quarried away by 1826.

ARTISTS, EXPEDITIONS AND NATIONALIST COMPETITION

↑ View from inside the peristyle court of the temple of Horus at Edfu. The temple was still buried almost up to the tops of the columns until it was cleared by Auguste Mariette in 1860, allowing Denon a perspective unfamiliar to visitors today. Modern buildings are visible within the court, while a group of figures sitting on top of a mound outside the temple gives a sense of the accumulation of debris.

Denon's account makes clear that the nature of the mission necessitated that the party press on at pace, his own mission to record the spectacular ruins that they encountered being secondary: 'We marched towards Thebes, the name alone of which fills the imagination with vast recollections. As if this city could escape me, I made a drawing of it the moment it came in view. We passed through it so rapidly, that scarcely was a monument discovered, when it was necessary to abandon it.' Nonetheless, he captured as much as he could. Murad led the French army on what might have been a wonderful tour of the country had Denon and his compatriots not been under constant threat of attack and he not had to witness the destruction wrought by both the Mamluks and the French, and the terror of the locals who scattered in all directions at the sight of the Europeans and their weapons. Despite all this, the scholar made over two hundred sketches in the course of the nine-month mission.

Towards the end of Denon's tour, while stationed in Qena, he was approached by a small group of savants who had been dispatched to inspect the agricultural and irrigation systems in the Nile Valley. They were not overly enthused by this task, however, and soon began exploring the landscape in search of ancient monuments. Denon told them of nearby Dendera and its wonderful zodiac ceiling, which would, some years later, be removed to Paris where, controversially, it remains.

↑ The temple of Qau el-Kebir (Antaeopolis) as seen by André Duterte, a fellow member, with Denon, of the French Commission of the Sciences and Arts. The temple stood close enough to the river that its waters had begun to undermine the ancient structure. By 1821 most of the temple was swept away by an unusually high flood.

→ A collection of antiquities painted by Duterte for publication in the monumental *Description de l'Égypte*, including a miniature shrine containing a figure with a the head of a human and body of a snake representing the goddess Renenutet, some fragments of relief, two ithyphallic figures lying on beds, some matting, textiles and a fragment of cartonnage.

Denon published an account of experiences entitled *Voyage dans la basse et la haute Égypte* (Travels in Upper and Lower Egypt) in 1802, two years after his return to France. He dedicated his work to the great commander:

TO BONAPARTE

To combine the lustre of your Name with the splendour of the Monuments of Egypt, is to associate the glorious annals of our own time with the history of the heroic age; and to reanimate the dust of Sesostris and Mendes, like you conquerors, like you benefactors. Europe, by learning that I accompanied you in one of your most memorable Expeditions, will receive my work with eager interest. I have neglected nothing in my power to render it worthy of the Hero to whom it is inscribed.

This was the first published account arising from Napoleon's expedition, and in no small part inspired the Commission to their ultimate goal: the great *Description de l'Égypte* published between 1809 and 1829. Denon's *Voyages* was published in numerous editions in French, as well as being translated into English and German, and so had an enormous impact on scholars across Europe. Battling illness, tripping over mummified remains and working sometimes in near total darkness with no idea of what was in front of them, Denon and his

ARTISTS, EXPEDITIONS AND NATIONALIST COMPETITION

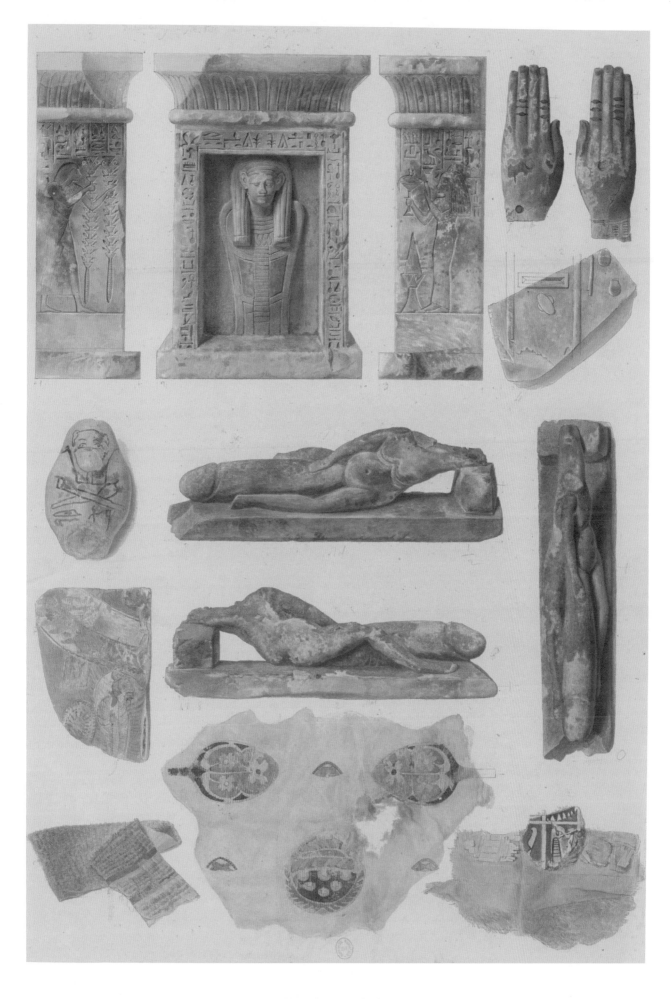

fellow savants produced staggering records. Denon himself lamented that his drawings were made most frequently 'on my knee, or standing, or even on horseback. I have never been able to finish any one of them as I could have wished, for this reason, that during the space of a whole year I could never find a table sufficiently straight and even, to be able to lay a ruler on it.' Perhaps their most enduring achievement was to document monuments that are now lost, such as the small southern temple of Amenhotep III at Elephantine. A rectangular inner chapel flanked by rows of square pillars on both sides and a row of papyrus cluster columns at the front was recorded in detail by the artists; by the time Champollion visited in 1829, it had been 'demolished in order to build barracks and warehouses for Syene'. Other buildings would survive a little longer, but nonetheless the savants' records of the Ptolemaic north temple at Esna, the temple that Cleopatra built for her son Caesarion at Armant, the town enclosure east of Dendera temple, the magnificent portico built by Alexander the Great and Philip Arrhidaeus at Hermopolis, the monuments of Hadrian at Antinoopolis and the so-called Roman tower at Alexandria remain of inestimable value for Egyptology. And yet for Denon himself, conducted through the country at the speed of the military march, there was a sense that there was so much more to see: 'I had seen a hundred things, while a thousand others had escaped me.'

← An enchanting view, painted by Edmé-François Jomard, of the larger of two temples at Qasr Qarun in the Faiyum Oasis, visited by the Commission at night. The temple was dedicated to Sobek-Ra, a hybrid of the crocodile-headed Sobek and sun-god Ra. A relief carving that may depict this deity is visible through the broken section of the pylon at a height that shows it to have been part of an upper floor, an unusual feature for an Egyptian temple.

Pascal Xavier Coste

1787–1879 French architect and explorer

Coste was the architect and designer of much of the infrastructure that lay at the heart of Mohamed Ali Pasha's modernization of Egypt in the first half of the 19th century. Although the new construction projects at times resulted in the irretrievable loss of ancient ruins, they are preserved in Coste's remarkably detailed technical drawings and maps.

↗ Coste's view of the obelisk of Senusret I at Matarea, site of ancient Heliopolis. This was an important site, as the cult centre of the sun-god Ra, but very little has survived, perhaps owing to the waning importance of the city as a centre of learning after the foundation of Alexandria and to unfavourable environmental conditions.

→ A panoramic view of the Memphite pyramid fields with the Step Pyramid of Djoser, the first stone pyramid, in the foreground. Coste was among the first to enter the Step Pyramid, it having been opened by Massara, a *dragoman* (translator) working for the French Consulate in Cairo, on 2 April 1820.

Pascal Coste was born in Marseilles, where he began his training in the studio of the architect Michel-Robert Penchaud before moving to Paris to study at the École des Beaux-Arts. There he met Edme-François Jomard, who had been a member of Napoleon's Commission of Arts and Science in Egypt and the editor of the resulting *Description de l'Égypte*. Coste owed his time in Egypt both to this connection and to the programme of modernization that had been launched by the Ottoman viceroy Mohamed Ali Pasha in 1805. Ali had a vision of an independent Egypt, ruled by its own hereditary dynasty, and launched ambitious reforms to the Egyptian economy, administration, infrastructure and military. He recruited European advisors and commissioned a series of grand buildings and factories, as well as embarking on other civic projects, such as creating canal systems to improve transport and agriculture.

Ali's reforms offered a great opportunity for wealthy foreigners to invest in this fast-developing nation. One such was M. Baffi, a French chemist who proposed the construction of a factory for the production of saltpetre, one of the principal chemical components of gunpowder – dovetailing neatly with Ali's military ambitions. Baffi set about finding the necessary personnel to undertake it, including an architect. The appeal reached Jomard, who in turn approached Coste.

Coste left Marseille on 17 October 1817 on the corvette *La Bella-Nina*, which belonged to Ali and was commanded by a Turkish captain with a crew of Turks, Greeks, Maltese and Italians. The ship arrived in Alexandria on 1 November, and Coste spent ten days there, taking the opportunity to study the ancient ruins, including Cleopatra's Needles and Pompey's Pillar. His records of these monuments demonstrate his technically minded approach; he sketched them situated in their landscape, and provided detailed descriptions and precise measurements evidently based on careful observation.

In February 1818 Baffi revealed to Coste his plan for the new development. The factory would consist of a series of basins into which impure saltpetre would be received and from which the water would then evaporate, leaving behind the purified form of the chemical. The land destined to be used for this purpose was a hamlet called Ezbet al-Ma'mal in the midst of the ruins of ancient Memphis. There is little doubt that the project accelerated the destruction of the ancient city mounds, which provided the main source of the raw material required for saltpetre production. They probably contained much valuable archaeological material that could have been salvaged, had techniques that would be invented decades later been available at the time. This development was symbolic of the threat that Mohamed Ali's modernization programme posed to the country's antiquities. The factory was completed in September 1819. Though the buildings themselves have since disappeared, the concrete floor is still visible and indeed used by the local livestock market.

ARTISTS, EXPEDITIONS AND NATIONALIST COMPETITION

1818.
Héliopolis

d'Égypte
    1819.

↑ Coste's watercolour sketch of the saltpetre factory he built at Memphis, drawn while the Nile was in flood . Although this was a major construction built less than two centuries ago – a brief moment in time by comparison with the monuments of ancient Egypt – the factory has almost completely disappeared now; only the concrete floor remains visible.

Coste produced a series of sketches of the area, along with a detailed map. These meticulous drawings are of great value in showing the situation at the site, which was changing rapidly, at that time. He visited the pyramid fields of Giza, Abusir, Saqqara and Dahshur, again taking measurements of the major monuments and compiling detailed descriptions to accompany his drawings. His plan of the Giza necropolis and section drawings of the Great Pyramid there and Step Pyramid at Saqqara are especially striking for their accuracy. At Saqqara he visited a group of 'catacombes' – evidently rock-cut tombs – and made detailed drawings of what appear to be statues of bulls hewn from the living rock itself. These tombs were lost until the 1990s, when a French mission directed by Alain Zivie rediscovered them. One of the tombs, belonging to a 19th Dynasty official named Netjerwymes, contains a stunning engaged statue of a cow, painted in glorious colours, representing the goddess Hathor who in this form was believed to dwell in the mountain, hence her depiction as a statue emerging from the rock.

After completing Baffi's project, Coste was asked by Mohamed Ali himself to build a gunpowder factory on the island of Rhoda to the south of Cairo and then a canal 75 kilometres (45 miles) long to connect Alexandria to the Rosetta branch of the Nile. This canal, still in use today, enabled cultivation to spread, freeing the city from the constraints that had hindered its growth for the preceding two centuries. In April 1820, the Pasha was afflicted by asthma and ordered by his doctor to bathe in the sea, and so asked Coste to build him a pavilion in the old harbour of Alexandria, which became the grand palace at Ras el-Tin. In May 1821 Coste undertook a voyage to Upper Egypt to inspect the works on the Sohag canal. This was a whistle-stop tour. Coste's diary records brief descriptions of the places he visited, but with precise dates and times, revealing his busy itinerary:

The 15th [of May], to Beny-Assam, where one sees the ruins of a Coptic town, and, towards the mountain, the tombs cut in the rock; afterwards, to Gebel-Cheyk-Tamaï situated on a rock in the Nile. At three o'clock, to Cheyk-Abadeh, upon the ruins of Antinoë, where one sees some columns either standing or fallen, with Corinthian bases and capitals, and a great number of fragments recumbent in the sun lying in the sand. At four o'clock to Achmouneyn, where a sugar refinery established by M. Brin, English, is found. 8 kilometres to the south are the ruins of the temple of Hermopolis-Magna where all that remains is a beautiful portico of twelve columns. Afterwards, to Malouy, a small town with four mosques and bazaars. In the evening to Gebel-Cheyk-Said, on a steep rock above the Nile, where there are some tombs cut into the rock.

All of this in a single day! Along with such brief descriptions of what he saw, Coste also made his characteristically detailed drawings.

In September 1827 Coste's time in Egypt was brought to a sudden conclusion: 'I was stung in the heel by a big yellowish scorpion, in my Cairo apartment. The sharp pain rose to the joints and settled on the liver. Dr. Dussap immediately made an incision in my heel where a very dark blood came out, which did not prevent the venom from spreading. The next day, in the morning, I was suffering from vomiting and was forced to go to bed. The pains diminished only after the application of numerous poultices of linseed, which finally calmed the irritation.' The head of the army's medical school in Cairo, Dr Antoine Clot (later Clot Bey), recommended that Coste leave Egypt for good, suggesting he would not survive if he stayed.

Coste published his map of Lower Egypt, dedicated to Mohamed Ali Pasha, in 1829, and his survey of the Islamic monuments of Cairo, *Architecture Arabe: ou Monuments du Kaire, mesurés et dessinés, de 1818 à 1825*, in 1837. But the majority of the drawings and notes he made in Egypt remained unpublished until the appearance, in 1878, of *Les Mémoires d'un artiste: Notes et souvenirs de voyage (1817–1877)*. His archive is enormous, comprising 4,577 documents, left to the Public Library of Marseilles. Most are drawings in pencil and ink, but there are also watercolours,

↓ Pair statue of a non-royal couple in limestone dating to the late 18th or early 19th Dynasty. Discovered at Saqqara in May 1822, according to Coste's note, the statue represents a man called Seba and his wife Werethener, and is now in the State Museum of Egyptian Art in Munich.

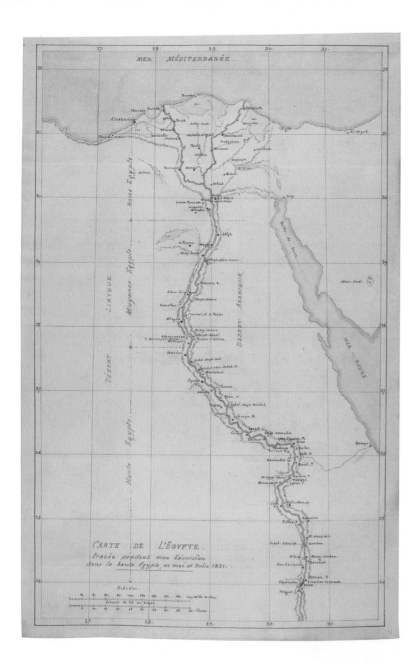

Coste's map of Egypt, 'traced during my excursion to Upper Egypt in May and June 1821'. Coste's employment as one of Mohamed Ali Pasha's foremost engineers demanded that he understand the geography of the country completely, in particular the course of the river. Coste's interest was primarily in contemporary, rather than ancient, Egypt, and his inclusion of the names of so many towns and villages, all of which any traveller venturing up the Nile would encounter, is especially helpful – descriptions of such journeys are relatively common, accurate maps less so.

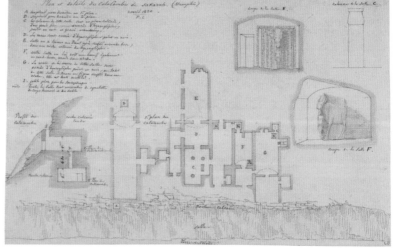

→ Coste's accurate plan and sample section of the catacombs at Saqqara in which, in two instances, he came across the striking sight of an engaged statue of a cow goddess, apparently emerging from the living rock. These tombs were lost after Coste's time and only rediscovered in the 1990s.

↑ 'Voyage to Egypt aboard the *corvette Bella Nina* belonging to the Pasha'. Coste departed from Marseille on 18 October 1817. The figure at far left of this drawing, seen sketching, is thought to be Coste himself.

manuscripts and photographs. Five volumes in the series 'Monuments de l'Afrique septentrionale' relate to Lower Egypt and only one to his voyage to Upper Egypt in 1821, an unusual balance explained by Coste having done most of the work for his employer in that region, while the interests of most of the other individuals represented in this book drew them more strongly to the Nile Valley.

In a curious side-note, Coste had sold some of his drawings to Robert Hay (see pp. 88–97), along with the right to publish them. The agreement required Hay to do so by 1830, but he was delayed by not initially having also acquired Coste's notes and by a breakdown in relations with his chosen engraver; eventually the agreement lapsed. Coste had kept copies, however, and some of them at least saw the light of day when they were included in his memoirs.

Through Coste's contributions to the modernization project, he perhaps had a greater impact on the country than any other individual in this book. Important, and even inevitable, though the industrialization of the country was, it is difficult to avoid the notion that Coste's work contributed to the rapid destruction of the remains of Egypt's ancient past, directly in the overbuilding on sites such as that of ancient Memphis – even if Coste was unaware of it – and indirectly in facilitating urban and agricultural expansion in many other parts of the country. The detailed and accurate records he left behind are thus of immense value for what they capture of Egypt at a time of rapid transition, the more so as Coste was as much interested in the modern landscape and buildings as the ancient, an unusual perspective for one who nonetheless can be considered an Egyptologist.

Frédéric Cailliaud

1787–1869 French traveller and mineralogist

Cailliaud worked for the French consul-general in Egypt at a time of intense competition between British and French interests in the country. In the search for antiquities he explored new territories in the deserts either side of the Nile and as far south as the frontier with Ethiopia, and was the first to correctly identify the site of ancient Meroë, the capital of the Nubian kingdom of Kush.

→ Drawing of a scene of Anubis tending to a mummy, whose spirit hovers above in the form of the *ba* bird. Cailliaud subsequently reworked this illustration with a view to publishing it, removing much of the detail that would become invisible when the image was reduced to fit along with several others on a single plate.

Frédéric Cailliaud was born in Nantes. He followed his brother into the jewelry-making profession, and his interest in precious stones led him first to Paris to study mineralogy, and then to tour Europe, observing the different traditions of gem-cutting. In 1813 he arrived in Rome, then travelled to Campania and Sicily, but following the collapse of Napoleon's empire the French withdrew from Italy, and Cailliaud himself moved on to Greece, Istanbul and finally, in 1815, to Egypt.

Upon his arrival in Alexandria Cailliaud met the French consul-general, Bernardino Drovetti, and was recruited into his network of scholars and explorers. In 1816 he embarked on a six-month journey with Drovetti to Wadi Halfa in Nubia, where they tried, unsuccessfully, to open the great temple at Abu Simbel. Drovetti introduced Cailliaud to Mohamed Ali Pasha, who appointed him the government's mineralogist and charged him with finding the lost emerald mines of the Eastern Desert, which had been exploited in particular during the Ptolemaic period. He travelled upstream, this time as far as the island of Philae, further familiarizing himself with the ancient monuments he had first visited with Drovetti. On Philae he copied the Greek inscriptions on the base of the obelisk that Giovanni Battista Belzoni (see pp. 136–43) would remove years later on behalf of the British consul-general Henry Salt and William John Bankes (pp. 68–73). Cailliaud then sailed northwards as far as Edfu before heading eastwards into the desert.

As we read of Cailliaud's travels through these unexplored regions we gain a vivid sense of the excitement that was conjured by the discovery of a previously unknown ruin. His delight at being the first person to visit a small, rock-cut chapel of Sety I at Kanais is palpable: 'A spectacle so unexpected I hailed with sentiments of joy; I might, perhaps, light on some fresh discovery, some work of those ancient Egyptians, whose indefatigable industry extended even into the desarts .... All the walls of this temple are covered with hieroglyphics, hollowed and sculptured in relief, and in fine preservation; the colours with which they are garnished yet retain an astonishing freshness.' But such moments of joy were accompanied, too, by discomforts and even the threat of disaster in the vast desert: 'After seven hours march, we encamped at the foot of a mountain .... During the night, we sustained a loss that might have deranged our plan, or, at least, have laid us under great difficulties. Three of our dromedaries were missing; the drivers did not perceive it till day-break, but following their tracks in the sand, they overtook them, at some distance, in the desert. These animals have a piercing sight, and as soon as the sack, holding their dourah, or food, was shewn them, they voluntarily returned.'

The mission proceeded towards the Red Sea until, at last, Cailliaud found what he had been seeking: 'As I was sitting on some pieces of rock, my eye suddenly glanced on a fragment of emerald, of a dark green. My surprise and joy made me forget all fatigue, and impatient to enter the gallery, I frequently encouraged the Ababdeh, and began

Pl. CXXXIV.

M.C

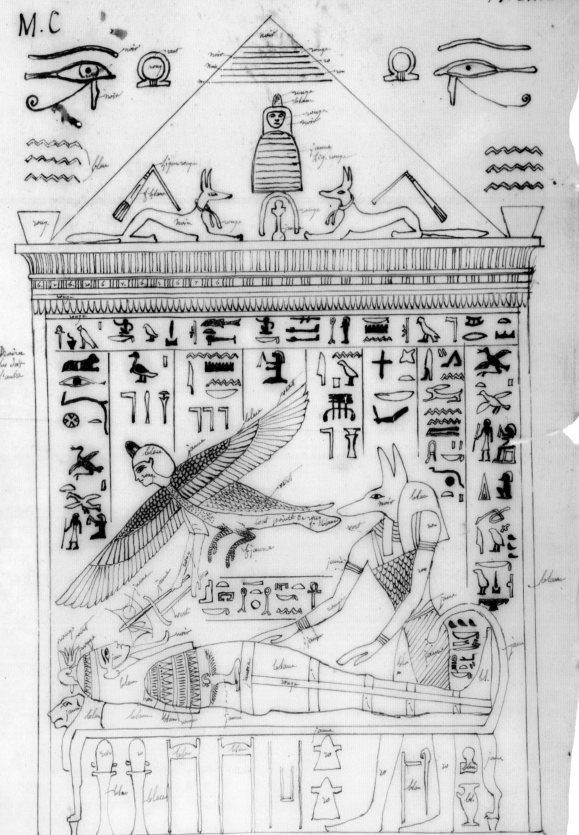

↑ Drawings prepared for Cailliaud's *Arts and Crafts*, showing three stages in the production of the final illustration, at right. The image shows a queen from a tomb in Thebes.

to labour with them; it was not long ere we all entered into the mine.' In his investigations of the emerald mine he reports perilous, unseen shafts, reluctant labourers, long periods with insufficient food and water and, ultimately, disappointment. Between November 1816 and March 1818 he organized three expeditions to reopen the mine, but they yielded only a very small quantity of emeralds – enough to persuade the viceroy that Cailliaud had located the Ptolemies' source, but not enough to convince him to recommence mining activities.

During his expeditions Cailliaud took the opportunity to spend time in Thebes, collecting antiquities for Drovetti and making drawings in the tombs, in and among which he made his home, as the locals did. His admiration of the ancient tombs was heartfelt; of one, he wrote that 'After traversing ... ten or twelve chambers, my astonishment was extreme, nor can any one, I think, Conceive the very profound impressions which a place like this will leave on the mind.' Although Cailliaud had was unable to read the hieroglyphic signs on tomb walls, his copies were very accurate and of great use to Jean-François Champollion (pp. 98–103). In some instances, they are also among the only records of tombs that have subsequently been lost, including that of the overseer of the granary, Neferhotep, which probably lay in the Dra Abu el-Naga area. It featured various scenes of the deceased and his family, including one showing them fishing and fowling. The location of a part of the latter scene *is* known: Cailliaud removed it from the wall of the tomb for his own collection of antiquities, and it is now in

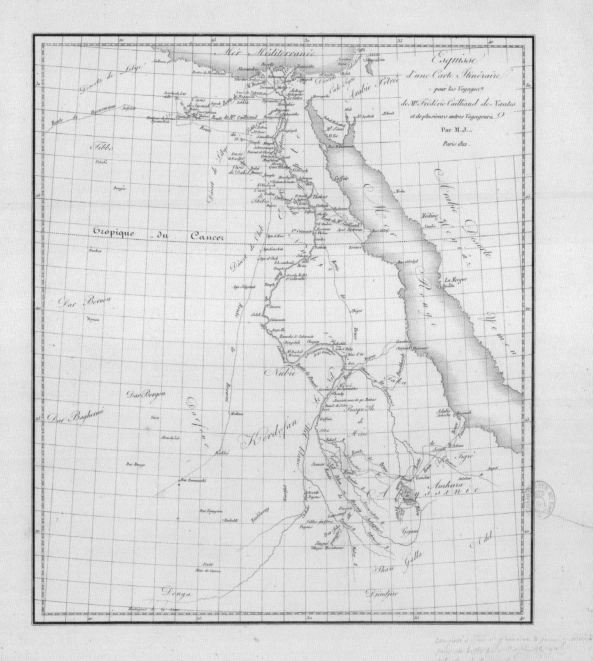

↑ Cailliaud's map of the places in the Nile Valley that he visited during his travels. It includes his routes across the Western Desert to the oases of Siwa in the north and those 'of Thebes', including Farafra, Dakhla and Kharga. More importantly, perhaps, it also provides a record of his travels to the south along the river in Sudan, passing through Gebel Barkal and Meroë ('80 Pyramides'), then on to the confluence of the Blue and White Niles, the kingdom of Sennar and beyond.

the Louvre in Paris. This was a great outrage to Giovanni d'Athanasi, who had recently opened the tomb on behalf of Henry Salt, and who had shared news of the tomb's existence with Cailliaud and allowed him to enter to make copies of the scenes. He was scandalized to find that Cailliaud had stolen a section of the wall: 'I was almost out of my senses on learning the ungenerous manner in which this gentleman had requited me of my civility; But out of pure pity I forgave him. It is almost inconceivable how he could have brought himself to publish anything relating to facts which do him so much discredit.'

Despite the tone of d'Athanasi's report, such activities were not uncommon at this time, and he was himself responsible for the removal of some of the most celebrated paintings to have survived from ancient Egypt: those of Nebamun. These are on display in the British Museum, and the tomb from which d'Athanasi took them is also now lost. His displeasure at Cailliaud's activities was perhaps related to the competition between the British and French consul-generals and their agents. Cailliaud met Henry Salt in the Valley of the Kings not long after Belzoni's discovery of the tomb of Sety I in 1817. Cailliaud made his own description of the tomb and the sarcophagus, which Belzoni had yet to remove. Cailliaud and fellow French agent Jean-Jacques Rifaud (pp. 144–49) had earlier warned Belzoni against trying to move the younger statue, only to find that the giant Paduan accomplished the task with the minimum of fuss. The year before, Belzoni had stopped at Philae and reserved some sixteen decorated blocks for Salt. By the time of his second voyage, he found that the words 'operation manquée' had been written on the blocks, evidently by one of the French agents operating in the area – who Belzoni eventually concluded was Cailliaud.

↓ Detailed notes on various gods and goddesses, including Ptah, Thoth and Sobek. Cailliaud made rough sketches of the ways in which each was depicted as well as their various accoutrements – staffs, fans, crowns and other symbols.

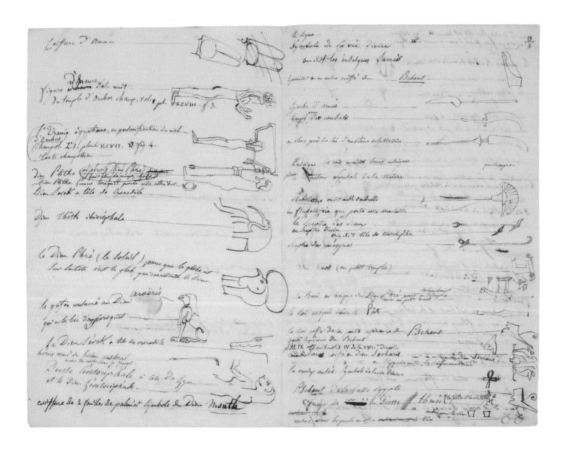

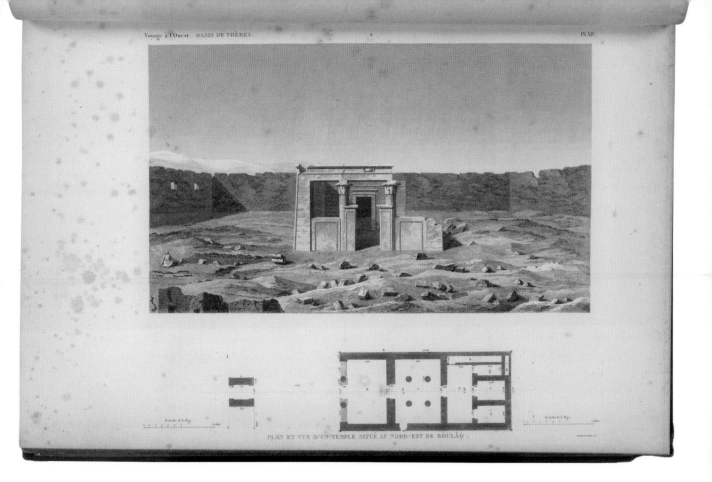

PLAN ET VUE D'UN TEMPLE SITUÉ AU NORD-EST DE BOULÂQ.

↑ Cailliaud's view and plan of the temple of Ghueita. The small temple lies within a magnificent walled fortress on top of a small hill, a few kilometres to the south of Kharga, one of the Western Desert oases. The earliest part of the temple dates to the reign of Darius I of the 27th Dynasty; the *pronaos* visible in Cailliaud's drawing and the columned hall beyond were built by Ptolemy III.

Cailliaud returned to Paris in February 1819. The Commission d'Égypte saw Cailliaud's work as a continuation of the Napoleonic expedition, and purchased his manuscript and collection of antiquities. His old friend and colleague Edme-François Jomard, editor of the *Description de l'Égypte*, was charged with publishing Cailliaud's account of his travels. The government sent Cailliaud back to Egypt, in particular to unexplored territories in the Western Desert and to the south of Egypt, to survey monuments, collect antiquities and map the terrain. He was assigned a midshipman named Pierre-Constant Letorzec, and together they set out for Egypt, arriving in Alexandria in October 1819.

Cailliaud and Letorzec's opportunity to explore Nubia was to present itself in March 1820. While in Cairo they learned that Mohamed Ali planned to send his army, under the command of his son Ismail, to Dongola to conquer and enslave the peoples of that region. Cailliaud asked Drovetti present him to Ismail, who agreed that he could travel under the protection of the Egyptian army. Few European travellers had ventured this far: Ismail's goal was the city of Sennar, some 300 kilometres (185 miles) beyond the point of the confluence of the Blue and the White Nile. One of the great, unclaimed prizes Cailliaud must have had in mind for himself was the identification of the ancient city of Meroë, described by Herodotus as 'the capital of all Ethiopia'.

In this desire Cailliaud was not alone, however. He found himself the victim of a conspiracy perpetrated by a group of Italians who claimed, falsely, that he was not in possession of genuine permits, so that they might pursue Meroë without competition. The schemers were thwarted

↑ Cailliaud's view of the northern group of pyramids at Meroë. Cailliaud correctly identified the pyramids as belonging to the ancient capital of the kingdom of Kush, a momentous discovery.

when Mohamed Ali confirmed the legitimacy of Cailliaud's papers, but by this time Cailliaud and Letorzec had fallen behind Ismail's army. This proved advantageous in some ways, however, as it meant that Cailliaud was free to study the monuments he came across on his journey south at his own pace. In accordance with the Commission's wishes, he made sketches of the ancient monuments at Semna, Kumma, Sai island, Sedeinga, Soleb, Sesebi, Kerma and Argo.

On 9 February 1821 they caught up with Ismail at Gebel Barkal. Cailliaud's rivals welcomed him, owing, Cailliaud believed, to their belief that they had triumphed. Their claim did not convince Cailliaud: 'Greeks and other Europeans ... to whom I was indebted for the fatigues and expenses of the journey of five hundred leagues which I had just lost, hastened to compliment me on my happy return; all offered me their good offices to the prince, and sought to show a satisfaction they were far from feeling. Moreover, they thought they had arrived at their ends. These ruins of Barkal, in their opinion, were incontestably those of the ancient Meroe ... but was this triumph really real? None had taken either measurements or drawings of these monuments; no astronomical observation had been made by them; their greatest work had been to truncate a few hieroglyphics to attach their names to them.'

On 12 April the news was brought that the province had surrendered. Cailliaud could now prospect for the gold and diamonds they hoped to find in the newly acquired territory. Ismail recommended that for this campaign the Europeans adopt Turkish dress and take on new names: Cailliaud would now be known as Murad Effendi and

Letorzec as Abdallah al-Faqir. They crossed the Bayuda Desert with the army for speed, rejoining the Nile at al-Baqir. It was here that, based on his calculations, Cailliaud believed they had arrived in the ancient territory of Meroë, and yet he saw no sign of what he was looking for: 'While the camels were being loaded, I thought in silence, undecided on the road I was to take. I ascended the elevated ground from which the view embraced immense plains, and I sought on all points of the horizon some remains of Meroe, some place where I could engage with the slightest glimmer of light. Hope: my eyes were tired in vain. This Meroe, I thought, has left no trace of her power and splendor? His temples, his pyramids, his monuments raised for posterity, his houses, everything has been reduced to dust like the men who lived in it?'

They stopped at the village of Saqadi where, as usual, their presence caused some consternation, discouraging Cailliaud from enquiring about ancient remains nearby. Reluctantly, he concluded that he was chasing a ghost, but awoke in the middle of the night unable to dismiss the possibility that Meroë lay only a few miles away. He set off at three o'clock in the morning to explore: 'Let's imagine the joy I experienced on discovering the summits of a crowd of pyramids, whose rays of the sun, still low on the horizon, gilded majestically the peaks! Never, never had a happier day had him for me! ... I pressed my camel; I would have liked him to cross the three leagues which still separated me from the ruins of the ancient capital of Ethiopia with rapidity. Finally, I arrived there: my first care was to climb an eminence, to embrace at a glance all the pyramids. I remained motionless with pleasure and admiration at the sight of this imposing spectacle.' Cailliaud's case was certainly much stronger than that of his rivals, who believed they had found Meroë at Gebel Barkal; the location of his ruins fit better with that given in the classical accounts. In any case, he had found something spectacular, and spent fifteen days there making drawings.

Cailliaud continued on with the army, studying the customs and practices of the locals and prospecting for gold. He did not, however, find reserves to satisfy the viceroy's wishes. Ismail Pasha sent him back with the gold they had managed to collect and to ask the viceroy to end the mission. This proved a fortunate turn of events for Cailliaud: when the army was recalled, the expedition stopped in Shendi and was ambushed by the former king of the region, Nimir, who had surrendered to them. Many of Ismail's men were killed as Nimir's rebels surrounded them during a banquet and set fire to their tents.

Cailiaud returned to France in 1822 and was awarded the Légion d'honneur in 1824. In the same year part of his collection of 500 objects was acquired by the Bibliothèque Nationale, and in 1826 he became curator at the Museum of Natural History in Nantes to which, along with the Archaeological Museum in the city, he left the remainder of his collection. He published several accounts of his travels, and intended to publish a synthesis of the remains of the ancient cultures he had seen but, while the plates appeared in a limited edition (most of the copies of which were lost when the building they were kept in collapsed), the text never appeared during his lifetime. Cailliaud's manuscript was rediscovered in 2005 and a new edition published by a team of scholars led by Dr Andrew Bednarski, finally doing justice to the work of one of Egyptology's great pioneers.

William John Bankes

1786–1855 British traveller, collector and antiquarian

Bankes visited Egypt as part of his Grand Tour of European and Eastern countries and quickly fell in with the British contingent involved with exploring and recording sites and monuments. A talented artist himself, he also enlisted the help of others who made some of the finest records of what he encountered.

→ A sketch of the Great Hall of the temple of Ramesses II at Abu Simbel, made early in 1819 by either Henry William Beechey or Louis Linant de Bellefonds. Bankes's expedition, his second journey up the Nile, made a prolonged stop at the temple, which Belzoni had opened eighteen months previously.

William Bankes was the eldest surviving son of Henry Bankes, a Member of Parliament for Kingston Lacy and Corfe Castle in Dorset. William was educated at the public Harrow School for boys before taking a place at the University of Cambridge. After serving as a Member of Parliament for Truro between 1810 and 1812, he embarked on a Grand Tour in the vein of many of his friends, including Lord Byron. He had a taste for adventure: he first visited Spain at the time of the Peninsular War, where he attached himself directly to the duke of Wellington's camp, before travelling on to Alexandria.

Bankes intended to make the classic journey up the Nile, but rather than wasting time in Cairo while his boat was prepared – as was the norm – he travelled overland to Sinai. There he visited the ancient turquoise mine at Serabit el-Khadim, and copied inscriptions in the temple of Hathor – an early sign that he had been gripped by the desire to document the ancient monuments he saw. By 16 September 1815 he was ready to set off on a trip that would last three months. He was accompanied by Giovanni Finati, an Italian traveller who acted as his *dragoman* (interpreter) and would join him for most of his travels throughout Egypt and the Near East over the following four years. Bankes would later repay the favour by translating Finati's memoirs, published as *Narrative of the Life and Adventures of Giovanni Finati* in 1830. This offers some of the best insights into Bankes's own travels.

On this trip Bankes reached as far south as Wadi Halfa in the region of the Second Cataract and visited Abu Simbel, which had been noted for the first time by a European, Jean-Louis Burckhardt, only a short time before. Bankes had met Burckhardt in Cairo, and received from him much good advice, including the recommendation that he should adopt the dress of the country. On his return journey Bankes stopped at Philae, where he found much to excite him, including an obelisk that he planned to remove to his home in England.

After this first adventure on the Nile, Bankes toured Eastern Europe, but he harboured a desire to return to Egypt, perhaps inspired by Belzoni's opening of the temple of Abu Simbel in the summer of 1817 and discovery just a few months later of the tomb of Sety I, one of the finest in the Valley of the Kings (pp. 140–43). Bankes arrived in Cairo in the autumn of 1818 and soon met Henry Salt, the British consul-general. Salt had trained as an artist and, having taken an interest in the decipherment of hieroglyphs, had begun to make copies of inscriptions. He was highly critical of the copies of texts published in the Napoleonic Commission's *Description de l'Égypte*, and saw an opportunity to improve on them. He and Bankes agreed to ascend the Nile together, penetrating further into Nubia than Bankes had managed previously, and this time the party was augmented by three additional artists: the Frenchman Louis Maurice Adolphe Linant de Bellefonds and two members of Belzoni's party, the physician Alessandro Ricci, who had been asked by the Italian giant to make copies of the decoration in the

ARTISTS, EXPEDITIONS AND NATIONALIST COMPETITION

↑ Although Belzoni had removed enough sand to allow the first entry into the temple in modern times, huge amounts still encumbered the rock-cut façade. Bankes's team freed up the colossus immediately to the south (left) of the doorway, uncovering an inscription left by a Greek mercenary, just below the statue's knee, showing that it was already buried to that height by the early 6th century BCE. This drawing was made by Beechey while the excavations were in progress.

tomb of Sety I, and Salt's secretary, Henry William Beechey, who had worked with Belzoni at Abu Simbel and in Thebes. The expedition artists generated vast quantities of drawings, a sense of competitiveness spurring them on; Salt wrote that they 'really vied with each other who should produce the best sketches, being generally occupied hard at it ... from nine o'clock in the morning till dark'. Belzoni himself joined them to expedite the removal of Bankes's obelisk from Philae.

Bankes's claim to the obelisk rested on 'the generosity' of Henry Salt, whose *firman* (permit) allowed its removal. According to Belzoni's account, he had originally laid claim to it on Salt's behalf, but Salt ceded it to Bankes. The expedition arrived to find that a counter-claim had been lodged by Salt's arch-rival, the French consul-general, Bernardino Drovetti, but Belzoni eventually prevailed. Unfortunately the pier from which the obelisk was to be loaded onto a boat collapsed, and Belzoni could only watch as the obelisk 'majestically' slid into the Nile. Finati recalled that Bankes was less impressed: 'Mr Bankes said little, but was evidently disgusted by the incident.' Nonetheless, the obelisk was retrieved from the water and was eventually erected at Bankes's family home in Kingston Lacy, Dorset, where it remains to this day.

The expedition made one of its longest stops at Abu Simbel. Despite having financed Belzoni's triumphant entry into the temple, Salt had never seen the site, and must have been amazed by its scale and grandeur. The party spent much time in freeing one of the colossal statues that adorn the front of the temple from the sand. They spent the greater part of their stop, however, in copying the finest of the inscriptions within. Finati recalled how the gloomy interior was 'lighted with from twenty to fifty small wax candles, fixed upon clusters of palm branches, which were attached to long upright poles, and spreading more than halfway to the ceiling', so as to enable the artists to work, 'even as they stood, almost naked, upon their ladders'.

Just before the expedition had set out from Cairo, Bankes had received a letter from Thomas Young, who was leading the British effort to decipher Egyptian hieroglyphs. Young had asked him to concentrate on copying the names of kings and gods, and explained how to identify them. At Abu Simbel, Bankes would find countless examples, including, importantly, the name of a king 'Psamettichus' halfway up the leg of one of the colossi. Bankes knew that kings of this name had ruled during the 26th Dynasty. He also realized that the name stood at such a height that it could only have been carved when the colossus was already half-buried. He reasoned that the statue must therefore have been created considerably earlier than the 26th Dynasty. He was right: an important deduction in reconstructing the history of the temple.

To this, and the Philae obelisk, Bankes added a third inscription that would play a significant role in the development of Egyptology. On his return journey, he discovered a king list decorating the walls of the temple of Ramesses II at Abydos. Bankes realized what he was looking at – a list of the names of Egypt's kings in sequence – and that it could furnish not only vital information on the history and chronology of Egypt, but also new material for use in the race to decipher hieroglyphs. He had no intention of removing it, instead making a careful copy. Tragically, the original was carelessly hacked out ten years later by the French consul-general Jean-François Mimaut, who took it for his private collection in France. After Mimaut's death in 1839 the king list was sold and entered the collection of the British Museum.

Following this expedition Bankes returned to England and would never again set foot in Egypt. However, he maintained his interest in Egyptology, even commissioning a third expedition, although he would not participate himself. He engaged Linant and Ricci to go even further south than they had reached on their great trip to look for Meroë. But Linant delayed, giving Frédéric Cailliaud (pp. 60–67), who was travelling in that region with the Egyptian army, the chance to scoop the discovery, to Bankes's displeasure. Nonetheless, the expedition eventually departed in the summer of 1821. On the upstream journey they copied the paintings from the tomb of Nebamun, which were in d'Athanasi's house awaiting transport to the British Museum. They also spent a few days between Elephantine and Aswan working on the chapels of Amenhotep III and Ramesses II; their records of these monuments have proven especially valuable as both were demolished the following year. On 5 September they reached Mograkka, the limit of the unfortunate journey taken two years earlier with Bankes, where in March 1819 their guides had fled, taking all the expedition's camels

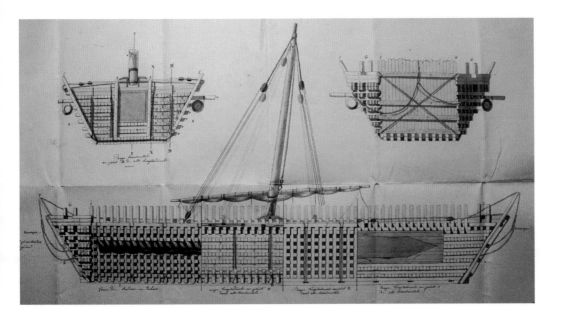

↑ Linant de Bellefonds's sophisticated technical drawings of the boat built to transport Bankes's obelisk from Alexandria to England.

with them, and the son of the local kashif had refused to let them go any further. This time Linant and Ricci went on to visit Kerma and New Dongola and passed the island of Nawi, where, according to the boat crew, the locals turned into crocodiles overnight.

Ricci and Linant eventually parted ways, and Linant visited Meroë, making drawings of the pyramids and even identifying the remains of the great temple of the nearby city. But he failed to recognize the ruins' importance, believing that the more impressive remains at Musawwarat were those of Meroë. Though he was mistaken, Musawwarat is nonetheless an extremely striking site, with its jumble of ramps and statues of elephants appearing out of nowhere in the most beautiful red desert, and Linant did archaeology a great service in his five days making drawings as the first European visitor at the site. There was something of a sense of nationalist triumph to this, as a graffito left by Linant mentioning his English associations demonstrates. Cailliaud, his French rival, visited a month later and left his own graffito in retaliation, a sure sign that Linant had claimed something of a prize.

Bankes waited anxiously for several years before finally receiving the drawings made by Linant, with which he was extremely pleased, though they were overshadowed by the publication of Cailliaud's own account of his *Voyage à Méroé*. After his father's death in 1834 Bankes restored his family home at Kingston Lacy. But the last years of his life were beset by scandal: he was charged twice with meeting a member of the same sex for 'unnatural purposes'. Following the second incident Bankes made arrangements for his house to be entrusted to others in the event that it might be forfeit in punishment of his crimes. In September 1841 he escaped conviction by fleeing the country, and remained in Europe for the rest of his life. He maintained an interest in antiquities and frequently sent acquisitions to Kingston Lacy, with instructions mostly dispatched from overseas but occasionally delivered in person during clandestine visits. He died in 1855, but his home and his collection, in particular the Philae obelisk, remain a fitting tribute to the legacy he left Egyptology.

← A top-hatted gentleman gazes up at the Philae obelisk, giving us a sense both of its size and of the awe it inspired – and continues to inspire – in visitors to Bankes's home at Kingston Lacy.

James Burton

1788–1862 British Egyptologist and traveller

Burton travelled to Egypt to take up a post as surveyor of the Eastern Desert for Mohamed Ali Pasha's government. While his missions in the desert were fruitless, during his time in Egypt he fell in with the leading British Egyptologists in the country and developed a keen interest in the ancient monuments. On his own travels he made important contributions to Egyptology through his work in the Valley of the Kings and his particularly fine copies of hieroglyphic inscriptions, published in four instalments as a valuable resource in the race to decipher the script.

→ An arresting painting by Burton of a scene from the tomb of Sety I (KV 17), known as 'Belzoni's Tomb'. The king (second from right), chaperoned by falcon-headed Horus, approaches Osiris (seated) and Hathor. Though the sketch is unfinished, Bankes clearly spent much time capturing the intricate details in all their technicolour glory.

James Burton was born in London and studied mathematics at Trinity College, Cambridge, completing his bachelor's degree in 1810. Burton had not excelled in his studies, and his father took him for an interview with a Captain Bush with a view to his entering the navy, but Burton was put off and instead took a job in the office of a London solicitor. This, too, failed to hold Burton's attention; but while his father might have despaired, Burton was fortunate to have the encouragement of a family friend, George Bellas Greenough, one of the founders of London's Geological Society. Greenough found Burton a position as assistant to Sir Humphrey Davy, a chemist who was at that time employed in Naples, testing new techniques to unroll ancient papyrus scrolls without damaging the delicate material. When he arrived in Italy, however, Burton found there was no job for him, as Davy had already recruited two assistants. He decided nevertheless to wait for Greenough, who was himself due to visit Naples, and stayed in the country for three years. Thanks to his connections, Burton was now mixing with other learned men on their travels, and in 1821 he and Greenough met John Gardner Wilkinson (pp. 110–19) and heard of his intention to visit Egypt, which fired Burton's imagination. Knowing of Burton's new-found ambition to travel, Greenough secured him a position as a mineralogist in Mohamed Ali's government. In preparation for the role, Burton took Arabic classes with Wilkinson and grew a moustache so as to fit in with the locals.

On 18 March Burton left Italy for Alexandria, arriving on 8 April 1822. Soon after reaching his destination he met the viceroy and set off on his first mission, to survey the Eastern Desert in search of coal. This ended without success, however, and Burton returned to Cairo. Greenough, suspecting that Burton was not up to the job, sent him an assistant, Charles Sheffield, who arrived in the company of a chemist, James Thornton. In 1823, Burton and his companions travelled back to the Eastern Desert with Wilkinson as part of a caravan of eighty-six camels. This expedition had more success: Burton located Mons Porphyrites, the source of porphyry, a fine red stone that the Romans were especially fond of using for sculpture. Again, however, they found no coal, and never would – it was a Frenchman who did, twenty years later. Burton decided to leave the Pasha's employ and, perhaps inspired by his conversations with Wilkinson, to devote himself to Egyptology (although Greenough's account suggests the Pasha had already come to the conclusion that Burton was not the capable man he needed heading the surveys).

At around this time Burton met William Thomson, a British soldier and adventurer better known in Egypt as Osman Effendi ('Effendi' is a Turkish title of respect, usually accorded to men of learned professions). Thomson helped Burton to buy the kind of clothes that would help him blend in among the Turks. Burton also took to smoking a long pipe, to complete the look. While in Cairo he met Robert Hay (pp. 88–97), who wrote of him: 'He is a pleasant and well educated man and takes great

Delgonel Tomb

pains to dress well in the costume of the country, and wears a most magnificent shawl turban. His face is rather thin, his nose aquiline and on the whole he makes a very good Turk, wears no beard, only mustaches.' Thomson also helped him with something that seems shocking now but was entirely ordinary among young, European (predominantly male) travellers in Burton's time: the purchase of slave girls. Several of Burton's peers also acquired female companions in this way, with varying degrees of enthusiasm and moral ambivalence. Burton, Hay and Edward William Lane (pp. 82–87) would eventually marry girls they acquired. But against a backdrop of increasing opposition against slavery during the 19th century the practice quickly disappeared.

In January 1825 Burton set off up the Nile to Luxor. Here he cleared sand from the monuments at Medinet Habu, Karnak and several tombs in the Valley of the Kings, one of which, thanks to excavations a century and a half later, would make his name.

Burton's intention was to compile information about the known tombs in the Valley and to create a map of their whereabouts. On 12 June 1825 he set up camp in the splendidly decorated tomb of Ramesses VI (KV 9), right in the centre of the valley. Slightly fewer than thirty tombs were known at this point, but Burton's notes make it clear that he was aware that the classical authors Diodorus Siculus and Strabo believed that there had once been as many as forty-seven. It was still less than a decade since Giovanni Battista Belzoni (pp. 136–43) had discovered the tomb that was now commonly given his name, along with several others, and Burton was perhaps inspired by the possibility of finding more. He gave each of the known tombs a letter of the alphabet, starting at the end of the valley where the late 19th and early 20th Dynasty tombs of Sety II ('catacomb B'), Tausret ('C') and the high official Bay ('D') are clustered. In cataloguing the tombs, he made dozens of sketches of their architecture and decoration, and undertook a little clearance and excavation work. He attempted to clear the entrance to the tomb he dubbed 'catacomb M', whose doorway was almost completely blocked. With the help of a team of local men, a tiny tunnel, just 20 centimetres (8 inches) high and 50 centimetres (20 inches) wide, was cut into the rock, allowing Burton access to three chambers on the main axis and to note the presence of several more. The tomb was choked with debris almost to the ceiling; Burton was unable to tell if the walls were decorated, and could not hope to measure the dimensions of the chambers with any great degree of accuracy. Nevertheless, it was clear that the tomb was very impressive, the largest room being filled with sixteen square-based pillars in four rows of four. Burton's sketch plan is nothing more than that; next to it he drew the cartouche of

↓ A *firman* (permit) provided to Burton by Mohamed Ali Pasha allowing him to travel through Egypt. The text is written in the Arabic script, but contains a mixture of Arabic and Turkish languages – the latter being the language of the Ottoman administration. Such permits were issued to all foreigners wishing to travel and work in the country.

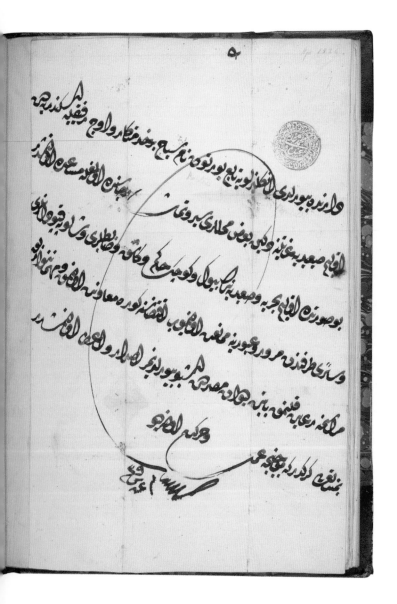

ARTISTS, EXPEDITIONS AND NATIONALIST COMPETITION

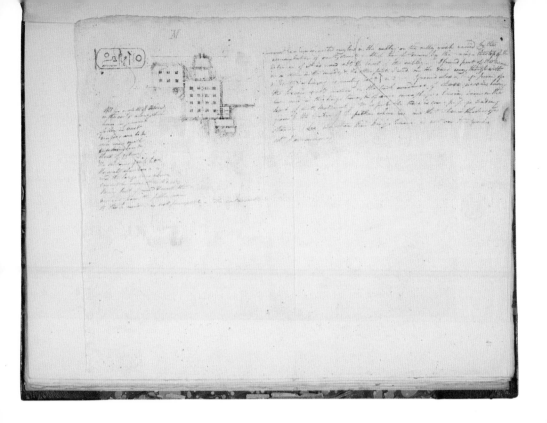

↑ A sketch of 'catacomb M', one of very few records of KV 5 until it was rediscovered in the 1980s. Recent excavations have shown it be much larger than shown here – in fact the largest tomb in the Valley of the Kings.

Ramesses II, which provided a clue as to the structure's date, but that king's own tomb had already been identified.

Although the tomb was later visited by Lane and Howard Carter (pp. 202–11), it was subsequently lost beneath debris and not relocated until the 1980s. With access to better technology, the American excavator Kent Weeks was able to penetrate further than any previous archaeologist, revealing the tomb to have been the largest ever built in Egypt. It seems to have been a mausoleum constructed for the sons of Ramesses II, hence the presence of that king's name. It is known today simply as KV 5. Though much larger and more complicated than anyone had suspected prior to Weeks's excavations – the tomb is now known to contain at least 130 separate chambers, with excavations ongoing – Burton's sketch plan has been shown to be remarkably accurate given the extremely difficult circumstances under which he was working. And although he had failed in his mission to discover coal in the Eastern Desert, he seems to have been able to bring some geological knowledge to bear in his investigation of KV 5, deducing that 'The catacomb must have been excavated very low in the valley or the valley much raised by the accumulation of earth, stones and rubbish brought down by the rains. I found a large piece of breccia verdántico, evidence of those quarries having been used in this king's time and of some sarcophagus having been in the tomb of this material.'

Following his sojourn in Luxor, Burton continued his journey upstream to Kom Ombo, Aswan, Philae and Abu Simbel, sketching throughout. Of all his drawings, those to which he paid perhaps most careful attention were of the hieroglyphic inscriptions he encountered, in preparation for his first – and, as it would turn out, last – substantial publication, the *Excerpta Hieroglyphica*. Consisting of sixty-four plates of facsimiles of tomb and temple decoration, the publication

Thebes

was intended to provide material to aid the efforts of those involved in the decipherment of hieroglyphs. It was published in four instalments between 1825 and 1828.

Burton's contribution to the decipherment did not end there. For a number of years he had been interested in locating a stone that, like the Rosetta Stone, bore a trilingual inscription. It had been reported by a British colonel named Leake at around the time of Napoleon's invasion. When the existence of the stone came to the attention of the British government, instructions were sent to the consul-general, Henry Salt, to locate it and transport it to England. Burton had been looking for it since 1822, but it was not until 1826 that he found it – or something like it; Greenough expressed doubt as to whether or not it was the same stone that Leake had seen – embedded in the wall of a mosque. Salt was authorized to do what he could to have it removed, and approached the Viceroy, Mohamed Ali, who agreed to let the British take it: 'I can refuse nothing to so dear a friend, so consider the stone yours.'

The Egyptian government seems then to have had a change of heart, declaring that the stone could not be removed from a place of worship. Burton took this to mean that the French, led by Bernardino Drovetti, had attempted to lay their own claim. A letter of Drovetti's strongly suggests that this was the case: 'The English have got the Rosetta Stone ... we must now be on the alert that they must not get this.' According to the customs of the time, Burton was perhaps entitled to feel as though the object should have been his; nonetheless, he was obliged to enter into discussions with Drovetti. At around the same time, Jean-François Champollion (pp. 98–103), who was already unpopular among the British for failing to acknowledge his rival Thomas Young's contribution to the decipherment of hieroglyphs, had arrived in Egypt, was shown the object and urged Drovetti to claim it for France. The British finally managed to remove it in 1829, but the Pasha intervened again, and it was eventually sent to Drovetti. It is believed to be the object sometimes now referred to as the 'Caristie Stone' after one of Napoleon's savants who had seen it during the French expedition in 1800, and is a part of the collections of the Louvre in Paris.

Burton continued to travel the country until his father, having heard nothing of him for some time, cut off his allowance. He returned to England with his Egyptian servants, one Greek girl, and a menagerie of animals including a giraffe, a dromedary, two antelopes, a hyena, an ibis, and several hawks and owls. Sadly the giraffe died in Cairo, depriving Burton of the much-needed money he had hoped to make by selling it in England. He sold his collection of antiquities through Sotheby's, but the firm went bankrupt shortly afterwards and he never received the money. Till the end of his life, Burton was supported by Robert Hay, as his own family had threatened to disown him. He spent much of the remainder of his life on genealogical research, trying to prove that he had a claim to the family estate. Burton died in 1862, survived by his Greek wife, Andriana Garofalaki, whom he had bought as a slave during his first years in Egypt.

Following his death, Burton's vast collection of papers relating to Egypt were given to the British Museum by his brother Decimus Burton, a celebrated architect. An inscription on his tombstone names him 'A zealous investigator in Egypt of its language and antiquities',

ARTISTS, EXPEDITIONS AND NATIONALIST COMPETITION

↖ Burton's camp in the Eastern Desert. Despite failing in his quest to find a source of coal, Burton did succeed in locating the Roman imperial quarries at Mons Porphyrites, famed for their red stone, and a second site that he (mistakenly) believed to be the Red Sea port of Myos Hormos.

↑ The first court of the Great Temple of Amun at Karnak, looking towards the ruined Hypostyle Hall (see p. 78). Burton must have been standing on top of the first pylon to sketch this view. The second pylon and the Great Hall behind it appear as little more than a heap of stones. The drawing constitutes an extremely valuable record of the state of the site before the great clearance and rebuilding of the late 19th century.

← One of three sketches made by Burton of a quarry at 'Alabastron', the name given by John Gardner Wilkinson to Akhenaten's capital city, now known as Tell el-Amarna.

and his papers show this to have been true. His notes and drawings reveal an insatiable curiosity and desire to capture a wide variety of different aspects of the monuments he encountered. It is his interest in hieroglyphic inscriptions that is perhaps most obvious, however, and his copies, many prepared for publication in his *Excerpta Hieroglyphica*, are generally excellent. His renderings of hieroglyphs are impressively accurate, giving one the sense that, even if Burton could not read the texts, he was at least able to recognize the signs, picking out the subtle variations from one to the next, crucial diagnostic features that allow the reader to recognize particular signs even if they are drawn or sculpted in slightly different ways by different hands – just as we can all recognize the letters of the alphabet in upper and lower case, despite the wide variety of different ways that people express them in their handwriting.

Edward William Lane

1801–1876 British Arabist and Egyptologist

Lane was the leading scholar of Arabic in Europe and made three prolonged visits to Egypt. He joined Robert Hay's expedition in 1827, but also travelled independently to Egypt's monuments. He prepared a monumental 'Description of Egypt' for publication, but it would only appear many years after his death.

→ Atmospheric view of the Grand Gallery inside the Great Pyramid of Khufu at Giza. Lane had intended this drawing to illustrate the relevant section of his *Description of Egypt*, but the book was never published.

Edward William Lane was born in Hereford and educated at the grammar schools of Bath and Hereford before following his brother into a career in engraving in London. His health declined while living in the capital, however, and he decided to find a way to spend time in warmer climes, a common doctor's order in the 19th century. He became fluent in Arabic, which he had begun to study when he moved to London, and journeyed to Egypt in 1825. His own recollections are preserved in his published writings, his notebooks and the journal of his sister, Sophia Lane Poole, who lived with Lane between 1842 and 1844. She published her account, *The Englishwoman in Egypt*, in two volumes in 1844 and 1846. Lane himself scrupulously destroyed his letters, on the basis that they were intended only for private audiences, but information about his time in the country can be supplemented by a biographical account written by his nephew, Stanley Lane-Poole, shortly after his death.

Lane's first voyage, aboard a brig named *Findlay*, took two months. Lane had high hopes as he caught his first glimpse of the country that would occupy him for most of the rest of his life: 'As I approached the shore, I felt like an Eastern bridegroom, about to lift up the veil of his bride, and to see, for the first time, the features which were to charm, or disappoint, or disgust him. I was not visiting Egypt merely as a traveller, to examine its pyramids and temples and grottoes, and, after satisfying my curiosity, to quit it for other scenes and other pleasures: but I was about to throw myself entirely among strangers; to adopt their language, their customs and their dress; and, in associating almost exclusively with the natives, to prosecute the study of their literature.'

Lane's preparation in his Arabic studies meant that he was able to immerse himself into the local culture, adopting the traditional Turkish dress and habits. His nephew wrote that he 'was able, as scarcely one other European has been, to mix among the people of Cairo as one of themselves, and to acquire not only the refinements of their idiomatic speech and the minute details of their etiquette, but also a perfect insight into their habits of mind and ways of thought. The Spirit of the East is a sealed book to ninety-nine out of every hundred orientalists. To Lane it was transparent.' The issue of dress was a sensitive one at this time, the British consul-general, Henry Salt, having issued a proclamation stating that the Consulate could offer no assistance to British subjects adopting Oriental dress should they fall victim to crime or find themselves embroiled in legal disputes. Lane mingled with the prominent British contingent, becoming well acquainted with Robert Hay (pp. 88–97) and John Gardner Wilkinson (pp. 110–19). The latter in particular became a lifelong friend, and the two referred to each other by adopted Arabic names: Wilkinson became 'Isma'eel', and Lane 'Mansoor'. Like many of his contemporaries, Lane took a slave girl, Nefeeseh, as a companion and would eventually marry her in 1840.

Lane visited the pyramids of Giza for the first time on 8 October 1825. He was not ready to undertake a thorough survey, but paid a

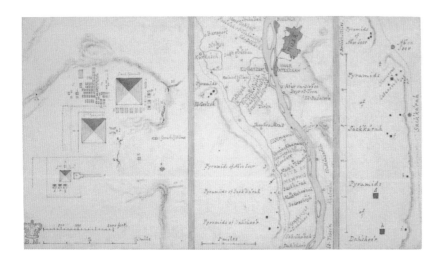

↑ Lane's three-part map showing (left) the Giza plateau and its major monuments; (centre) the Nile Valley between Cairo ('Musr', the old city) and the site of Memphis and its pyramid fields; and (right) a detail of the previous map showing the distribution of the pyramids of Abusir, Saqqara and Dahshur, the squares marking their locations and relative sizes.

↗ View looking into the Great Hall of Abu Simbel. Lane visited the site on 26 May 1826 in very hot weather: 'Within three hours after sunrise, I found this sand almost too hot to tread upon ... the heat of the confined air was quite unsupportable.'

→ Lane's view of the second court of the temple of Ramesses III at Medinet Habu, where he saw 'many small monolithic columns of granite; the remains of a spacious Christian church.' This structure was destroyed by the Antiquities Service later in the century.

'flying visit, to take the edge off his ardent curiosity'. He climbed to the summit of the Great Pyramid during the night, and was rewarded with 'a sight such as one hardly sees twice in a life time ... the moon rose and lighted up the eastern side of the nearer pyramid with a magic effect. Two hours more and the sun had revealed the plain of Egypt, and Lane had been already amply rewarded for the dangers and trouble of his journey from England by one of the most wonderful views in the world.' He would later spend a fortnight at the site, studying the pyramids and surrounding monuments. For the duration he stayed in one of the ancient tombs, evidently undisturbed by the 'usual accumulation of bones and rags, and even whole bodies of mummies'; his nephew assures us that 'the contemplation of these details gave Lane no unpleasant sensations; he merely observed that the skulls were extraordinarily thick.' Lane himself remarked that, though at first the interior looked 'rather gloomy', when 'the floor was swept, and a mat, rug, and mattress spread in the inner apartment, a candle lighted, as well as my pipe, and my arms hung about upon wooden pegs driven into crevices in the wall' – the paintings had been effaced long before – 'I looked around me with complacency, and felt perfectly satisfied.'

On 15 March 1826 Lane set out on his first journey up the Nile. He was an 'indefatigable' sightseer, taking the heat and sandstorms in his stride, as well as the *'Efreets* (demons) who conjured sand-pillars: 'Lane encountered one of these pillars of sand in one of his walks, and following the instructions of his guide he accosted the 'Efreet with the cry of "*Hadeed*" ("iron"), and the sprite passed at a respectful distance.'

As an Arabist, Lane was perhaps better able than most of his contemporaries to ponder the local toponyms, searching for clues to help him to match the places he visited with the sites the classical writers had seen. He was not always right, however; he was convinced that the 'Memnonium', now generally thought to be the Ramesseum in Luxor, was at Abydos: 'Here we find a vast edifice, of high antiquity, buried nearly to the roof with rubbish and the drifted sand of the desert. It is doubtless the building to which Strabo and Pliny have given the name of Memnonium, of the palace of Memnon.' His description of the building, now one of the great sights for visitors to Egypt, is fascinating, for at this time it was virtually inaccessible and most of its beautiful reliefs were yet to be revealed: 'The epithet "El-Med'foo'neh" (or "the buried"), which is sometimes given to the neighbouring village of El-'Ar'abah, more properly applies to this building. No entrance is visible from without; but in two parts, where the roof has fallen in, we may descend into the interior. Here, also, the sand has accumulated so high that we have to crawl for some space on our hands and knees, among the capitals of the columns which support the roof.'

ARTISTS, EXPEDITIONS AND NATIONALIST COMPETITION

← The temple at Luxor was concealed to a depth of 6 metres (20 feet) above the base of the first pylon, according to Lane. Visiting the temple then would have been a very different experience from today. He describes 'what was once a vast, open court ... now crowded with modern buildings ... After having crossed a small open space in front of the mosque, we wind through a narrow lane between low and half-ruined huts.'

Although Lane preferred to work alone, he met with fellow European artists during his travels, including James Burton (pp. 74–81) and, on more than occasion, Linant de Bellefonds. During a prolonged stay in Thebes from July to October 1826, he assisted Robert Hay (pp. 88–97) in his survey of the Valley of the Kings. Lane's description of the natural road that wound its way to the valley conjures a sense of his frame of mind as he navigated this 'barren and secluded' place: 'Not a blade of grass, nor even a noxious weed, is seen throughout the tedious route; which is well calculated to prepare the mind for the traveller for the contemplation of the solemn and mysterious tombs.'

Lane's intention was to compile a monumental 'Description of Egypt', so named in homage to the publication of the great Napoleonic expedition's work. This was essentially an account of his travels, but embellished with masses of detail on the urban landscape of Cairo, the natural environment, the Nile, agriculture and the recent history of the country, in particular the period of Mohamed Ali's rule. It was primarily, however, a work of Egyptology, focusing on the ancient ruins so abundant wherever he went. He prepared the manuscript following his first visit to Egypt and presented it to London publisher John Murray, who accepted it for publication in 1831, but the book was delayed and eventually rejected, perhaps owing to the high cost of production that Lane's inclusion of a large number of illustrations and inscriptions in various scripts including Arabic, hieroglyphic and Greek would demand. The alternative for aspiring authors at this time was to finance the cost of publication themselves, but Lane was not a wealthy man. His widow sold the manuscript to the British Library after his death, and it was not until the 21st century, when his biographer, Professor Jason Thompson, prepared the text for modern publication, that his great masterpiece finally appeared.

Lane did, however, publish an expanded version of one of the chapters in his 'Description' following a second trip to Egypt. *Manners and Customs of the Modern Egyptians* appeared in 1836 and formed a companion to Wilkinson's *Manners and Customs of the Ancient Egyptians* (1837). For this work Lane focused on the lives and customs of the people he encountered while in Egypt. Lane then concentrated his efforts on the Arabic language, producing a translation of *One Thousand and One Nights*, and devoted his final visit to Egypt, from 1842 to 1849, and the remaining years of his life to the compilation of a vast *Arabic–English Lexicon*. Lane died in 1876, before he could complete this last great project, but Stanley Lane-Poole took over the endeavour and published it in eight volumes.

Lane was an Arabist first and foremost, and placed perhaps more emphasis than his contemporaries on aspects of contemporary culture in Egypt. This is reflected in a number of his drawings, which emphasize modern conditions rather than the ancient architecture. These add interest to his sketches; for instance, his drawing of the second court of the temple of Ramesses III at Medinet Habu is of enormous value in showing the remains of the Christian basilica that stood there until the temple was cleared by the Egyptian Antiquities Service from the middle of the 19th century onwards, and of which nothing now remains.

Robert Hay

1799–1863 British traveller, antiquarian and collector

Hay made two extended visits to Egypt, in 1824–28 and 1829–34, putting together a team of artists to create a record of the monuments he encountered. His account remains of great value to modern scholars as it captured many sites that have since been lost or damaged.

↗ View looking southwards up the Nile from the island of Philae, with the west colonnade at left.

→ The remains of the Ptolemaic 'birth-house' at Edfu, with the pylon of the great temple of Horus visible in the distance. From the Late period onwards, such buildings were used to celebrate the birth of a god and were therefore connected with the cycle of death and rebirth.

Robert Hay was born in Duns Castle, a historic house in Berwickshire, in 1799. He started his working life in the navy as a midshipman, and in this capacity travelled to Alexandria in 1818. But after inheriting the estate of Linplum from his brother James the following year – ensuring that he would never be in want of money again – he turned instead to solo exploration. In 1824 he embarked on a leisurely journey southwards through Europe towards the Middle East. It is not clear to what extent he had determined to undertake any serious scholarly endeavour in Egypt, although he may have been inspired by Giovanni Battista Belzoni's *Narrative of the Operations and Recent Discoveries within the Pyramids, Temples, Tombs, and Excavations in Egypt and Nubia* (p. 143), which had been published in 1820. Certainly at some point he made it his mission to improve on the surveys undertaken with official government-level backing by Napoleon's savants and subsequently Ippolito Rosellini, with Jean-François Champollion (pp. 98–103). While in Rome, Hay engaged the services of an artist, Joseph Bonomi, indicating that he already had some intention to make a record of his travels. He also met Sir William Gell, a classical archaeologist and fellow traveller, who encouraged him to visit the renowned Egyptologist John Gardner Wilkinson (pp. 110–19), who was working in Luxor in the south of Egypt. Such connections were key for these early travellers. Upon arriving in Cairo, Hay sought an introduction to James Burton (pp. 74–81), who not only showed him around the local sites, but also, crucially, assisted him with the preparations for an expedition up the Nile. This mission, in its duration and focus, and above all its product – a staggeringly comprehensive record of ancient sites and monuments – would become one of the great early achievements in Egyptology.

One other meeting of Hay's in Cairo was to be of great personal significance for him. It was common at this time for European men travelling in Egypt to acquire female companions. Hay was no different, and visited the slave market. Here he came across Kalitza Psaraki, a woman from Crete who had been captured by Ottoman Turks, along with 900 other woman and children, and transported to Cairo for sale. Hay planned to liberate as many of these prisoners as he could, but he was persuaded against this course on the grounds that their freedom would not last long without ongoing financial support. Instead he bought only Kalitza and one other girl, Nefeeseh, who was taken into the care of one of his colleagues, Edward William Lane (pp. 82–87). In 1828 he and Kalitza married. The union seems to have been a happy one; in 1829 Hay wrote: 'I should counsel all travellers never to travel with any other companion than a wife.'

Hay's first expedition lasted four years. The journey upstream involved few lengthy stops by comparison with the journey back, in the style that had become well established among serious travellers: the first pass served as reconnaissance, and the second was planned carefully to allow the team to seriously investigate key monuments.

ARTISTS, EXPEDITIONS AND NATIONALIST COMPETITION

1 Gebel Sheik abd el Gourna
2 Halwet el Hoba
3 Sbug Ismail
4 Bab e Gaafa
5 El Jorn
6 Koom el Fesaad
7 Gusr Deghage or Dsuke Asumuldfun
8 El Beraba
9 Hotan abn Daraa
10 Beer os Shalonia
11 El Assaseef
12 Deir Sekaio
13 Bab el Gamousa
14 Bab el Goria
15 Bab Minia
16 Bab Biar
17 Bab el Loulee
18 Bab el Assafia
19 Bab om el Minafed
20 Bab el Effine
21 Assafit ed Deghage
22 Kaharetet abd el Gouria
23 El Deir er Roume
24 El Howi
25 Assafeet es Sondouk
26 Bowabet e Deir
27 Drar et Tuffel
28 Beer abd el Nebbe
29 Convent of S. Athanasius

MEDINET-ABOU

Baeban el Molook is composed of the Coptic word baeban signifying CAVE and the Arabic word Molook signifying Kings —

5 1326 in height.

Valley in which are these Tombs at about the distance of mile and a half from the entrance

TOMBS OF THE KINGS or Baeban el Molook

Valley of the Tombs

Valley of the position of the Kings

Plan of Gournou forming part of West Bank of Thebes

← Detailed map of the Theban necropolis, apparently by Hay's colleague Frederick Catherwood. The area includes the Valley of the Kings at bottom right; the major known tombs are marked. Of the local toponyms listed at top left, some are still in use today – by archaeologists at least – but many are not.

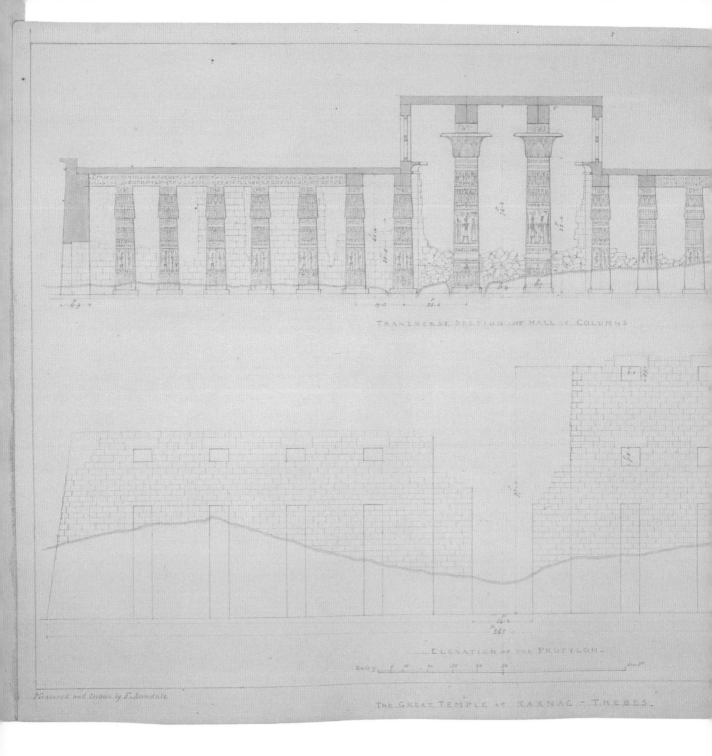

TRANSVERSE SECTION OF HALL OF COLUMNS

ELEVATION OF THE PROPYLON.

Scale of

Measured and Drawn by F. Arundale.

THE GREAT TEMPLE AT KARNAC - THEBES.

↑ Technical drawing by Francis Arundale of the Great Temple of Amun at Karnak. Above is a transverse section through the 'Hall of Columns' (i.e. the Hypostyle Hall), showing both its architectural elements and the collapsed masonry and accumulated debris. Beneath is an elevation of the first pylon, built during the 30th Dynasty.

Nonetheless, on their journey south Hay, Bonomi and their companions stopped for a short while at Dendera, where a beautiful temple to the goddess Hathor stands, and spent six weeks at the celebrated temple of Abu Simbel. Here they would clear one of the colossal heads of Ramesses II, draw the architecture and make copies of the inscriptions, all the while struggling with its immense scale – the temple stands a staggering 30 metres (98 feet) high, and must have been a remarkable sight as it emerged from centuries' worth of debris.

Most of Hay's first expedition was spent in Thebes, in particular the west bank of the river, best known today for the Valley of the

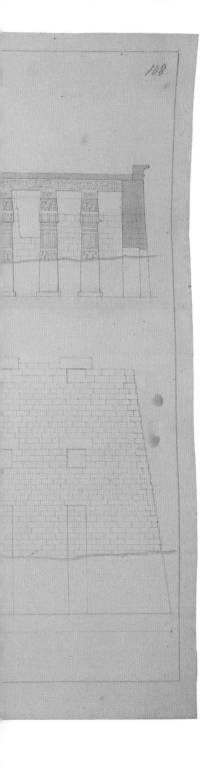

↗ A monumental granite gateway at the temple of Hatshepsut at Deir el-Bahri. The gateway itself stands proud, but the walls around it are badly ruined. The larger, inscribed stone blocks to the left date from the time of the temple's construction, but the mudbricks heaped up behind are the ruins of a Coptic monastery.

Kings but also littered with thousands of tombs belonging to officials, courtiers and artisans, as well as the mortuary temples of kings and queens. He would remain here from October 1825 to February 1827. However, his relationship with Bonomi was deteriorating. Bonomi was frustrated with his low pay in the light of his reputation, which had grown since they had embarked on their journey; meanwhile Hay felt that the artist was using the expedition to enhance his own career. In the middle of 1826, Bonomi left the team and was replaced by Lane.

The party pressed on, visiting Abu Simbel once more and then the ancient city of Amarna. Wilkinson, who had by this time become a good friend and colleague of Hay's, had several years earlier discovered the beautifully decorated tombs of the famed heretic pharaoh Akhenaten's courtiers here. Wilkinson had revealed his discovery to Burton, and they had since visited the site together twice, but when Burton led Hay to the site, he was enraged: 'This piece of knowledge has been kept a secret, and has been guarded with as much care as ever miser watched and fondled the largest treasure ever told!'

↑ Detailed drawing, with notes and measurements, of the exquisitely decorated east wall of the tomb-chapel of Khnumhotep II at Beni Hasan. The scene shows the tomb owner on a papyrus skiff hunting birds, his wife kneeling in front of him. The tomb represents one of the masterpieces of Egyptian painting.

→ Unfinished drawing of the pillared hall of the tomb of Neferhotep, a chief scribe of Amun who lived during the later 18th Dynasty. The tomb, now known as (TT) 49, appears in its unexcavated state; among the debris are what appear to be human remains – not an uncommon sight at uncleared tombs.

ARTISTS, EXPEDITIONS AND NATIONALIST COMPETITION

← View across the first court of the temple of Edfu, with the remains of modern mudbrick buildings in the foreground. The sketch is very similar to that made by Denon (p. 49) two or three decades earlier. The elevated viewpoint is the result of a great accumulation of debris reaching almost to the columns' capitals.

↙ A group of European men in Turkish dress – almost certainly Hay and his party – recline around a low table, smoking waterpipes. The large masonry blocks suggest that they are in an ancient monument, but the exact location is unknown.

↓ Scene from Tomb No. 2 at Beni Hasan, which belonged to Amenemhat, a local governor in the time of Senusret I. The deceased sits at left, receiving a huge number of offerings, also listed above.

Hay left Egypt in 1828. Lane had returned to England, leaving him short of an artist, and he was anxious to secure funds for an expedition to Abu Simbel. He had also received news that his youngest brother had died; more happily, he was to be married to Kalitza on the island of Malta, her native Greece having gained its independence. But he would return the next year, mounting a second expedition to the Nile Valley that lasted from 1829 to 1834. This time he engaged the services of the artist Charles Laver, who was recommended by Lane and who in turn recommended Owen Browne Carter, an architect. This trio was responsible for the illustrations comprising the main body of the only substantial work Hay would ever publish, *Illustrations of Cairo* (1840). Hay continued to search out artistic talent, recruiting the English draughtsman Francis Arundale and artist Frederick Catherwood. He even persuaded Bonomi to rejoin the team – on a much higher salary.

Illustrations of Cairo sold badly, at enormous financial cost to Hay, a setback that seems to have deterred him from publishing anything further. And yet he towers over the field of Egyptology perhaps more than any of the other early copyists. This is in part due to the immensity of the record that he left behind, the professional artists that he engaged having produced forty-nine enormous volumes in addition to his own personal diaries; but perhaps also in part because these manuscripts have passed into legend. The vast collection of drawings and notes made over the course of nearly a decade during his two expeditions is now kept in the British Library, and has remained one of Egyptology's best-kept secrets.

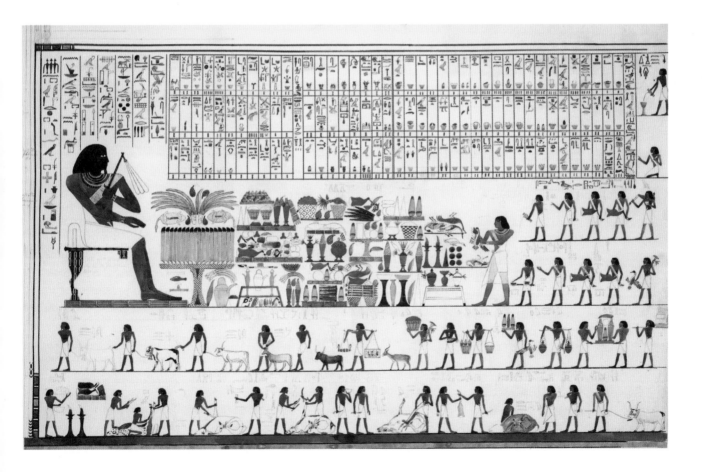

Jean-François Champollion

1790–1832 French linguist and Egyptologist

Champollion devoted his life to the study of ancient languages and more than any other individual was responsible for the decipherment of the hieroglyphic script.

→ A page from Champollion's manuscript for the *Grammaire Égyptienne*, showing hieroglyphic symbols grouped according to form: insects, plants, animals and birds.

Jean-François Champollion was born in Figeac in south-western France and studied at the Lyceum in Grenoble. By the age of sixteen he had written a paper at the Academy of Grenoble in which he asserted – correctly – that Coptic was a later version of the ancient Egyptian language that had been written in hieroglyphs, as Athanasius Kircher (pp. 16–21) had proposed (though Champollion rightly rejected many of his other conclusions). He continued his education at the Collège de France and the École Spéciale des Langues Orientales Vivantes in Paris, studying under the great linguist Silvestre de Sacy between 1807 and 1809. Sacy had been the first Frenchman to attempt to read the Rosetta Stone inscriptions, identifying in 1802 three names in the Demotic script, including that of Ptolemy.

In the years that followed, Champollion continued his intensive study of ancient languages, familiarizing himself with a bewildering variety of ancient writings in Hebrew, Arabic, Syriac, Chaldean, Chinese, Ethiopic, Sanskrit, Zend, Pahlevi, Parsee, Persian and even Mexican scripts. Most crucial of all would turn out to be his work on the Coptic language. The word 'Coptic' derives from *Aigyptos*, the name given to the land of the pharaohs by the ancient Greeks. It probably derives from the even earlier ancient Egyptian *Hut-ka-Ptah*, meaning 'the temple of Ptah', which was one of the names given to the ancient capital city of Memphis. It survives in corrupted form as the modern word 'Egypt'. The Greek language came to be widely used in Egypt following the establishment of the Ptolemies, who were Macedonian Greek in origin, as the country's ruling dynasty. The Greek script was adopted by the Egyptians to write their own language, but, as its alphabet could not adequately express all the sounds in the Egyptian language, six or seven characters were added, creating, in the 2nd century BCE, a new script: Coptic. Following the Arab conquest of Egypt in the 7th century CE Arabic was established as the principal language and script of Egypt, but Coptic continued to be used by the minority of Christians who remained unconverted to Islam. It is still in use today by worshippers of the Christian faith in Egypt. It has thus never been 'lost' as a language in the way that the phases of ancient Egyptian written in the hieroglyphic script were. That Coptic contained traces of that same ancient language was not universally accepted in Champollion's time, but his recognition of the Coptic connection and mastery of the language put him at an advantage over those who did not have the same depth of knowledge.

The Rosetta Stone, which his tutor had examined, was to become key to Champollion's own advances in understanding the hieroglyphic script. The stone was found in July 1799, when the Napoleonic expedition was in the course of rebuilding an old Mamluk fort just outside the town of Rashid near the Mediterranean coast. An officer named Pierre-François Bouchard found a slab of stone bearing ancient inscriptions that had apparently been used as part of the foundations

4° Des <u>Insectes</u> tels que l'abeille, le Scarabée &c;

5° Des <u>Plantes</u>; telles que diverses Espèces de <u>Lotus</u> et de <u>Roseaux</u> &c;

Mais on n'employait dans les inscriptions moins détaillées peintes sur les Sarcophages ou les Stèles, que des couleurs totalement conventionnelles pour les images d'êtres appartenant au Règne animal ou au Règne végétal.

Ainsi les images de Quadrupèdes, ou de portions de quadrupèdes, des Reptiles et des plantes étaient peintes en Vert et quelquefois rehaussées de Bleu.

20. Les ailes et la partie supérieure du corps des <u>Oiseaux</u> Son coloriées en <u>bleu</u>, le reste du corps en vert et les pattes en <u>bleu</u> ou en <u>Rouge</u>:

of the fort when it was built in the 15th century CE, its historical significance evidently having been of no import to the builders. This stela was the record of a decree dating to 27 Match 196 BCE, shortly after the coronation of Ptolemy V, and announced the establishment of a religious order for the worship, as a god, of the new pharaoh. But the stela's significance lies not in what it records, but the way it was recorded. The inscription was written three times, in three different scripts: ancient Greek, which could be read easily by contemporary scholars, and two scripts that were used to write ancient Egyptian, hieroglyphs and the less formal, cursive Demotic (meaning 'of the people', from the ancient Greek *demos*). Bouchard immediately realized what this meant: if it was the same text in each script, then the Greek could be used to decipher the hieroglyphs and the Demotic, and potentially any other Egyptian inscription. After Napoleon's defeat in 1801, the Stone became the property of the English government and was removed to the British Museum, and so Champollion had to rely on academic papers and copies to study the object.

In 1808 Champollion was able to demonstrate significant progress by equating fifteen signs in the Demotic with Coptic, correctly recognizing several signs and their phonetic values. In 1809 he began teaching in Grenoble and became chair in history and geography from 1818 to 1821. From this time on he was able to devote himself fully to the study of the ancient Egyptian language and the decipherment of the hieroglyphic script.

The hieroglyphic script is often described as being a 'code' that needed to be 'cracked', giving rise to the mistaken idea that there was an underlying system that, once identified – and the 'key' obtained – would lead suddenly to a comprehensive ability to read the ancient texts. In reality the decipherment was a long process of chipping away at the problem, Champollion and others gradually coming to recognize more of the rules of the script, adding slowly to the lists of signs whose value was known, words that could be translated, and aspects of the underlying grammar understood so that sense could be made of long passages of text. Many mistakes were made along the way.

If there is one point at which Egyptology took a single great step forward in the decipherment, however, it was the publication of Champollion's *Lettre à M. Dacier relative à l'alphabet des hiéroglyphes phonétiques*, the latter being the secretary of the Académie des Inscriptions et Belles-Lettres. This text of forty-four pages was published in October 1822 and revealed many new readings of the phonetic values of certain signs and the names of rulers, and a table of concordance of hieroglyphic signs and their counterparts in Demotic and Coptic.

Champollion had read an earlier version of the letter to a gathering of scholars at the Académie in September that year. By chance Champollion's main rival, the Englishman Thomas Young, was in Paris at the time and present to hear the announcement. Young, a brilliant polymath, had made major contributions in various scientific fields and was also a scholar of languages, inventing the term 'Indo-European' to describe the family of languages that includes English. He began his work on the Egyptian scripts in 1814. He had made a number of significant advances, establishing that the Demotic and hieroglyphic

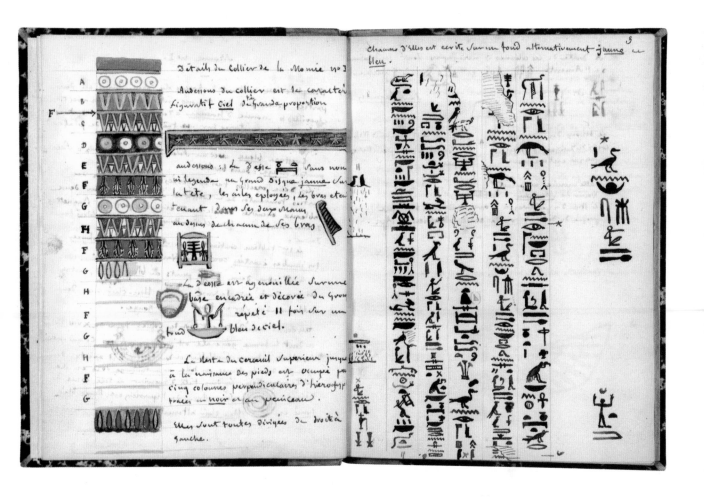

↑ Champollion's notes for the *Grammaire Égyptienne*. At left is a series of decorative designs from a coffin, and at right his copy of an inscription dedicated to a man called Gem-Hapy, son of Ahmose.

scripts were related, and recognizing that Demotic was not purely alphabetic – an important step forward. He also correctly identified the names 'Ptolemy' and 'Berenike' in the hieroglyphic inscription on the Rosetta Stone. He still laboured under the misunderstanding at this point that the hieroglyphs were purely ideographic, but hypothesized that the signs had been adapted to write these Greek names phonetically. Though his comprehension was incomplete, this idea allowed him to identify correctly the phonetic values of the hieroglyphic signs used to write these names, which could of course then be read elsewhere in the text. Champollion initially rejected this idea, maintaining that the signs were not phonetic but had only ideographic values. Young published his theory and readings in an article for the *Encyclopaedia Britannica*; when Champollion later revised his view, accepting that some hieroglyphic signs did have phonetic values, he made no acknowledgment of Young's prior claim to this breakthrough. This slight did not go unnoticed among the British, perhaps fuelling the rivalry between the two camps, which played out most spectacularly in Egypt itself. Nonetheless, even the British accepted that Champollion had made significant advances, rapidly expanding the number of signs and words that could be read. In 1824 Sir William Gell wrote to John Gardner Wilkinson (see pp.110–19), who was by then the leading scholar of the Egyptian language and had studied the texts *in situ* in Egypt, saying of Champollion's announcement that he had 'now superseded the old school of Young

Scene from the tomb of Ramesses IV, showing deities personifying aspects of the geography of Egypt. Champollion would have had ample opportunity to familiarize himself with such scenes, since he and his companions made this particular tomb their base in the Valley of the Kings.

14. Dans le premier Système applicable aux Caractères, Sculptés en Grand, on cherchait, par des teintes plattes, à rappeler à peu près, la couleur naturelle des objets représentés : Ainsi les Caractères figurants le Ciel (1) était peints en bleu, la terre (2) en Rouge ; la Lune (3) en Jaune, le Soleil (4) en Rouge, l'Eau (5) en bleu ou en Vord (6)

15. Les Figures d'Hommes en pied. Sont peintes, sur les grands monuments d'après des règles assez constantes : Les chairs sont en Rouge plus ou moins foncé, les coiffures en bleu et les tuniques blanche, les plis des draperies étant indiqués par des traits rouges

16. On donnait ordinairement des chairs jaunes aux figures de Femmes et leurs Vêtements variaient en blanc, en Vord ou en Rouge.

Les mêmes règles sont suivis dans le coloriage des hiéroglyphes désirés ou petit sur les Stèles et les Sarcophages ; mais les Vêtements sont tous de couleur Verte.

A continuation of Champollion's handwritten classification of hieroglyphic signs. The top group signifies the sky, the sun, water and mountains, while the remaining three show people involved in various activities, including a woman in childbirth

who remains the founder while Champollion has finished all the columns & friezes of the hieroglyphical edifice. He has turned all the cats Lions zigzags owls &c into letters .... I cannot give you a dissertation on it but the thing is quite settled.'

Despite his strong Republican leanings, Champollion's successes secured him the patronage of Louis XVIII and Charles X, and in 1824 he was sent on a mission to study the great collections of Egyptian antiquities in the museums of Turin, Leghorn, Rome, Naples and Florence. In 1826 he was appointed curator of the Egyptian collections at the Louvre, which were opened to the public the following year. Finally, in 1828, he visited Egypt.

Champollion's year-long expedition was intended as a comprehensive survey of Egypt's ancient sites and monuments. It was to be supported by King Charles X of France and Leopold II, grand duke of Tuscany. The Tuscan contingent was led by Ippolito Rosellini, who had become professor of oriental languages at the University of Pisa in 1824 when only in his mid-twenties. He had met Champollion when the latter visited Florence in 1825, and Rosellini visited him in Paris in 1827. Rosellini had become Champollion's first disciple, and the two became great friends.

The Franco-Tuscan expedition arrived in Alexandria on 18 August 1828 and by November had reached Thebes, where Champollion stayed for only four days, one of which was spent entirely in the Valley of the Kings. The expedition journeyed up the Nile as far as the Second Cataract, the region of the present-day border between Egypt and Sudan. On the return downstream they would spend several months in Thebes, copying the decoration on the monuments including the tombs of the Valley of the Kings, one of which, the tomb of Ramesses IV, they made their temporary home. The expedition members gathered a vast quantity of notes and drawings, and Champollion was able to make significant improvements to his understanding of the ancient language. They also removed a significant quantity of antiquities, including a panel from the tomb of Sety I now in the Louvre and 10,000 francs' worth of items purchased in Cairo with funds from the French government. In addition, Mohamed Ali Pasha offered the expedition the two obelisks that stood outside the temple of Luxor, though in the end only one was removed. It now stands in the Place de la Concorde in Paris.

Champollion died while preparing his account of the expedition, which appeared between 1835 and 1847 as *Monuments de l'Égypte et de la Nubie d'après les dessins exécutés sur les lieux, sous la direction de Champollion-le-jeune* (Monuments of Egypt and Nubia, after the drawings executed on the spot under the direction of Champollion the younger). Rosellini's account, *I Monumenti dell'Egitto e della Nubia* (Monuments of Egypt and Nubia), was published between 1832 and 1844. Monumental in both subject matter and scale, both of these works remain a valuable record of the Franco-Tuscan expedition and the monuments it encountered. Along with the notes and drawings made for the official publications, the informal diaries and sketches of a number of the team members, among them Nestor l'Hôte (pp. 104–9), survive, revealing varied perspectives on the great Champollion's only expedition to Egypt.

Nestor l'Hôte

1804–1842 French artist

L'Hôte developed an interest in ancient Egypt at a young age and became a protegé of Champollion. He joined the Franco-Tuscan expedition of 1828–29, where he made an immense number of drawings, many of which appeared in the subsequent publications by Champollion and Rosellini.

NESTOR L'HÔTE.

→ L'Hôte's view from inside the temple of Ptah at Gerf Hussein, 90 kilometres (56 miles) south of Aswan, built in the time of Ramesses II. The magnificent square pillars with engaged Osirid figures are no longer visible: when the construction of the High Dam at Aswan created the vast Lake Nasser to the south, the exterior parts of the temple were moved to the site of New Kalabsha, but the interior was left in place and is now underwater.

Hippolyte Antoine Nestor l'Hôte was born in Cologne, Germany. In 1814 the family returned to France to live in Charleville, where l'Hôte studied archaeology and drawing. He also read Vivant Denon's *Voyage dans la basse et la haute Égypte* (Travels in Upper and Lower Egypt), published in 1802 (p. 50). When he was twenty years old, he wrote a treatise on archaeology, which he submitted to his teacher, M. Duvivier, curator of the antiquities department of the Ardennes. In essence this was a review of the writings of a range of scholars, including Jean-François Champollion (pp. 98–103). L'Hôte had written to the great decipherer of the hieroglyphic script in preparing his study; Jean-François was travelling in Italy, but his brother, Jacques-Joseph, responded amiably to l'Hôte's enquiries and sent him copies of Champollion's *Précis du système hiéroglyphique* and perhaps the *Lettre à M. Dacier*.

L'Hôte was appointed to a post at the *Revue encyclopédique* (Encyclopaedic Review) in Paris in 1827. Champollion was one of the editors, and when l'Hôte was invited to attend their monthly meeting he took the opportunity to speak to his hero, plucking up the courage to show him a copy of his treatise. Champollion was impressed, and in due course invited l'Hôte to join his great Franco-Tuscan expedition to Egypt. L'Hôte was just twenty-four years old when, on 21 July 1828, he set off on board the *Églé* with Champollion and Rosellini.

Throughout the journey, l'Hôte sent home detailed letters as well as recording his experiences in his journal and, above all, in his sketches. Shortly after arriving in Alexandria, he realized that he had forgotten to bring the thick paper best suited to watercolours and wrote home to request some: 'Watercolour is the most expeditious way to do in a moment studies of effect and tone that make a pleasant and true nature of this country. If you had the opportunity to send it, there would be so many more drawings in my collection, which increases every day, because I do not omit, every morning, at sunrise, to go on an excursion in the city or surroundings with the notebook under the arm.'

L'Hôte made numerous portraits of the locals he encountered, and of the setting of the monuments the expedition was there to study. His drawings are often impressionistic, and his delight in re-creating the landscapes meant that he frequently captured views of the sites from rare vantage points, such as an image of the temple of Luxor in the far distance beyond a tree-lined stretch of the Nile. He was not a great admirer of the art of the Ptolemaic period, and was unafraid to say so. Of the reliefs showing Cleopatra breastfeeding her son Caesarion in the temple of Armant, he declared: 'These scenes are interesting in various ways but their execution seems to reflect, more than any other monument of the era, the degeneration of Egyptian art. The exterior and interior bear the imprint of a style that has fallen into a primitive character. The reliefs there are exaggerated and bloated, and the hieroglyphs of a heaviness and a thickness such that it is difficult to distinguish forms.'

↑ Osirid pillar from the interior of the great temple of Abu Simbel. L'Hôte's sketch shows the bright colours in which it would originally have been painted. This figure shows the deified Ramesses II in the guise of Osiris, wearing the double crown of Upper and Lower Egypt.

L'Hôte was often frank about the disappointments of finding ancient monuments degraded or even entirely lost. Of a visit to the far side of the river from the town and temple of Esna, he wrote that though 'we hoped to find a temple there, we only found the dust. For consolation, we could discover on a remainder of basement the cartouche of a Ptolemy: it was enough to note the time of the building and decrease perhaps the regret of its loss, but it is not less a monument destroyed, and a testimony of more barbarism that must necessarily destroy the remains of the old Egypt.' In this same entry, we learn something of the trials and tribulations of travelling by river: 'We returned, somewhat disappointed, only to find another surprise awaited us: a great movement reigned aboard, all the crew was busy transferring into vases full of water. We were told that as soon as we left, the boat, which had probably been going for some time without being noticed, had suddenly filled up to the point of sinking.'

And it would sometimes get worse: 'Crocodiles are common in this part of Egypt. The locals cite one in particular which is remarkable for its size. It qualifies as the "Grand Vizir" according to the hierarchy of the size of these animals. The king of the crocodiles lives around Armant and Ombos where he holds his court. Of the Vizir, he seemed, from a distance from which we could see him, to measure more than twenty-five paces in length. He comes habitually to wait in the sun on a large island of sand situated in the middle of the river south of Thebes. In his size and the contrast of the colour of his body with the sand he gives the impression of a fallen tree trunk with all the roughness of the bark. This formidable reptile removes, says one, the cattle that graze without distrust on the banks of the river or whoever will go there, and does not even care for the human species; women and children are each year his victims. Or at least that's the story.'

L'Hôte also complained of the challenges of keeping their Egyptian crew happy, particularly as regards their payment. The continuation of their journey, the First Cataract having been passed, involved protracted negotiations with the crew, who protested at the hardships they had had to endure and demanded improved terms, which they got before the expedition could proceed southwards:

16 Dec 1828

In the morning 8 boats arrived from Nubia were arranged to receive us. One of them, larger than the others, carried the headquarters: MM Champollion, Rosellini and Ricci and the dragoman, with the canon(!). The other members of the commission were divided into groups of three plus a domestique on each boat. Each craft was covered with a tent and mats on hoops to serve as a shelter for the travellers and their equipment.

ARTISTS, EXPEDITIONS AND NATIONALIST COMPETITION

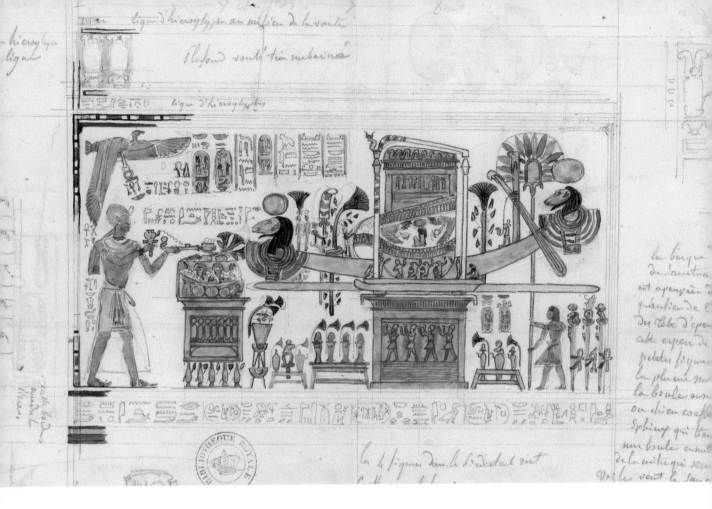

↑ Scene showing Ramesses II making a libation and offering incense to the sacred bark of Amun-Ra, from the sanctuary of the temple of Wadi es-Sebua in Lower Nubia. L'Hôte has partially coloured his pencil sketch and added notes all over the page in an attempt to record all the fine details.

The embarkation of all this world and the material was as usual, with as much haste and embarrassment as if it were an attempt to flee from the sacking of a city; it was a confusion, a crisis, a melee to lose the head, but this misfortune is almost inevitable when one wants to finish with such a considerable move, and with Arabs, no less clumsy than apathetic. Finally towards noon our flotilla was able to set sail, and it was only after the departure that everyone was able to restore some order in his new home.

L'Hôte produced a huge quantity of drawings during the expedition, many of which were published in both Champollion's *Monuments* and Rosellini's *I Monumenti*. He painted many more, however – 500 by the time they returned to France in 1831 – and wrote more than 200 pages of letters to family and friends. His writings shine a light on some of the less well-known aspects of life on expedition, for instance a festival at Girga: 'During this time these gentlemen had brought in dancers who were engaged in all their exercises and made great movement; the tent was open and the crowd of curious obstructed the entrance. R and L each took one to their room and did what modesty prevents me from saying.'

In 1838 l'Hôte returned to Egypt, this time alone. The letters he wrote to the prominent French scholar Jean-Antoine Letronne were subsequently published as *Lettres écrites d'Égypte en 1838 et 1839* (Letters Written from Egypt in 1838 and 1839) in 1840 with the addition

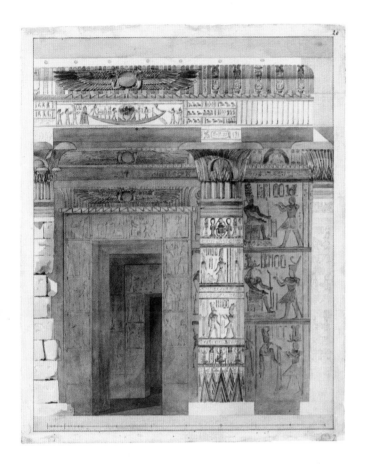

↑ L'Hôte's reconstruction of the Roman portico of the temple of El-Hilla on the east bank of the Nile, opposite Esna. It was completely destroyed in 1828, not long before l'Hôte's visit; he perhaps based his reconstruction on what remained, or on the notes of others.

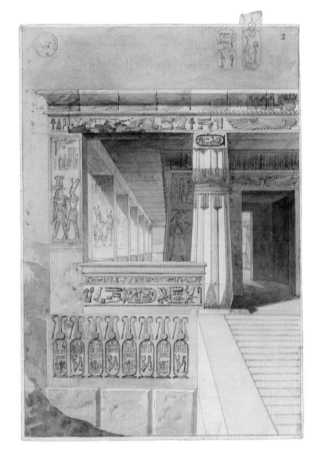

↑ L'Hôte's reconstruction of the sanctuary of the temple of Amenhotep III, Elephantine. The temple was destroyed in 1822, a few years before l'Hôte's first voyage to Egypt. To the left of the column base is a renewal text of Sety I, with a row of cartouches of Ramesses II beneath.

↖ View looking northwards from the hilltop site of Qasr Ibrim, with the ruins of a Meroitic fort in the foreground. The site's elevation made it naturally defensible, and it was occupied for many centuries. It is now an island in the middle of Lake Nasser.

← The temple of Ramesses II at Gerf Hussein, Lower Nubia. The freestanding parts were re-erected following the flooding of the region and can now be seen on the island of New Kalabsha.

of Letronne's notes. This trip was plagued by difficulty, both political and personal: not only did l'Hôte encounter Egyptians hostile to Europeans, but he also contracted dysentery and, on his return journey, some water entered the hull of his ship, damaging his notes and obliging him to return to Egypt again. This he did in 1840, leading to the publication of another volume, *Lettres d'Égypte en 1840–41* (Letters from Egypt 1840–41), in 1841. Sadly l'Hôte died the following year, his decline perhaps hastened by Egypt's hot climate and the strains of travel. The greater part of his work, and in particular the sketches he made while travelling the Nile with Champollion and Rosellini, was never published. It remains a testimony to his talents as an artist, his letters a powerful evocation of life alongside perhaps the greatest of all Egyptologists. His own legacy remains important, and would bear fruit not long after his lifetime: Auguste Mariette, the great French excavator and founder of the Egyptian Antiquities Service and National Museum, was a relative of l'Hôte's, and his interest in Egyptology was first ignited when he saw l'Hôte's papers.

John Gardner Wilkinson

1797–1875 British Egyptologist

Wilkinson lived and worked in Egypt in the 1820s, staying in the country for longer than most European travellers. He amassed a vast quantity of notes and drawings in the course of his study of the ancient Egyptian language and culture, and published several major works of lasting impact that have ensured his legacy as the first great British Egyptologist.

→ Wilkinson's detailed map of the Theban necropolis and surrounding landscape. The great sweep of the cliffs behind the temples of Deir el-Bahri, the causeways extending from the temples down towards the cultivated land, and the great temple enclosures are all clearly visible. The oval-shaped mounds at bottom right describe the shape of Amenhotep III's immense man-made harbour, the Birket Habu.

John Gardner Wilkinson was born in the village of Little Missenden, Buckinghamshire. Both of his parents died by the time John was ten years old, and he was educated at Harrow in his teenage years. There he came under the influence of the headmaster, George Butler, a friend and student of the linguist Thomas Young. Wilkinson went up to Exeter College, Oxford, in 1816, but left in 1818 without a degree and in 1819 embarked on Grand Tour of Europe. While in Italy he met Sir William Gell, an English archaeologist and illustrator who persuaded him to give up the idea of joining the army in favour of joining the race to decipher the hieroglyphic script. Gell also showed Wilkinson Young's system of hieroglyphic transliteration, which was to serve Wilkinson well from the moment he arrived on Egyptian soil.

Wilkinson reached Alexandria on 22 November 1821. He was underwhelmed by his first sight of the ancient capital, ruined as it was, but nonetheless spent time visiting the antiquities that were still visible, making notes and copying inscriptions. He observed that the obelisks of Cleopatra 'have … the names of Dr Young's Mespheres (Tuthmosis III) in the central lines'. He then began his journey south, crossing the Delta to the Rosetta branch of the Nile by the Mahmoudiya Canal, which had been built under the supervision of Pascal Coste (pp. 54–59). On 19 December 1821, his boat neared Cairo, and Wilkinson was presented with a splendid vista, with the pyramids in view to the right and minarets of Cairo to the left. He wasted no time making illustrious contacts, meeting the British consul-general Henry Salt (for whom Gell had provided Wilkinson with the customary letter of introduction), who in turn introduced him to the Pasha. Salt accompanied Wilkinson on his first visit to the pyramids. Wilkinson measured and climbed all three, leaving his name at the top of Khafra's, the most difficult to climb since its smooth outer casing was still present. While in Cairo he also met the Scot Osman Effendi, who taught him to dress as a Turk – which meant sporting a pair of voluminous trousers, a shirt, three jackets, a pouch holding a copy of the Quran, a Turkish sword, a long, drooping moustache and a turban atop a shaven head. A burdensome costume it might have seemed, but those who adopted the attire noticed that the locals' attitude towards them improved dramatically.

In February 1822 Wilkinson began his first journey up the Nile, with Frederik Ludwig Norden's *Travels in Egypt and Nubia* as a guide (p. 33). He and his travelling companion, James Samuel Wiggett, made it as far as Semna, a few miles beyond the Second Cataract. They planned to spend an extended period in Thebes on the return journey, but Wiggett suffered a serious case of dysentery, necessitating a swift return to Cairo, and then, once he had recovered sufficiently, to Europe. Rather than accompanying his friend home, Wilkinson stayed in the Egyptian capital and turned his attention towards the serious study of hieroglyphs. He renewed his acquaintance with James Burton (pp. 74–81), whom he had briefly met while in Italy.

ARTISTS, EXPEDITIONS AND NATIONALIST COMPETITION

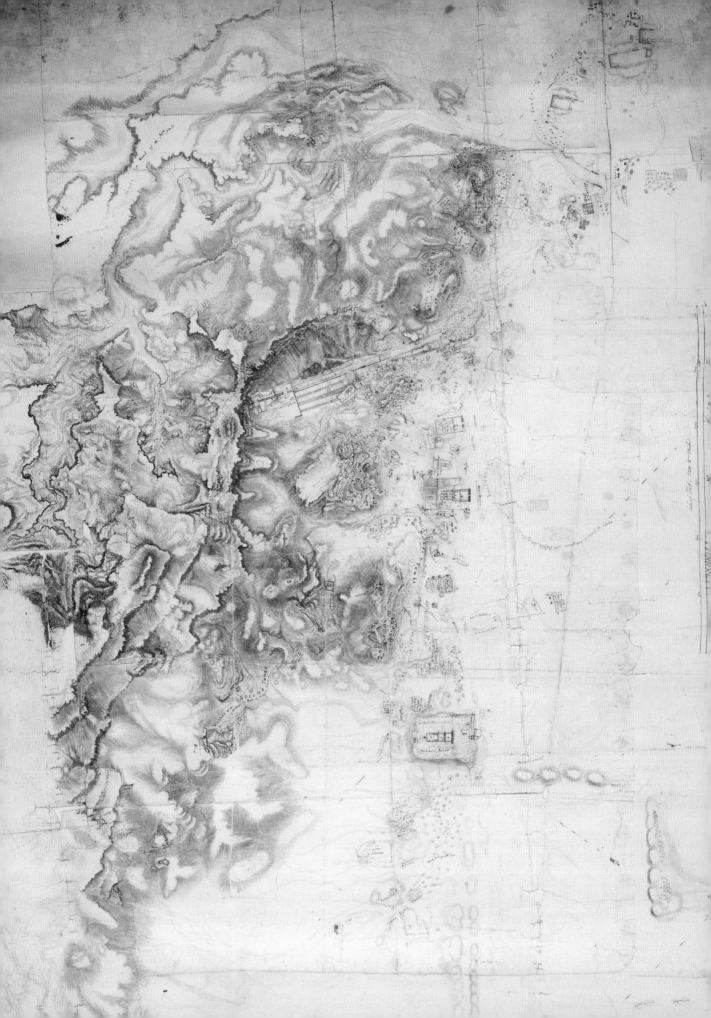

↑ Locals and their animals at the edge of the river, with the pyramid of Meidum in the background.

Burton moved into a spare room in Wilkinson's house in the predominantly Turkish Hasanain district of Cairo. They avoided the Frankish quarter favoured by Europeans, some of whom, Wilkinson felt, had arrived in Egypt having failed to make anything of themselves at home to take advantage of Mohamed Ali's enthusiasm for employing foreigners for the expertise he supposed they had. Wilkinson and Burton preferred to distance themselves from such people and were shocked, therefore, when Henry Salt issued a proclamation advising that no protection could be offered to British subjects adopting Turkish dress. This seemed bizarre, given that dressing as locals made it far easier for Europeans to avoid harassment. Salt was eventually forced to backpedal, claiming that the proclamation applied only to those in the service of the Pasha and not to independent travellers. In any case, the episode reveals the extent to which British visitors to Egypt felt they had or should have the protection of the consulate, which allowed them to travel and carry out their researches with more confidence and success than they could have done otherwise. In this way the combined efforts of the consulate and the traveller-scholars contributed significantly to the colonization of the country, albeit by 'softer', non-military means. Wilkinson and Burton each at times pretended to be Muslim, though this was a risky business – the punishment for renouncing that faith being death. Perhaps Wilkinson's motivation had something to do with his female slave, who initially refused to have anything to do with him, it being a sin for an 'infidel' to take

ARTISTS, EXPEDITIONS AND NATIONALIST COMPETITION

a slave. While anti-slavery sentiment ran high in England at this time, many European travellers to Egypt eventually became comfortable with the practice.

Not content to stay in Cairo, Wilkinson travelled extensively, first accompanying Burton on his expedition to the Eastern Desert in 1823. During this trip they identified Mons Porphyrites, a settlement established around the porphyry quarries to supply Rome with large quantities of this beautiful red stone, and Mons Claudianus, the site of a white granite mine. On 28 February 1824 he set off up the Nile for the second time, intending to reach Aswan, but he was delayed for eight weeks by illness, and then by a series of revolts of the *fellahin* – Egypt's rural settlers – against the rule of Mohamed Ali. Wilkinson and the other English travellers on the Nile at the time escaped serious harm, but must have been thoroughly disquieted by effects of the violence, witnessing such horrors as human corpses being eaten by dogs at the riverside. John Madox, a traveller who would later publish a two-volume account of his *Excursions in the Holy Land, Egypt, Nubia, Syria, &c: Including a Visit to the Unfrequented District of the Haouran*, reported that in Qena he found 'all the English who had lately been in Upper Egypt, viz. Captain Pringle, and Messrs. Wilkinson, Parke, Scoles, Westcar, and Catherwood. We were all delighted at meeting, and congratulated each other on our fortunate escape.'

Wilkinson nonetheless continued his researches as best he could and visited the Faiyum Oasis for the first time, making a map of the region. The following year he continued his investigation of the areas to the west of the Nile by travelling to the western oases, which had still at this point only rarely been visited by Europeans and were somewhat unruly and with different customs from the rest of Egypt.

Around this time Wilkinson went to Amarna. This royal city had been recorded by Napoleon's savants, but Wilkinson was apparently the first to visit the tombs, whose walls were decorated in the naturalistic style of the period, unlike any other in the pharaonic canon. He was fascinated by the unique depiction of the Aten, a manifestation of the sun-god, and the prominent and frequent appearance of a king and queen who were shown with very unusual – even grotesque – features.

→ Wilkinson's view of the 'Memnonium', the mortuary temple of Ramesses II better known now as the Ramesseum. Until the construction of the High Dam at Aswan, the Nile floodwaters often reached the temples in the Theban necropolis; the river is in fact several kilometres away.

Their names, Akhenaten and Nefertiti, were unknown to Wilkinson, who was unsure what to make of what he had seen. When he showed Burton the tombs in 1826 he, too, was bewildered, and Wilkinson swore him to secrecy. Robert Hay (pp. 88–97) was later – quite justifiably – angered by this most unscholarly reluctance to share the discovery. Although the ancient name of the site and its king would remain unknown for decades, Wilkinson was responsible for establishing the name by which we know the place today, Tell el-Amarna, which is in fact a conflation of the names of two villages, et-Till and Beni Amra.

Wilkinson also visited the site of Beni Hasan, slightly further north of Amarna on the same side of the river, where the tombs of the Middle Kingdom 'nomarchs' – local governors – are found. Here he was captivated by the images of birds and animals and scenes of people engaged in a huge variety of activities, which helped sow the seeds of the idea for his book *Manners and Customs of the Ancient Egyptians*. The decoration in the tombs was to suffer badly in the decades to come, and the drawings Wilkinson made here, some of the earliest and best from the site, are especially valuable to modern scholars.

From the mid-1820s Wilkinson began to settle in Thebes, building a fine house on the hill of Sheikh Abd el-Gurna in the midst of the 'Valley of the Nobles' on the West Bank. The house made use of the tomb of Amethu called Ahmose (TT 83), a governor of the town and vizier during the reign of Tuthmosis III. Wilkinson added a pigeon house, grand mudbrick tower and surrounding wall to enclose a garden and courtyard, obscuring the monumental rock-cut portico of the original sepulchre. It became a magnet for European travellers: Hay lived there for a time, as did Edward William Lane (pp. 82–87) and, much later, Karl Richard Lepsius (pp. 126–31). It lay only a little way from that belonging to Giovanni d'Athanasi, an agent of Henry Salt, where his most recent acquisitions were often on display. As wood was in short supply, the remains of mummy cases were used as fuel; the acrid smoke of their fires smelled of the bitumen used to embalm the bodies. Brightly decorated coffins were also used to construct doors, shutters and shelves in d'Athanasi's house. The traveller G. A. Hoskins wrote of Wilkinson's home that: 'On Thursday evenings ... the artists and travellers at Thebes used to assemble in his house, or rather tomb I should call it; but never was the habitation of death witness to gayer scenes. Though we wore the costume, we did not always preserve the gravity of the Turks; and the saloon, although formerly a sepulchre, threw no gloom over our mirth. The still remaining beautiful fragments of the painted roof were illuminated by the blaze of waxlights; and the odour of the mummies had long ago been dispelled by the more congenial perfume of savory viands.'

It was from this base that Wilkinson embarked on one of his most important projects: the creation of a topographical map of Thebes, numbering the tombs of Gurna and also the royal tombs. In 1827 he strolled through the Valley of the Kings and painted numbers at the entrances to the twenty-one tombs that had been discovered in the main part of the valley to that date, starting with the closest to the valley entrance – the tomb of Ramesses VII, which he designated KV 1. He gave those in the Western Valley separate numbers (WV 1–4),

ARTISTS, EXPEDITIONS AND NATIONALIST COMPETITION

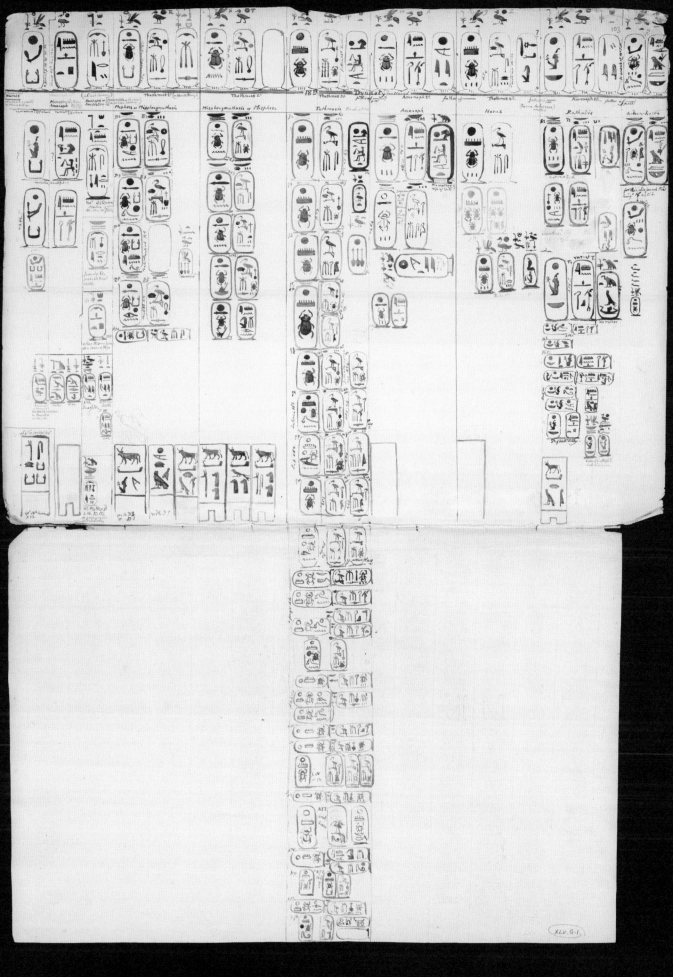

↑ Two drawings by Wilkinson, from the tomb of Neferhotep, chief scribe of Amun. The upper drawing depicts a funerary procession, while the lower scene shows the deceased and his wife receiving bouquets at the temple of Amun at Karnak, complete with obelisk, flagpoles, and a tree-lined quay fed by the river. This rare depiction has been crucial in helping archaeologists to establish the temple's appearance in the late 18th Dynasty.

but they were subsequently incorporated into the main sequence as KV/WV 22–25. Wilkinson thus provided the foundation for the identification system that is still in use in the valley today: all tombs discovered since have been assigned a number building on this sequence. Wilkinson's main focus in Thebes, however, was on copying the decoration in the tombs of non-royal individuals (or 'nobles') in the area. Here he found a great variety of scenes of the sorts of activities the deceased hoped to enjoy in eternity, which he understood to be a reflection of the reality of their day-to-day lives. This allowed him to develop further his ideas for *Manners and Customs of the Ancient Egyptians*.

Wilkinson published his *Topography of Thebes, and general view of Egypt. Being a short account of the principal objects worthy of notice in the valley of the Nile [&c.]* in 1835. Although principally a description of archaeological and other sites in Egypt, it also contains useful

digressions into various subjects including the name of Thebes, the etymology of the word 'pharaoh', the 'manners and customs' of the people, the chronology of the kings of Egypt, and an appendix on 'things required for travelling in Egypt'. The latter is full of guidance that would resonate with many of our Egyptologists. He recommended, for instance, that 'the traveller, if unacquainted with Arabic, should either provide himself with a servant at Malta, who understands that language, or afterwards look out for one at Qaherah on his arrival in the Frank quarter, where several of the natives may be found who are in the habit of accompanying European travellers, and speak Italian and sometimes French', and provided a list of essential equipment that they should procure before embarking on their mission. This included: 'a camp stool and drawing table ... drawing paper, pencils, and Indian-rubber .... For observations, a sextant and artificial horizon, or rather Captain Kater's repeating circle, chronometer, large and small telescope, siphon barometer, thermometers, &c. with a good measuring tape'. The list of medical necessities would alarm any modern traveller: 'a lancet, diachylon and blistering plaster, salts, rhubarb, cream of tartar, ipecacuanha, sulphate of bark, James's powders, calomel, laudanum, sugar of lead, or sulphate of zink, nitre, oil of peppermint, and other common medicines'. Finally, the serious traveller should be armed with a full portfolio of scholarly resources: 'The choice of his library will depend, of course, on his occupations or taste; I shall only, therefore, recommend Larcher's Herodotus, M. Champollion's Phonetic System of Hieroglyphics, Pococke, Denon, Hamilton's AEgyptiaca, Modern Traveller, and Colonel Leake's or my own Map of Egypt, with that of Mr. Parke and Mr. Scoles of Nubia; to which may be added Browne, Belzoni, Burckhardt, Ptolemy, Strabo, and Pliny; but of these three last, as well as of Diodorus, extracts will suffice, if he considers them too voluminous.'

Over the course of his twelve years in the country, Wilkinson gained an unrivalled appreciation of its monuments and in particular of the

↑ Wilkinson's reconstruction of the 'pavilion' of Ramesses III at Medinet Habu. Shown still partially buried by the sands, this was in fact a fortified gatehouse, or *migdol*, built in the style of Asiatic fortresses of the period and highly decorated.

ancient script and language. Champollion's great breakthrough in the *Lettre à M. Dacier* confirmed the Frenchman as the leading scholar in the field (p. 100), but Wilkinson was not far behind and at an advantage in having access to a far greater quantity and variety of inscriptions. He was even able occasionally to correct Champollion, perhaps the only scholar in the world capable of doing so at the time. He found fault both in the Frenchman's notorious belief that he alone was capable of copying or reading the signs, and in some of his conclusions, which Wilkinson believed were sometimes arrived at too hastily: 'He seldom hesitated but made a dash according to probability, this was his fault.'

ARTISTS, EXPEDITIONS AND NATIONALIST COMPETITION

Ultimately, however, Wilkinson admired him greatly and recognized his tenacity and skill: 'But he frequently made a happy hit where the sense was obscure & where another would have given it up.'

Wilkinson returned to England in 1833 with a huge amount of material to digest and publish, but still he was drawn to Egypt; he would visit the country a further four times before the end of his distinguished career. But it was during his first, twelve-year stay that he laid the foundations for his legacy: he was the first to read many royal names, and to put the dynasties and kings into order; his *Topography of Thebes, and general view of Egypt* represented the first survey of the surviving sites and monuments from a topographical and archaeological point of view, a colossal achievement; and he was the first to document thoroughly the tombs at Beni Hasan and to visit the royal tombs at Amarna. His *Manners and Customs of the Ancient Egyptians*, published in three volumes in 1839, was such a success that it earned him a knighthood – the first to be bestowed on an Egyptologist. It remained the best general survey of ancient Egyptian culture for half a century. All of this Wilkinson achieved without the government backing that funded and protected the great expeditions of Napoleon's savants, Champollion or, later, Lepsius. He largely avoided the politics that surrounded the efforts of the representatives of the various European powers, particularly the British Henry Salt and the French envoy Bernardino Drovetti. His modus operandi was more in keeping with those of Robert Hay and his associates, James Burton and Edward William Lane, but unlike them Wilkinson succeeded in publishing his work, ensuring that it had a greater impact during his lifetime and beyond.

↗ A more polished version of the scene at left as prepared for publication, with Wilkinson's scribbled notes removed, and further details of the decoration added.

Hector Horeau

1801–1872 French architect

Horeau drew some of the plates for Frédéric Cailliaud's Voyage à Méroé, *published in six volumes between 1826 and 1827, though he would not visit Egypt himself until 1839. He made many drawings on his travels, including imaginative reconstructions of the ancient landscapes as they might have been when the great monuments were at their peak, informed by his architect's vision.*

→ View looking west of the first pylon of the temple of Luxor. By the time of Horeau's first visit to Egypt in 1839, one of two obelisks that had stood in front of the temple had been removed; it now stands in the Place de la Concorde in Paris. The temple would remain half-buried in sand, as here, until it was cleared in the 1880s.

Hector Horeau was born in Versailles and trained at the École des Beaux-Arts between 1819 and 1822. His first experience of Egyptology was a commission to draw the plates for *Voyage à Méroé*, published in six volumes between 1826 and 1827 by Frédéric Cailliaud (pp. 60–67). It was not until 1839, however, that he was to visit Egypt itself as part of a wider tour of Eastern countries. Horeau's itinerary took him on the by then standard route from Alexandria to Cairo, then up the Nile, ultimately reaching as far south as Abu Simbel.

Horeau was captivated by the monuments he saw, both ancient and modern, declaring that 'No nation on the Earth belonging to the ancient world or the modern erected more giant or splendid monuments than the ancient Egyptians .... In addition to the grave and eternal Egyptian monuments, rise the graceful Arab buildings which, in the seventh century of our era, sprang up with the Mahometan religion. Elegant minarets dart into the air to summon the true believers to prayer from heaven.' Horeau recognized the continuity between pharaonic buildings and their successors, noting that fragments of ancient buildings could often be seen in the fabric of mosques, but seems also to have suffered from a sense of nostalgia at their ruin. His attitude towards the country's later inhabitants was not entirely uncommon among our travellers but seems a little unfair today: 'Alas! the men, the rulers who successively fell on Egypt made human hell of this privileged contra, a miserable population vegetates in a country which was the granary of abundance of so many conquerors, and this cradle of the civilization of the world seems to be able to recover only because it has fallen to the last degree of misery and degradation.'

Horeau's drawings, sketched in colour, meticulously re-created the monuments that he encountered. His views of the front of the first pylon of the temple of Luxor exemplify his skill: the hieroglyphs on the obelisk are reproduced with great accuracy and clarity, and those on the face of the pylon conveyed with similar attention to detail despite the oblique angle from which Horeau painted them. He was one of the first artists of his calibre in Egypt to take advantage of the new technology of photography – which, sadly, would eventually supersede drawing and painting altogether – ordering a number of daguerrotypes from the photographer Pierre-Gustave Joly de Lotbinière in Thebes and using them to assist him in his drawings. These drawings were published in his *Panorama d'Égypte et de Nubie, avec un portrait de Méhémet-Ali et un texte orné de vignettes* (Panorama of Egypt and Nubia, with a Portrait of Mehemet-Ali and a Text Adorned with Vignettes) between 1841 and 1846.

This was a lavish, beautiful volume, dominated by Horeau's images of ancient monuments but also containing his observations and explanations of other aspects of the country that he came across during his journey. A sketch of a group of Egyptian dancers, reproduced as an engraving in the published volume but in glorious colour in the

ARTISTS, EXPEDITIONS AND NATIONALIST COMPETITION

↑ Horeau's imagined view of the ancient city of Thebes. He has paid attention to such details as the furniture on the flat roof and the monumental flagpoles, but has combined elements from different eras, making it difficult to locate the vantage point. The viewer seems to be looking southwest from perhaps the fourth pylon, with the temple of Khonsu beyond, connected to the temple of Luxor in the distance via the avenue of sphinxes.

original, is accompanied by his description of their performance – 'these young girls of nature, with transparent clothes, do not hide their emotions; what they experience they express to the audience and cause them to feel it' – and provides a few bars of musical notation for some of the music he heard, which was accompanied by 'chanting in unison and clapping of hands'.

Some of Horeau's scenes of the local landscape and activities are positively idyllic, such as those of the towns of Mallawi ('Melawi el Arich') and Assyut ('Syout'), or a scene of shipbuilding on the banks of the Nile at Derr; others, like his view of the slave market, less so, though it illuminates this thankfully forgotten aspect of life in Egypt that was

ARTISTS, EXPEDITIONS AND NATIONALIST COMPETITION

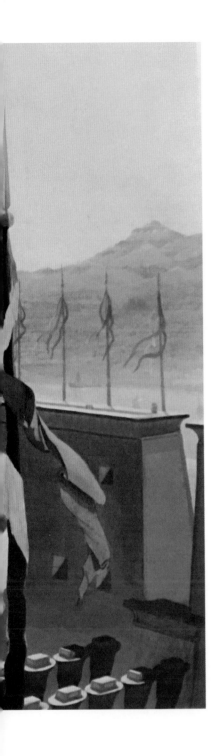

Sketches of column capitals, which became very elaborate during the Ptolemaic and Roman periods. This no doubt appealed to Horeau's architectural sensibilities.

nonetheless part of the Egyptian experience for some of our explorers. Indeed, Robert Hay and Edward William Lane found their wives there.

Horeau is perhaps most celebrated for his contribution to the history of architecture. None of his buildings has survived, but in any case he is best known for his visionary designs that were never realized, including a submission for the Great Exhibition in London and another for a tunnel running underneath the channel between England and France. His interest in architecture is reflected in his drawings of the ancient monuments he saw in Egypt and Nubia, particularly in his series 'Comparaison des différents ordres Egyptiens'. The architect's sense of vision is also evident in his imagined reconstructions of Thebes and Edfu as they would have appeared in ancient times, perhaps the most striking of all his drawings.

Comparison of Horeau's original sketches with the illustrations as published in his *Panorama* is fascinating. Some were reproduced in glorious, full colour, others in the form of black-and-white engravings. The originals are clearly the work of a gifted artist and accurate observer, but are scruffier, perhaps more hurried and more impressionistic than the published versions, which are altogether cleaner, clearer and, where coloured, more vivid. The latter lose something, however, of the immediacy and character of the drawings

↑ The temple of Montu built by Cleopatra at Armant. (Compare with Denon's view on p. 47.) The seven columns of the temple would stand until the 1860s, when the stone was removed for the construction of a sugar factory. Six featured images of Cleopatra and her son, Caesarion, all of which were lost.

↖ View across the first court of the temple of Edfu, from the entrance towards the *pronaos*. This is the opposite view to that on pp. 49 and 97.

← The east side of the island of Philae, with the kiosk of Trajan at left.

that were created on the spot, and in some cases the arrangement of peripheral elements in his scenes, especially human figures, was changed for the publication. The gorgeous view of the approach to the temple of Ramesses II at Wadi es-Sebua ('Asseboua') was changed greatly for the published version, in which the number of people, along with their actions and placement within the composition, was adapted.

Horeau's *Panorama* attracted an impressive list of subscribers, which included his fellow Egyptologists Luigi Cherubini (a member of the Franco-Tuscan expedition), Jacques-Joseph Champollion-Figeac (brother to Jean-François) and Léon Dubois (a curator at the Louvre). They would undoubtedly have been pleased with the results of their investment, but it is in Horeau's original drawings, now kept by the University of Oxford's Griffith Institute, that the sense of his expedition really comes alive.

Karl Richard Lepsius

1810–1884 German Egyptologist and linguist

Lepsius led the Prussian expedition sponsored by King Frederick William IV to record the monuments of Egypt and Sudan. His survey was published in twelve folios that are still consulted today and known to Egyptologists simply as the Denkmäler *(Monuments).*

→ Sketch by Ernst Weidenbach of Friedrich Otto Georgi writing a letter in a tent at Gebel Barkal. Both men were members of Lepsius's Prussian expedition to Egypt and Nubia.

Karl Richard Lepsius is one of the giants of Egyptology, immortalized by the publication of his *Denkmäler aus Aegypten und Aethiopien* (Monuments of Egypt and Ethiopia), the latter referring not to modern-day Ethiopia but to the ancient territory to the south of Egypt referred to as Aethiopia by the ancient Greeks. Possibly the largest Egyptological work ever produced, its title is apt: as a record of the ancient monuments in that part of the world it requires no qualification, for it was intended to be definitive and succeeded in that aim. It is monumental, too, in its scale: its twelve large and unwieldy volumes even have their own room in some libraries. Yet it remains magisterial, unsurpassed and indispensable. Any enquiry into the sites and monuments it covers begins with a reference to 'LD', the simple convention by which it is known to all Egyptologists.

Lepsius was born in Naumburg an der Saale in 1810. He studied classical archaeology at universities in Leipzig, Göttingen and Berlin and then left for Paris, where his interest in Egyptology seems to have begun with his study of the ancient Egyptian language under a colleague of Jean-François Champollion (pp. 98–103). In 1836, Champollion's *Grammaire égyptienne* was published posthumously. Although he had first published his system of decipherment several years earlier, in his now famous *Lettre à M. Dacier*, it had not yet been fully accepted within the scholarly world, and several competing systems were still under consideration. It was Lepsius who finally showed beyond doubt that Champollion was correct, through systematic study of the *Grammaire* and scrutiny of ancient texts, modifying and refining Champollion's theory in several important ways in the process. He made copies of numerous inscriptions from the Egyptian objects in museums and universities in Paris, and subsequently visited the major Egyptian collections in England, Holland and Italy. In fact he must have seen the majority of Egyptian antiquities then outside Egypt – and with the careful insight of one who could actually read the ancient texts, still a very rare thing at this time.

It was inevitable that Lepsius would eventually make the journey to visit Egypt itself. When he did, it was as the leader of the best-organized expedition to the country ever attempted, modelled on the Napoleonic expedition of half a century earlier and in all ways designed to supersede it. Although Egyptology is a scholarly discipline, by no means all those who have contributed to it have been scholars; indeed, many of the individuals featured in this book were not. Lepsius unarguably was, however, and this expedition, which resulted in the publication of the *Denkmäler*, was the culmination of years of academic preparation. He was commissioned by the Prussian King Frederick William IV, and joined by the surveyor Georg Erbkam and the painters Ernst and Max Weidenbach and Johann Frey, although the latter was forced to return home by the 'injurious climate' and was replaced by

Mai m II Pfingstfeiertag.
Georgi

Friedrich Otto Georgi. In addition, the English artist Joseph Bonomi joined the team. Bonomi had gained valuable experience drawing Egyptian monuments in the course of his travels with Robert Hay (pp. 88–97), and had developed a sophisticated understanding of Egyptian art.

The expedition members met in Alexandria on 18 September 1842. Arriving in Giza a few weeks later, they began a thorough study of the site and the other major pyramid fields at Abusir, Saqqara and Dahshur. Lepsius commented that 'The inexhaustible number of important and instructive monuments and representations, which we met with in these Necropoli, the most ancient that have existed in any country, surpassed every expectation we had been entitled to hold concerning them.' Lepsius was careful not to duplicate, unnecessarily, the work of the preceding expeditions of Napoleon's savants, Champollion or Rosellini, but he was often able to improve on them and was sometimes scathing in his appraisal of their efforts, writing of the Giza plateau that 'the French-Tuscan expedition, in particular, did little more than pass through it'. His approach was methodical: his team first produced a comprehensive plan of each site, assigning codes to each of the visible monuments, some of which, such as the 'L' numbers given to mastabas at Saqqara, or those assigned to the sixty-seven pyramids they surveyed – the first such systematic numbering of these monuments – are still in use today. Limited excavations were undertaken to facilitate the careful recording of all aspects of the monuments, including their architectural plans and decoration schemes. This proved necessary to access the 130 non-royal tombs they recorded in and around the pyramids: 'A great many of these sepulchral chambers, richly adorned with representations and inscriptions, could only be reached by excavations.'

After spending six months surveying the northern pyramid fields, the expedition journeyed upstream, stopping at Hawara, the site of a pyramid and the fabled 'labyrinth' that Lepsius was able to attribute, correctly, to the 12th Dynasty pharaoh Amenemhat III. They carried on to Beni Hasan, investigating the tombs of the nomarchs of the same period, and Thebes, where they spent twelve 'over rich, astonishing days', little more than a preliminary visit ahead of a much longer stay on their return downstream. They then spent a little time at the island of Philae before continuing further south. The Napoleonic expedition had gone no further than the First Cataract, which for much of Egypt's ancient history was its southern frontier; that of Champollion and Rosellini had made it only as far as the Second Cataract, taking in the territory that the Egyptians had periodically established as their own and in which they had built numerous fortified towns. Lepsius went far further, however, into modern-day Sudan to the heartland

↑ A watercolour and a pencil sketch of Lepsius, accompanied by a servant, riding a camel. The pencil sketch is dated 23 June 1844 and refers to Dongola, suggesting it was made in the Third Cataract region, around the old capital of the Makurian kingdom. The watercolour includes a distant view of three pyramids that seem closer to the Memphite pyramids of Egypt than those of Sudan.

Detailed technical drawings of mastaba tombs in the Giza necropolis. At top, the tomb of the Prophet of Ra in the sun temple of Neferirkare and Khuwiwer; two statues of the deceased flank a recessed false door. Beneath is a 6th Dynasty tomb belonging to the overseer of the Great Court, Ihy.

of the kingdom of Kush, pharaonic Egypt's principal southern rival. Here, hundreds of miles from Egypt's ancient southern border at Aswan, his expedition found monuments that had apparently been inspired by those in Egypt but were not entirely Egyptian – most spectacularly, the pyramids of Meroë.

On its return northwards, the expedition spent several months in Thebes, where Lepsius excavated in the tomb of Ramesses II in the Valley of the Kings and at that pharaoh's mortuary temple, the Ramesseum. His team also made accurate copies of inscriptions and artworks in a selection of non-royal tombs, including that of Rekhmire (TT 100), and in the temples of Luxor and Karnak on the east side of the river. Lepsius was enraptured by the wealth of archaeological remains that they encountered: 'I should be afraid of being almost oppressed

by the overwhelming number of monuments, if the mighty character of the ruins of this most royal city of all antiquity did not maintain, and daily renew, our interest to the highest possible degree. While our investigations of the numerous temples, from the Ptolemaic and the Roman period, immediately preceding that, had in fact become almost fatiguing, here, where the Homeric forms of the mighty Pharaohs of the 18th and 19th Dynasties stand out before me in their dignity and splendour, I feel as fresh again as at the commencement of our journey.'

Lepsius finally returned home in 1846. The final volume of the *Denkmäler* would not appear until 1859, and the five volumes of accompanying text were not published until after his death. The four years his expedition spent in Egypt were a glorious triumph, and its product one of Egyptology's great landmarks.

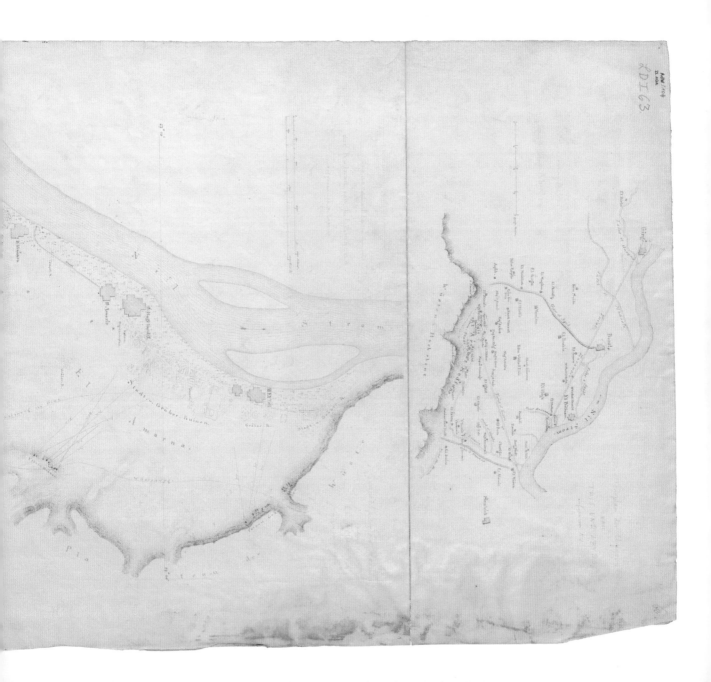

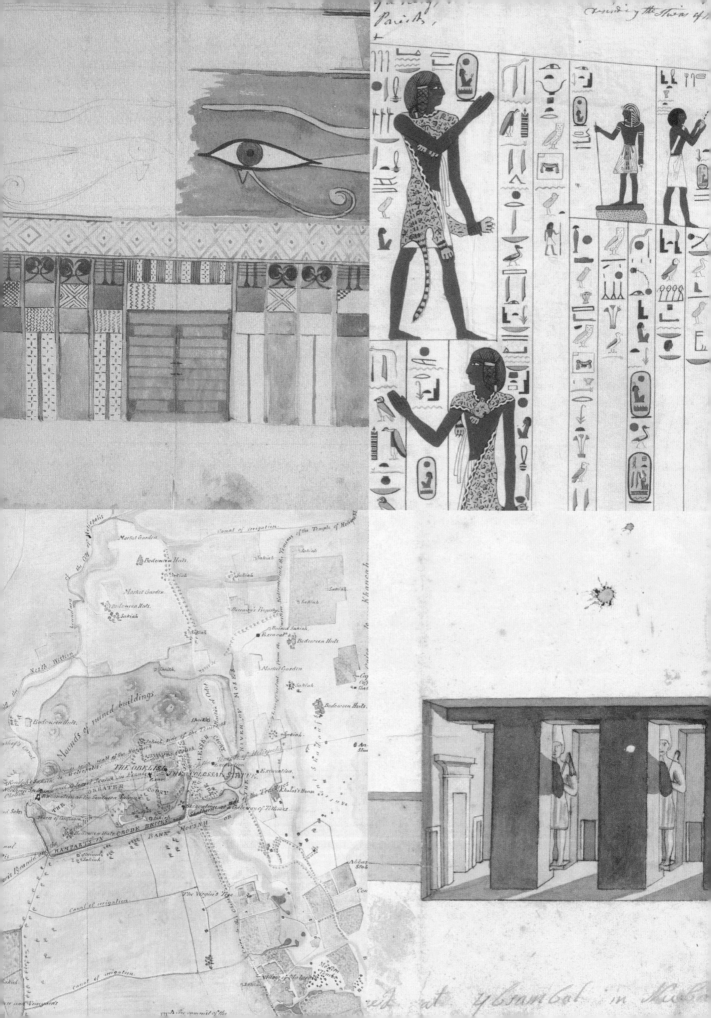

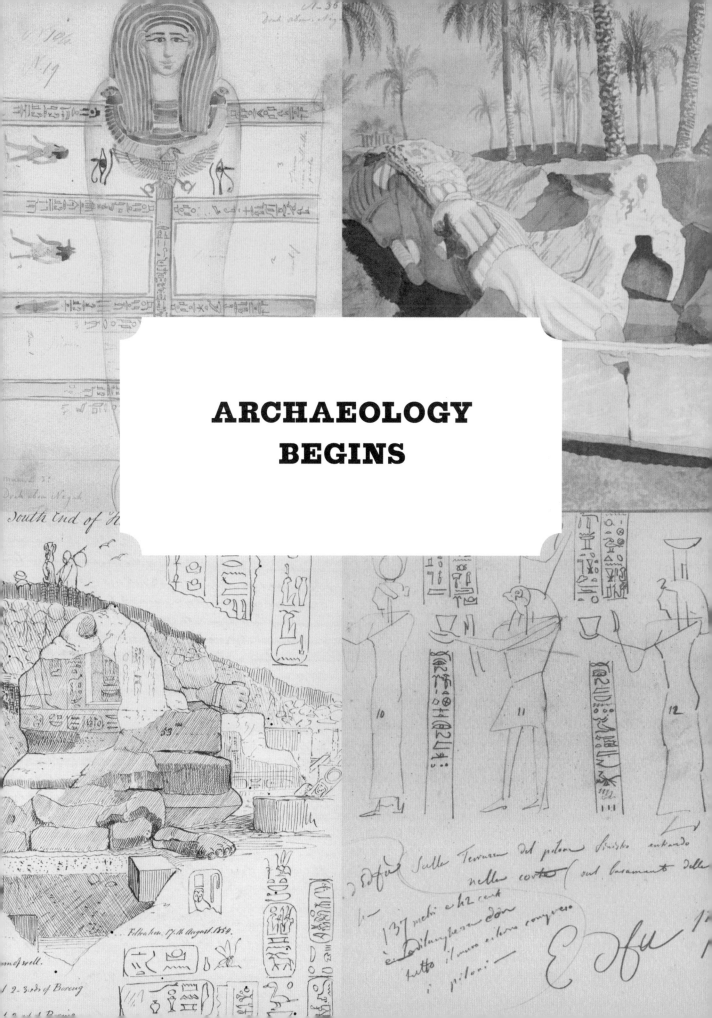

ARCHAEOLOGY BEGINS

'My functions in Egypt are to see that no one destroys the monuments of antiquity, and at the same time to create a museum for the Vice-Roi.'

AUGUSTE MARIETTE

Egyptology in the first half of the 19th century was dominated by the first serious studies of the ancient ruins and a sudden rush to discover more for the glory of the dominant European powers. Excavations were sponsored in the name of acquiring artefacts for the collections of the great European museums – there was no thought that such antiquities should remain in Egypt. As the century progressed, these treasure-hunting missions gradually became more scientific endeavours, and Egypt increasingly asserted a claim to its ancient past, creating a national Antiquities Service.

The French consul-general Bernardino Drovetti and his British counterpart Henry Salt operated as direct rivals in the 1810s and 1820s. Each amassed large and important collections, in part by commissioning agents to carry out excavations, among them Jean-Jacques Rifaud (pp. 144–49) and Frédéric Cailliaud (pp. 60–67) for Drovetti, and Giovanni Battista Belzoni (pp. 136–43) and Giovanni d'Athanasi for Salt. These digs were barely documented, and there is no question that they altered the archaeology at such crucially important sites as Karnak dramatically and irreparably. Drovetti and Salt's interest in purchasing antiquities encouraged more of the same at sites throughout the country. The artefacts they procured ultimately made their way into the Egyptian Museum, Turin, the British Museum, London, the Louvre, Paris, and the Ägyptisches Museum, Berlin. It was not until 1835 that steps were taken to control the flow of antiquities out of the country, when Mohamed Ali Pasha issued a decree banning the export of antiquities without a permit. All objects already in the possession of the government, and all those discovered during future excavations, were to be deposited in a newly established museum in the Ezbekia district of Cairo. Nonetheless, permits were still issued, sometimes for the export of very large quantities of antiquities, and the system was full of loopholes to be exploited, such as shipping via Suez rather than Alexandria. Worse, although the new museum was to be modelled on European standards and headed by a well-qualified Egyptian, Rifa'a el-Tahtawi, the collection was regarded as second-rate, and was gradually denuded when Mohamed Ali's successor, Abbas Pasha, began giving objects away as gifts. The collection eventually shrank to the extent that it could be housed in a single room in the Citadel in Cairo, and the final blow was dealt when Abbas's successor, Sa'id Pasha, gave all that remained to the Archduke Maximilian of Austria-Este (the objects would eventually be transferred to the Kunsthistorisches Museum in Vienna, where they remain).

It was a Frenchman, and indeed a former treasure-hunter, Auguste Mariette, who took up the cause of protecting Egypt's ancient monuments. After Nestor l'Hôte (pp. 104–9) died in 1842, Mariette, his cousin, was given the task of organizing his papers. This ignited in Mariette a passion for Egyptology. He became a junior curator at the Louvre, and travelled to Egypt in 1850 to obtain Coptic, Syriac and Arabic manuscripts for the Bibliothèque Nationale, and pharaonic objects for the Louvre. When he arrived, he found himself thwarted in the first of these aims by the Coptic pope who, angered by the removal of such manuscripts by British agents, had ordered that all that remained be protected in Cairo. Turning to his second objective, Mariette began prospecting at ancient sites. At Saqqara he noticed the head of a sphinx poking out of the sand, and was reminded of Strabo's description of the *dromos* leading to the temple of Serapis: he had located the fabled Serapeum, entering the subterranean galleries where the sacred bulls were buried. This work was undertaken with the correct permit, but Mariette revealed himself a master in the covert removal of antiquities, which he arranged to ship to Paris as per his mission. He would go on to excavate at Giza where, in 1853, he discovered the 'valley temple' of Khafra and the now-famous diorite statue of the king protected by Horus in the guise of a falcon. That same year he shipped a colossal quantity of antiquities to Paris – 7,000 objects in 230 cases. His achievements made him a hero in France, but unpopular with the authorities in Egypt, especially Abbas Pasha, who learned of the Louvre's gains through the European press. On his next visit to Egypt in 1857, perhaps unsettled by claims made by the Egyptian authorities and rival foreign excavators that his activities were tantamount to theft, Mariette seems to have gained an acute awareness of the destructive consequences of unrestricted excavation, and he proposed a series of measures to protect the country's ancient sites and monuments. Fortunately, this was received by a new ruler of Egypt, Sa'id Pasha, who authorized the creation of a 'Service des Antiquités' and appointed Mariette as its first director.

Mariette was endowed with the power to conscript vast numbers of labourers for excavations and was fortunate to have the assistance of a series of talented deputies, including Luigi Vassalli (pp. 164–67) and the capable Egyptians who acted as *reis* – foremen – of the labourers. Under Mariette's direction, numerous spectacular discoveries were made: the detailed autobiographical inscription of Weni at Abydos; the beautifully painted statue of Rahotep and Nofret at Meidum; the 'Meidum geese' masterpiece in the tomb of Nefermaat; the strikingly lifelike wooden statue of Ka-aper, the 'Sheikh el-Beled', from his tomb at Saqqara; and the treasure of the 17th Dynasty queen Ahhotep from Thebes.

Mariette's intentions were more honourable, perhaps, than those that had gone before him, but his excavations were still almost uncontrolled and very poorly documented – although more information might have been salvaged had his library in the Boulaq suburb of Cairo, including his notebooks, not been destroyed by flooding in 1878. While control of Egypt's sites and monuments still lay firmly in the hands of Europeans – perhaps even more so following Mariette's appointment – the idea of protecting the antiquities for Egypt had taken hold. And at least by now the antiquities discovered would remain in Egypt in the national collection, which, from 1863, had a new home in an old building in Boulaq that had belonged to a steamboat company and was now remodelled with an ancient temple façade. During the second half of the 19th century, some archaeologists – such as Joseph Hekekyan (pp. 150–63) and Luigi Vassalli – began to work much more methodically, scientifically even, in their investigations of the ancient ruins. Egyptology was heading in the right direction.

Giovanni Battista Belzoni

1778–1823 Italian explorer and engineer

Belzoni, a former circus strongman, removed antiquities from Egypt's archaeological sites on behalf of the British consul-general, Henry Salt. He also carried out his own excavations and discovered numerous tombs in the Valley of the Kings, most importantly that of the founder of the 19th Dynasty, Sety I.

→ Belzoni's illustrations of brightly coloured collars.

Giovanni Battista Belzoni was born in Padua and studied engineering in Rome. In 1803 he moved to London to join his brother Francesco and found employment as a circus strongman: he was an impressive 2 metres (6 feet 7 inches) tall. But a meeting with Ismael Gibraltar, an agent of Mohamed Ali Pasha, in 1814 was to set him on a new career path. Gibraltar told Belzoni that the Pasha was looking for skilled engineers and technicians to assist in his grand project to modernize the country; sensing an opportunity, Belzoni talked up his expertise in hydraulics and proposed that a new kind of waterwheel might be built to improve the country's irrigation. On 19 May 1815 he left for Alexandria. It was not long before he met the explorer Jean-Louis Burckhardt and the French consul-general Bernardino Drovetti, and in 1816 Burckhardt recommended him to the British consul-general, Henry Salt (probably at the cost of good relations with Drovetti). Alongside his engineering knowledge, a mixture of persuasiveness and determination allowed him to navigate the perils and pitfalls of dealing with the Egyptian administrators and the population he would need as his labour force.

Belzoni's great physical strength, in a time before mechanized lifting technology was readily available in remote regions, proved a boon to his value to the consul-general in the retrieval of heavy stone monuments. The first task assigned to him by Salt was to remove a colossal bust of Ramesses II from that king's mortuary temple, the great Ramesseum at Thebes. The French agents of Drovetti had assured him that this was an impossible task, yet Belzoni removed the statue, known as the 'Younger Memnon', with the minimum of fuss: in fifteen days it had been transported to the Nile ready for its journey northwards, ultimately to London.

Belzoni then visited Aswan and Nubia intending to open the temple of Ramesses II at Abu Simbel, but faced with uncooperative locals and a shortage of money and food he abandoned the effort after just seven days. He returned downstream to Karnak, where – while waiting for the Younger Memnon to be transported to Cairo – he discovered twenty lion-headed goddess statues at the temple of Mut, six of which were intact. At this time he also carried out his first work on the Theban West Bank, discovering, in the western branch of the Valley of the Kings, the tomb of Ay, a pharaoh of the late 18th Dynasty, who had been a senior member of the administration under Akhenaten and Tutankhamun and became king when the latter died with no heirs. But Belzoni was unable to identify the tomb's intriguing owner, and so was somewhat disappointment with its contents, writing 'I cannot boast of having made a great discovery in this tomb'. A short while later he found a second tomb in the same area, which contained the mummies of eight individuals, probably belonging to a family of 22nd Dynasty date. Such discoveries would make headlines around the world today, but Belzoni would not be satisfied until he had found the tomb of a great royal, and so he focused his efforts on the main branch

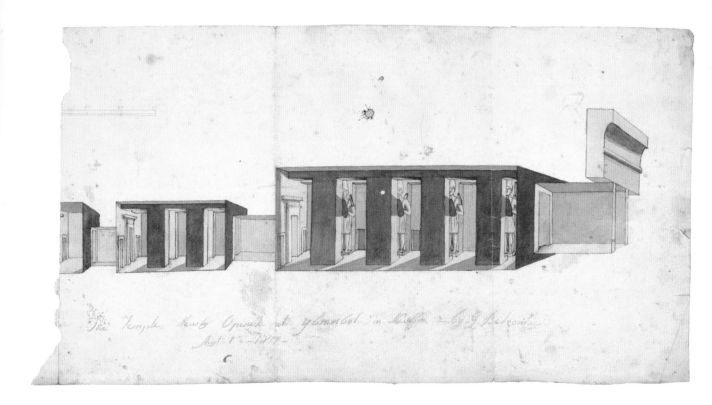

'The Temple Newly Opened at Ybsambul in Nubia – by G. Belzoni. Aug 1 1817.'

↑ 'The Temple Newly Opened at Ybsambul in
Nubia – by G. Belzoni. Aug 1 1817.' Isometric section
drawing by Belzoni of the interior of the great temple
at Abu Simbel, which he had opened for the first
time since antiquity.

of the valley. He was swiftly rewarded with success, discovering the
tomb of Mentukherkhepeshef, a son of Ramesses IX. He also found
an undecorated tomb that contained two mummies, each with one
arm across the chest, indicating that they were queens, probably of
the 18th Dynasty, although their identity remains a mystery.

Belzoni subsequently returned to Cairo and thence to Alexandria
with the Younger Memnon to see it off on its journey to England.
In February 1817 he returned to Thebes. He intended to excavate at
the temple of Karnak, only to find that Drovetti's agents had secured
exclusive permits to dig: 'From the moment these personages came
to Thebes, I had a continual series of disagreeable circumstances to
encounter, which I could not describe, were I to attempt it. Suffice it
to say, that the Bey, who had the command of the whole country, made
it a particular point, I have no doubt, to thwart our views .... The petty
advantage taken on this occasion soon showed me the characters of
the persons I had to deal with. I do not mean the first two agents alone,
who had arrived in Thebes, but those who had given them instructions,
and others who were sent after them, consisting of European renegades,
desperadoes, exiles, &c.'

Belzoni abandoned Karnak and crossed to the West Bank,
where he resumed his exploration of the tombs in search of papyri
and mummies. His reports convey the claustrophobic experience,
surely worsened by his great size:

*Of some of these tombs many persons could not withstand the
suffocating air, which often causes fainting. A vast quantity of dust
rises, so fine that it enters into the throat and nostrils, and chokes the
nose and mouth to such a degree, that it requires great power of lungs
to resist it and the strong effluvia of the mummies. This is not all; the*

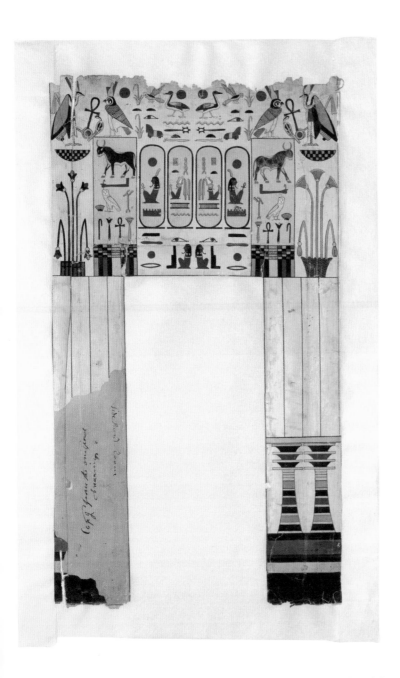

↑ Belzoni's copy of inscriptions on a doorway leading to a side chamber in the tomb of Sety I. The apparently elaborate design above the doorway comprises the names and epithets of the king, while the lotus and papyrus motifs symbolize Upper and Lower Egypt.

entry or passage where the bodies are is roughly cut in the rocks, and the falling of the sand from the upper part or ceiling of the passage causes it to be nearly filled up.

After getting through these passages, some of them two or three hundred yards long, you generally find a more commodious place, perhaps high enough to sit. But what a place of rest! surrounded by bodies, by heaps of mummies in all directions; which, previous to my being accustomed to the sight, impressed me with horror. The blackness of the wall, the faint light given by the candles or torches for want of air, the different objects that surrounded me, seeming to converse with each other, and the Arabs with the candles or torches in their hands, naked and covered with dust, themselves resembling living mummies, absolutely formed a scene that cannot be described. In such a situation I found myself several times, and often returned exhausted and fainting, till at last I became inured to it, and indifferent to what I suffered, except from the dust, which never failed to choke my throat and nose; and though, fortunately, I am destitute of the sense of smelling, I could taste that the mummies were rather unpleasant to swallow ....

Once I was conducted ... through a passage of about twenty feet [6 metres] in length, and no wider than that a body could be forced through. It was choked with mummies, and I could not pass without putting my face in contact with that of some decayed Egyptian; but as the passage inclined downwards, my own weight helped me on: however, I could not avoid being covered with bones, legs, arms, and heads rolling from above. Thus I proceeded from one cave to another, all full of mummies piled up in various ways, some standing, some lying, and some on their heads.

Politics, however, continued to interfere with Belzoni's excavations, and the governor of Upper Egypt prohibited the English from gathering artefacts, probably under pressure from Drovetti. On 23 May Belzoni left for Abu Simbel, to try again to clear the temple. The undertaking took a month but this time yielded success: he and his team entered the temple on 1 August. The temperature inside was over 50 °C (122 °F) but, alas, there was no sign of the treasure that they had believed they would find. Belzoni carved his name on the north wall of the interior of the temple, where the statues of four deities were seated, unmoved by the passage of thousands of years since they were first sculpted into existence.

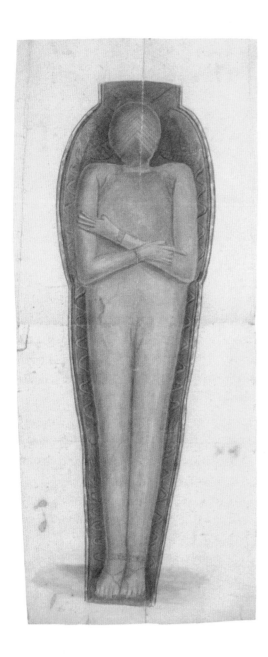

↑ Drawing of a mummified body inside a coffin. It is believed to be that of a man named Butehamun, now in the Egyptian collections in Brussels.

By the time the temple was cleared, the ban on the British missions in Thebes had been lifted, and so Belzoni headed back to the Valley of the Kings. Here, over the course of just a few weeks, he would make a most remarkable sequence of discoveries. Aware that the classical authors had described many more tombs in the valley than were known in modern times, he resolved to begin uncovering the missing ones. In October, he found the tomb of the first king of the 19th Dynasty, Ramesses I. It had a beautifully decorated burial chamber, 'tolerably large and well painted' in Belzoni's estimation, with a red granite sarcophagus in the centre. Belzoni found two mummies inside the sarcophagus, but neither was that of the king. The tomb seemed not to have been completely finished: one would normally expect further chambers in the tomb of a king, and the decoration on the sarcophagus had not been carved into the stone, as was the norm, but applied in yellow paint, and with numerous errors. As the founder of the dynasty, and therefore not of royal blood himself, Ramesses may have come to the throne late in life and ruled only for a short period of time, which might explain why his tomb was not grander.

In any case, Belzoni clearly still was not satisfied and moved his team a little further up the same branch of the valley. Here, at last, he made a discovery of the magnitude he had hoped for: the tomb of Ramesses I's successor, Sety I, one of the greatest of all pharaohs, who re-established Egypt's territory in Syria–Palestine and commenced massive building projects, notably at the sites of Karnak and Abydos (although all this was unknown to Belzoni at the time – he believed the tomb to belong to a 'Psammuthis'). This was the longest tomb ever constructed in the Valley of the Kings, its passages stretching over 450 feet (137 metres), and beautifully decorated throughout. Fragments of the king's burial equipment littered the floor of the tomb, including the remains of numerous shabti figurines, small statues that acted as the servants of the deceased in the afterlife.

The single most spectacular discovery in the tomb was that of the king's sarcophagus. It was found in the vaulted burial chamber, not in its intended position but lying over a staircase leading to a roughly cut passageway (the end of which was only, finally, reached in 2007). The lid had been removed and smashed into fragments, some of which Belzoni found close to the tomb entrance, and the king's body was missing. What remained was the sarcophagus box, a masterpiece of craftsmanship made from a single enormous piece of translucent Egyptian alabaster and decorated with finely carved hieroglyphic texts and accompanying images from various religious texts, principally the 'Book of Gates'. This text divides into twelve sections, one for each hour of the night. The gates themselves were depicted on the sarcophagus at fearsome scale, guarded by snake-like creatures with names such as 'Bloodsucker' and 'He Whose Eyes Spew Fire'. The deceased king would have to pass through all of them on his journey to the afterlife.

Belzoni removed the sarcophagus from the tomb, and it was transported to Alexandria, and from there to England on the steamship *Diana*. Although Belzoni had acted on his own initiative in the Valley of the Kings, he was still the agent of Henry Salt, and so the sarcophagus became part of Salt's collection and was destined to be sold when it reached England. Relations between Salt and Belzoni had become

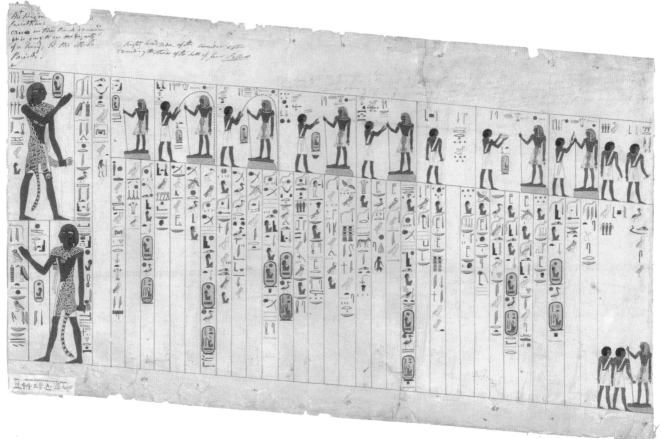

↑ Belzoni's record of a scene from Corridor G, beyond the stairs leading down from the four-pillared hall, showing priests performing rites before royal statues.

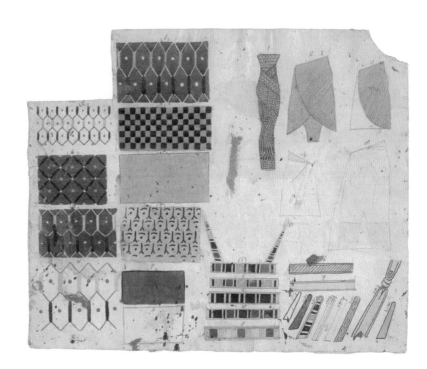

→ Part of Belzoni's index of patterns, here showing a series of diaper and chequer motifs, and various kilts as worn by male figures.

strained by this point, Belzoni wanting – quite reasonably – greater credit for his discoveries. An arrangement was reached between the two: Belzoni would receive half the proceeds of the sale over and above £2,000 (the equivalent of approximately £115,000 today). The sarcophagus was exhibited at the British Museum in 1821, where it attracted considerable attention. The museum authorities deliberated for two years over whether to purchase the Salt collection, and for how much. Eventually they settled on the sum of £2,000 – considerably less than Salt had spent in amassing it. That offer did not include the sarcophagus, however. In what, for many, has become a notorious blunder on the part of the museum, they declined to purchase it on the grounds that it was too expensive. Instead it passed into the hands of a London architect, Sir John Soane. Soane possessed a considerable collection of Egyptian antiquities, which he kept at his home in Lincoln's Inn Fields. In 1822 he had attended an exhibition of Belzoni's drawings of the tomb and used them to create a replica of parts of it, which the sarcophagus would complete.

Belzoni took a loan from a bank so that he could excavate independently of Salt, opening the pyramid of Khafra on the Giza plateau in 1818. He then returned to Thebes but found that all the best excavation sites had been divided between Drovetti and Salt.

Later that year, he accompanied William John Bankes's expedition to remove the Philae obelisk (pp. 68–73). Once more, the British interests conflicted with the French, who had laid a claim to the obelisk. The Aga was summoned to Belzoni's boat to give his verdict as to who first claimed the obelisk, which turned out to be in Belzoni's favour. But disaster struck as they attempted to load the obelisk onto their boat: 'The obelisk was now ready to be embarked, when the following accident happened, which was entirely owing to my own neglect, by trusting a single manoeuvre to some who speak more than they can execute. I had left the care to others of making a sort of temporary pier of large blocks of stones ... the pier appeared quite strong enough to bear at least forty times the weight it had to support; but, alas! when the obelisk came gradually on from the sloping bank, and all the weight rested on it, the pier, with the obelisk, and some of the men, took a slow movement, and majestically descended into the river, wishing us better success. I was not three yards off when this happened, and for some minutes, I must confess, I remained as stiff as a post. The first thing that came into my head, was the loss of such a piece of antiquity; the second was, the exultation of our opponents, after so much questioning to what party it belonged; and, lastly, the blame of all the antiquarian republic in the world.'

Removing the obelisk was an incredible feat – both in the rescuing of it from the water over the course of two days and then getting it across the First

↓ A somewhat naive drawing of a colossus in Nubia, perhaps from the great temple at Abu Simbel. A cartouche on the shoulder features symbols that do not correspond to any known royal name – understandable, perhaps, given that Champollion had yet to decipher the ancient script.

H4547A

↑ Belzoni supervising the removal of the 'Younger Memnon' from the Ramesseum for transport, ultimately, to the British Museum; illustration from the *Fruits of Enterprize Exhibited in the Travels of Belzoni in Egypt and Nubia* by Sarah Atkins (1823). The bust here is given distinctly classical features rather than the more Egyptian appearance it presents in reality.

↗ A watercolour by George Scharf of a man advertising 'Belzoni's Egyptian Tomb'– his model of the tomb of Sety I on view in Piccadilly, London.

Cataract, 'the greatest fall, or rather descent, of water' in the Nile. The obelisk had arrived in Luxor by 24 December 1818, leading to an argument with Drovetti in Thebes; Belzoni's servant was beaten and Belzoni himself threatened and, although Belzoni had had the better of his competitors on so many occasions, this proved to be the last straw. It was clear he could no longer work in Egypt. He collected the sarcophagus of Sety I and left Upper Egypt for good on 27 January 1819, testifying in the trial of Drovetti's agents in Cairo before leaving Egypt in mid-September.

In 1821, he put on an enormously popular and influential exhibition at the Egyptian Hall in London's Piccadilly that included two full-scale replica chambers and an enormous model of the tomb of Sety I over 15 metres (50 feet) long, and displayed many antiquities, which were sold at the hall in 1822. His account of his exploits, *Narrative of the Operations and Recent Discoveries within the Pyramids, Temples, Tombs, and Excavations, in Egypt and Nubia*, published in 1820, was also enormously popular, inspiring many of those who would visit the country in the following years, and represents a fitting culmination of his career. Belzoni set out for West Africa in 1823 with the aim of reaching Timbuktu, but contracted dysentery in the kingdom of Benin and died in December that year. He achieved a huge amount in a very short time, perhaps more than any other individual at this time of immense discoveries.

Jean-Jacques Rifaud

1786–1852 French archaeologist

Rifaud was a French excavator in the employ of the French consul-general Bernardino Drovetti. He is rivalled only by Belzoni as the discoverer of the great masterpieces of sculpture now in major European museums, but his personal reports sadly fall short of the standards not only of modern archaeologists but also his own contemporaries.

Jean-Jacques Rifaud was born in Marseilles, where he trained as a sculptor and apprenticed as an engraver before being conscripted into the French army. He fought in Spain, where he was taken prisoner or perhaps deserted. He travelled to the Levant and then on to Egypt, where his earlier training was to serve him well. He quickly became associated with the French consul-general Bernardino Drovetti, with whom he travelled to Abu Simbel in 1816 along with Frédéric Cailliaud (pp. 60–67). They attempted, but ultimately failed, to open the great temple, a feat that would be achieved by Giovanni Battista Belzoni (pp. 136–43). Nonetheless, Drovetti and Rifaud left their mark at the site, each carving their names onto a pillar in the first room of the small exterior temple. Drovetti left graffiti at several other sites in the region, although in one instance his name is spelt incorrectly as 'Droveti', suggesting he was not responsible – the likeliest culprit is Rifaud, whose somewhat slapdash letters are riddled with similar mistakes.

Between 1817 and 1823 Rifaud undertook a vast amount of excavation and clearance work in the Luxor area; Cailliaud described him as 'a character truly zealous in the search of antiquities'. By this time Drovetti had secured a permit to excavate at Karnak, site of three vast temple complexes of the Egyptian gods Montu, Amun and Mut, within each of which were the remains of dozens of buildings and hundreds of fine statues. Importantly, the concession denied others – particularly Drovetti's rival, the British consul-general Henry Salt, and his own agent, Belzoni – the opportunity to excavate the temple.

Rifaud's excavations at the site were a revelation, unearthing spectacular monumental sculptures. Many of these are now in the Egyptian Museum of Turin, which purchased Drovetti's first collection of antiquities in 1824. They include statues of the pharaohs Tuthmosis I, Horemheb with the god Amun, and Ramesses II standing between Amun and Mut, as well as several depicting the lion-headed goddess Sekhmet and one of the god Ptah. Rifaud carved inscriptions into a statue of Tuthmosis III and colossus of Sety II to tell the world that he was their discoverer. Perhaps the most famous of all his discoveries was that of an unusual granodiorite statue of Ramesses II wearing the blue crown and a curiously benign, smiling expression.

Rifaud's exploits in Thebes were not without mishap – of a very serious nature, in one instance. In the last days of December 1818, he and Drovetti were visiting Luxor, leaving the Karnak excavations in the charge of a deputy. Rifaud should perhaps have kept closer watch: the excavations were allowed to reach a depth of 10 metres (33 feet) without the sides being shored up. They collapsed, burying a group of children who had been employed to carry debris away. Most were rescued, but six were killed. The locals, including children, might otherwise have been working in the fields to help their families make ends meet, and archaeological excavations offered a good opportunity to make money, but this incident also speaks to a relationship between the

→ Lithograph from *Voyage en Égypte*, in Rifaud's characteristically naive style. This must be a record of the granite doorway leading to the third terrace of the temple of Hatshepsut at Thebes, but it contains several inaccuracies. Compare with Robert Hay's infinitely superior drawing on p. 93.

Portique en granit rose, au devant d'un des hypogées de gournak (Thebes)

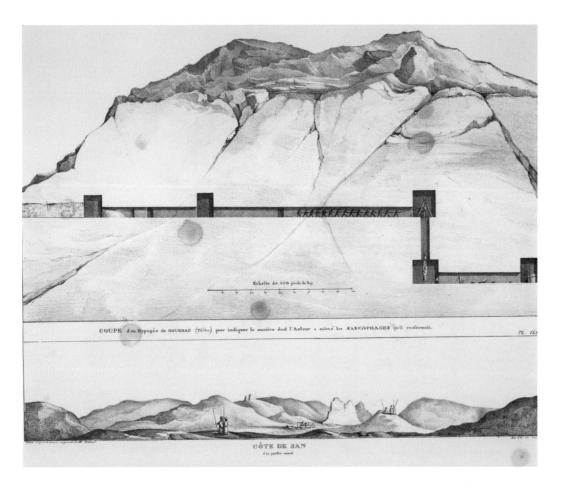

COUPE d'un Hypogée de GOURNAC (Thèbes) pour indiquer la manière dont l'Auteur a enlevé les SARCOPHAGES qu'il renfermait.

Echelle de 100 pieds de Roy.

CÔTE DE JAN
à la partie ouest

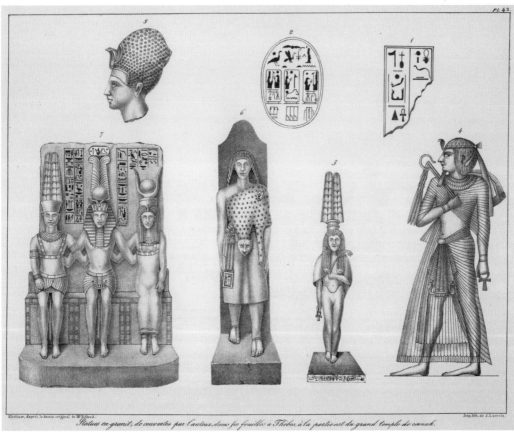

Statues en granit, découvertes par l'auteur, dans ses fouilles à Thèbes, à la partie est du grand temple de carnak.

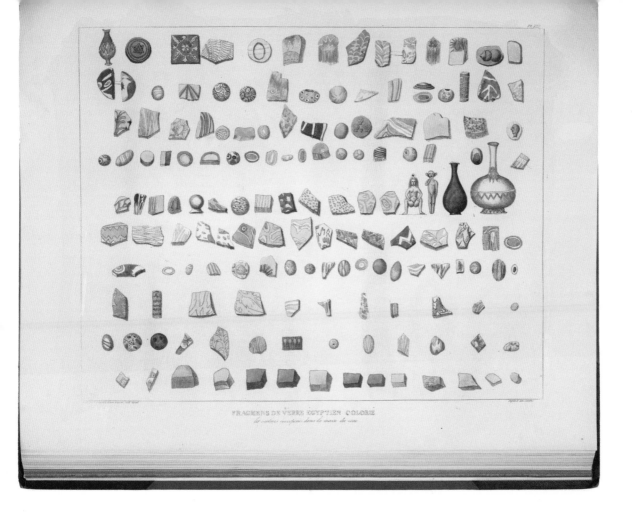

↑ Fragments of coloured Egyptian glass. Plate 130 of Rifaud's *Voyage en Égypte*.

↖ Plate 137 from Rifaud's *Voyage en Égypte* shows a section of a tomb cut into the hillside, 'for indicating the manner in which the author raised up the coffins which it contained'. Fifteen men are shown hauling on a rope and pulley above a tomb shaft, in which an anthropoid coffin is making its way to the top.

← Plate 42 from Rifaud's *Voyage en Égypte* shows a series of objects identifiable as pieces now in the collection of the Egyptian Museum in Turin, including the head of the famous seated statue of Ramesses II.

Egyptian population and the Europeans for whom the gains – of some of the finest sculptures to have been produced in the ancient world, which they would remove from Egypt for their own museums – were ultimately much greater.

In 1823–24 Rifaud visited the Faiyum region and attempted to open the pyramid of Amenemhat III at Hawara. He succeeded only in making a large scar on its north side. In Rifaud's defence, this pyramid has proven notoriously difficult to investigate, as its burial chamber lies beneath the water table; William Flinders Petrie (pp. 178–83) was able to enter only with the greatest difficulty, and it has remained inaccessible since. When the harvest meant no workmen could be spared, Rifaud took the opportunity to survey Lake Qarun and to look for the fabled 'Labyrinth' – in fact the mortuary temple connected to the pyramid of Amenemhat III – that had been described by Herodotus: 'Though the pyramids were greater than words can tell, and each one of them a match for many great monuments built by Greeks, this maze surpasses even the pyramids.' The complex was in fact located right next to the pyramid, although very little of it was left by the time Rifaud made his visit, thanks to stone-robbing and Roman building activities.

By the middle of 1825 Rifaud had moved to Tanis in the north-eastern Delta, another site that was ripe for the removal of large sculptures. On the second day of work he uncovered a superb seated statue in grey granite and another in the same material some 6 metres (20 feet) high. The main temple at Tanis, a counterpart to the temple

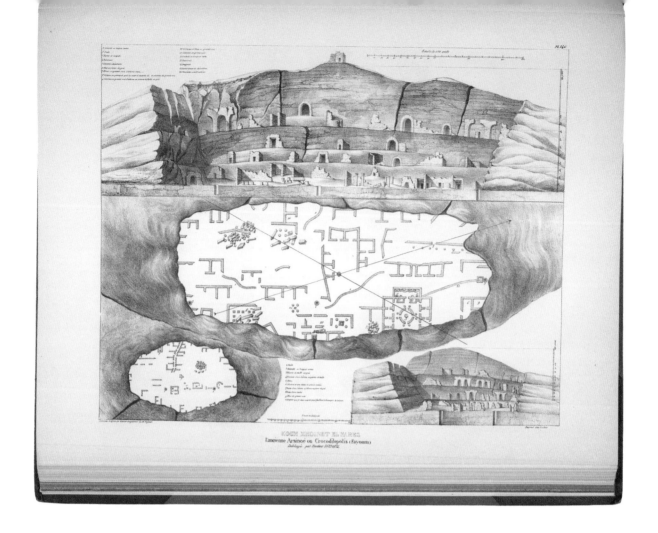

KOUM MEDINET EL FARES
l'ancienne Arsinoé ou Crocodilopolis (Fayoum)
Archéologie par Bertré RIFAUD

↑ The eastern part of the mound of Kom Medinet el-Fares, the ancient site of Crocodilopolis (later Arsinoë), out of which the modern city of Faiyum has grown. It was excavated by Rifaud in the 1820s. Very little is known about the site today.

of Amun at Karnak from the 21st Dynasty onwards, remains littered with very fine and large statues, mostly of Ramesses II. Many were simply too large for Rifaud to remove, though at his request Drovetti sent money and provisions, including five gun-carriage wheels, to carry some of the smaller pieces away.

By 1826 relations between Rifaud and his employer had begun to sour. Drovetti accused Rifaud of complaining about him to Salt and the Swedish–Norwegian consul-general Giovanni Anastasi – Rifaud had indeed met both – and reprimanded him for not taking better care of the antiquities held in store during his absence in Turkey. Rifaud, for his part, was still awaiting 4,000 of 10,000 *piastres* promised for his work in Thebes (completed in 1823). He was broke, battling illness and grieving for his youngest son, who had recently died. Frustrated with his situation – even describing Egypt, where he had lived for over a decade, as 'a country where ... people's morals collapsed' – he chose to return to Europe, arriving in Marseilles in 1827.

Rifaud published an account of his experiences as *Voyage en Égypte, en Nubie et lieux circonvoisins, depuis 1805 jusqu'en 1827* (Travels in Egypt and Nubia and Surrounding Places from 1805 until 1827), but his ambitions for the project, which he envisioned as a major scholarly work that would correct the errors of the Napoleonic *Description de l'Égypte*, were not fulfilled. Though he had laid the groundwork for a monumental publication – during his time in Egypt

↑ Rifaud's drawing of 'newly circumcised children going from house to house receiving the customary gifts' in Thebes. His drawings were not reliably accurate, but this one is nonetheless interesting for the jumble of modern and ancient buildings it shows in the immediate vicinity of the temple, including a pylon belonging to the temple of Luxor.

Rifaud had amassed 6,000 drawings and 14 volumes of manuscripts, along with an impressive collection of antiquities and specimens of flora and fauna – no more than three-quarters of the intended plates were ever published, and none of the text ever appeared. Rifaud had perhaps overestimated the quality of his drawings in particular, which, published in the form of lithographs, serve only to emphasize the talents of others working in the country at the same time; they do not stand up to those of his peers, such as William John Bankes (pp. 68–73), Frédéric Cailliaud, James Burton (pp. 74–81) and Robert Hay (pp. 88–97). The landscapes have a style that verges on the naive, but while this lends them some character it was fatal for his aspiration to provide useful material for scholars.

The archaeological material in Rifaud's collection comprises landscapes, architecture, a small number of plans and sections, and groups of objects of various kinds including statues, most of which were 'decouvertes par l'auteur' and include some of the best-known of the pieces he found. His drawings of glass fragments (reproduced in colour, otherwise a rarity) and column capitals show an attempt at analysis, and the plans and sections some sense of the basics of archaeological recording, but his depiction of sculpture and in particular his rendering of human forms and hieroglyphic signs is no better than parody, and certainly could not have been relied upon by those involved in the decipherment of the texts. It is striking that, while some of Rifaud's contemporaries were able to capture the minute details of individual hieroglyphic signs even if they were unable to read the texts, Rifaud's clumsy efforts reveal a mind unaware that such details were vital for distinguishing one sign from the next and unable to recognize them. Further, his captions lack detail. Though he rarely fails to mention that he was the discoverer of given pieces, his limited descriptions (such as merely 'statues en granit') are decidedly poor by comparison with the copious notes made by others alongside their drawings. In this regard, he falls well short of his intention to rectify the errors in the *Description*.

Perhaps owing to the absence of any usable records of his excavations and to the poor quality of his output, Rifaud has been largely forgotten by Egyptology, but he was a greatly significant figure for his involvement in the formation of the major museum collections in Europe, particularly that of Turin. His excavations made his name but were unscientific, his only aim being the retrieval of objects. We cannot know the full extent of the impact his excavations had on the landscapes in which he worked, but their duration and the quantity of items he removed suggest it was probably significant. In any case, Rifaud should be remembered as the discoverer of numerous monuments and in 1831 was awarded the Légion d'honneur, the highest French order of merit for civilians.

Joseph Hekekyan

1807–1875 Armenian civil engineer and geologist

Hekekyan undertook two surveys at ancient Heliopolis and Memphis to understand better the rate of deposition of alluvium in the floodplain either side of the Nile. His methodical approach was ahead of its time, and he uncovered much important archaeological material in the course of his geological study.

→ Hekekyan's 'Elevation of the Colossus of Ramses The Second'. The statue, found lying face down, was excavated by Giovanni Battista Caviglia from 1821; Hekekyan's drawing shows it upright, but since that time it has lain on its back. Hekekyan was especially interested in the statue's pedestal, believing its base reflected the ground level at the time of the statue's erection in the reign of Ramesses the Great.

Joseph Hekekyan was born in Constantinople. His father was an interpreter in the service of Mohamed Ali Pasha. He was trained in England in various technical trades, including engineering and hydraulics, and so when he arrived in Egypt in 1830 he was well-equipped to contribute to the Pasha's modernization programme. In 1837 he was appointed advisor to the government, playing a role in the construction of roads, bridges and canals, but he was discharged from his duties in 1850 when the new ruler of Egypt, Abbas I, issued a dictat that all Christians in official service should be dismissed. He found private employ under businessman and philanthropist Leonard Horner, who had an interest in geology. On Horner's behalf he undertook fieldwork at the sites of ancient Heliopolis and Memphis. His forward-thinking approach mean that these surveys are among the finest examples of scientific investigation of the ancient capital to this day.

Horner was a founding member of the London Institution, which would eventually become University College London. He had read the observations on the levels of the Nile, as recorded in ancient times and observable in the present, made by Karl Richard Lepsius' (pp. 126–31) in the great Prussian Egyptologist's letters, and Horner's geological leanings led him to take an interest in the rate at which layers of soil had been deposited on the Nile floodplain over thousands of years. The river is the single most important feature of Egypt's natural environment. It provides a source of drinking water, a channel of transport and communications and, most importantly, thanks not only to its waters but also the silts they deposit on the land each year during the annual inundation, a narrow strip of immensely fertile land on its banks. This allowed the ancient Egyptians to grow crops, providing a reliable and sustainable source of food, which in turn allowed settled civilization to flourish. And yet the workings of the river were far from the minds of most Egyptologists, who, since the decipherment of the ancient language, were generally preoccupied with the abundance of inscriptions available to them as new textual material was discovered. While Horner's interests lay elsewhere – he wanted to use securely dated Egyptian monuments to fix the timescale for changes to land and sea levels – his line of enquiry could provide archaeologists with a methodology to reconstruct Egyptian history, allowing them to establish how towns and cities came to be built, rebuilt or moved; how long it might take for a monument to be buried by detritus; and when such monuments came to fall or disappear.

In 1851 Horner secured funding from London's Royal Society to excavate at locations where ancient monuments might be used to establish the timescales involved in the geological processes he wanted to observe. He engaged Hekekyan to undertake the work, beginning at the site of ancient Heliopolis in the Matariya district of Cairo in 1851. Here he opened a series of excavations beginning close to the obelisk of Senusret I, on which a benchmark calibrated to sea level had been established by French surveyors in 1846. Horner believed the obelisk,

ARCHAEOLOGY BEGINS

ELEVATION OF THE COLOSSUS OF RAMSES THE SECOND,

Showing its Foundations and Pavements, the Section of the Soil on which it stands, and its relations to the Levels of the River, of the Inundations, of the Alluvial Deposits, and of the Pavements of Modern Buildings erected in its close vicinity.

The sections marked with red dots represent Rubbish-Soils. The parts of the Statue coloured red are those which are wanting.

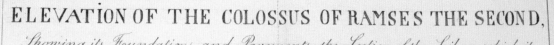

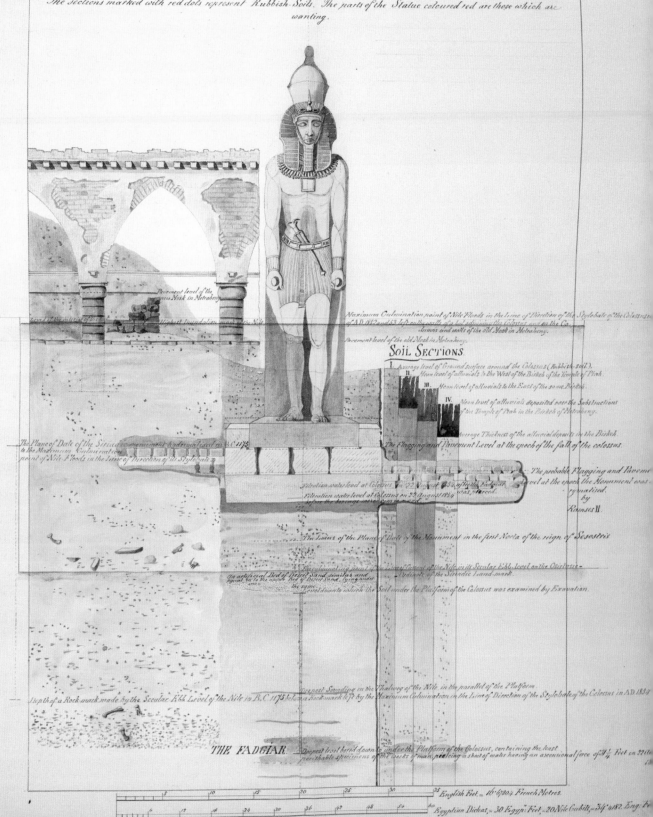

→ Several pages of Hekekyan's incredibly detailed notes, including sketches and maps of Memphis and Faiyum.

which had apparently remained standing since it was first erected, would provide an indication of the level of the floodplain in that area during the reign of that king. But Hekekyan quickly realized that the ground had already been churned by earlier excavations, and that the deposits therefore did not represent an intact geological sequence. In search of less disturbed ground, he began digging in an area close by and found the pedestal of another obelisk. Further excavations were carried out for the purposes of collecting soil samples and little more archaeological material was found, apart from some stone fragments possibly from one or more colossal sphinxes. Nonetheless, his records are of great importance for the study of the site, although his work there was almost completely forgotten until the 1990s. Heliopolis remains relatively poorly understood, the encroachment of modern buildings having prevented systematic archaeological investigations from being carried out in all but a few parts of the site.

Hekekyan's papers are a masterpiece of scientific archaeological documentation, reflecting an approach and expertise that were well ahead of their time. He was guided by an eleven-point list of requirements set out by Horner, including the instruction that 'If any fragments of human art are to be found in the soil passed through … [effort should be made] to preserve them, marking each specimen … with a number referring to a catalogue descriptive of the sinking.' Horner was evidently mindful of the importance of the archaeology, even if it took second place to his geological interests.

Before he began to take any geological samples at the sites, Hekekyan produced detailed and accurate maps of their topography.

↓ Sketch showing the colossus of Ramesses II as Hekekyan found it, lying face down in the mud, just in front of its pedestal.

ARCHAEOLOGY BEGINS

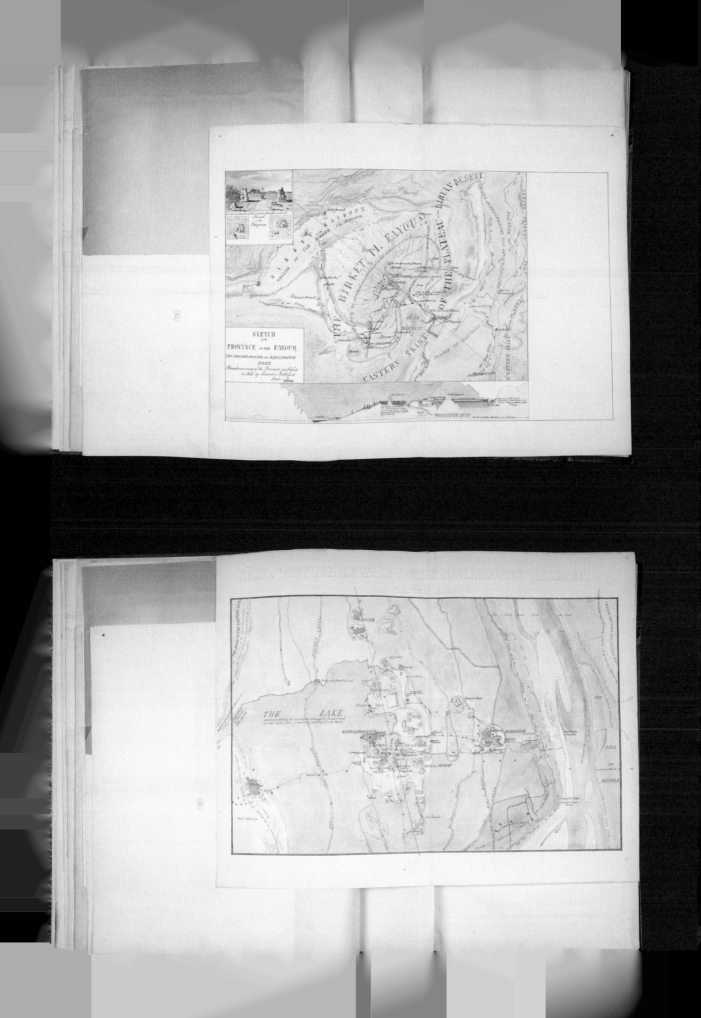

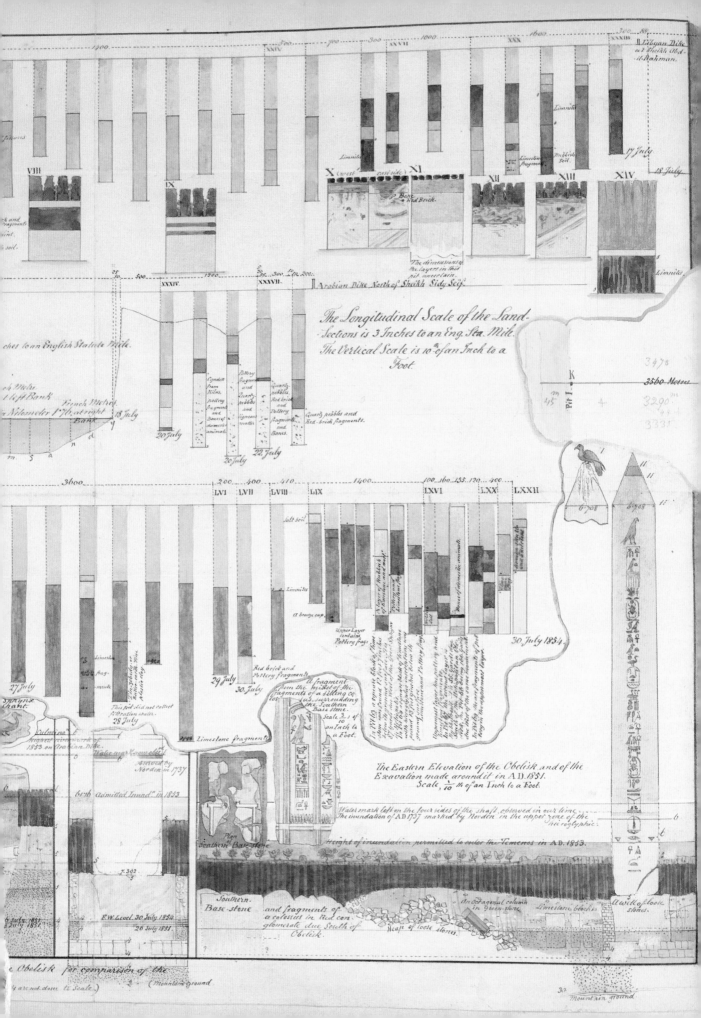

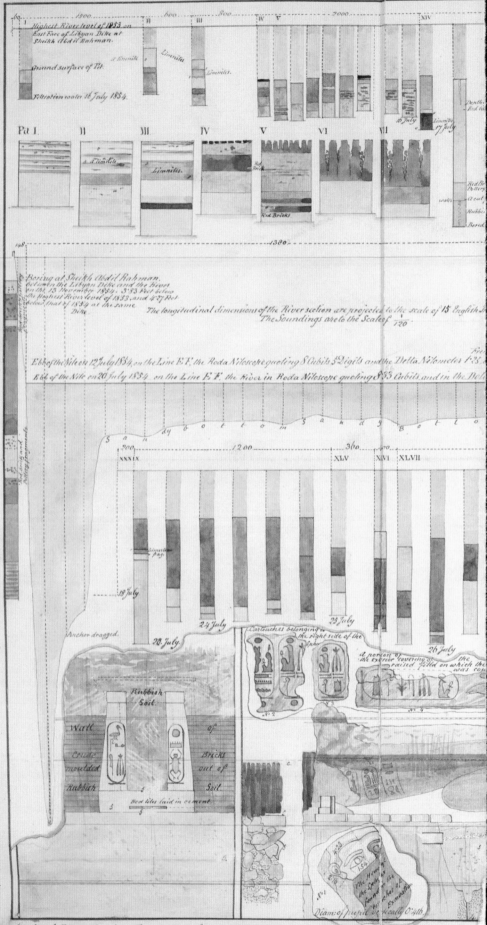

→ Diagrams and notes made by Hekekyan following his excavations. They show the stratigraphy of the soil at Heliopolis (left) and a wider area of the Nile Valley (right). Hekekyan used the position of the obelisk and sphinx fragments at Heliopolis to estimate the level of the valley floor and Nile floods at the time these monuments were erected.

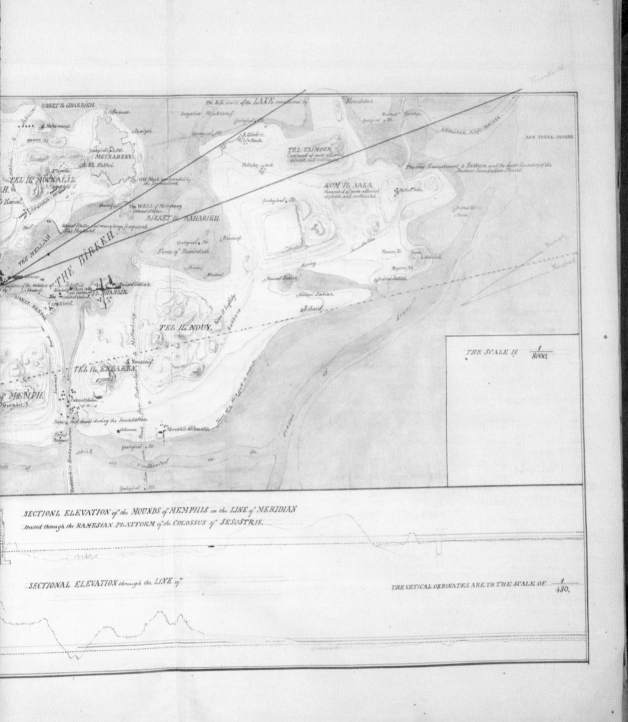

BIRKET IL GHARRIEH.

The N.E. limit of the LAKE mentioned by Herodotus.

METRAMENY

TEL IL MOKALIL.

THE BIRKEH.

TEL TAIMOEN.
Composed of pure alluvial deposit, and cultivated.

KOM IL AALA.
Composed of pure alluvial deposits and cultivated.

AHALIDEE AND MOSSA.

KOM TORRA MOSSA.

The WELL of Helesheny

BIRKET IL BAHARIEH.

Farm of Damirdash

TEL IL NOUY.

TEL IL ERBAEEN.

MEMPHI

THE SCALE IS $\frac{1}{8000}$.

SECTIONL ELEVATION of the MOUNDS of MEMPHIS on the LINE of MERIDIAN
traced through the RAMESIAN PLATFORM of the COLOSSUS of SESOSTRIS.

SECTIONAL ELEVATION through the LINE of

THE VETICAL ORDINATES ARE TO THE SCALE OF $\frac{1}{480}$.

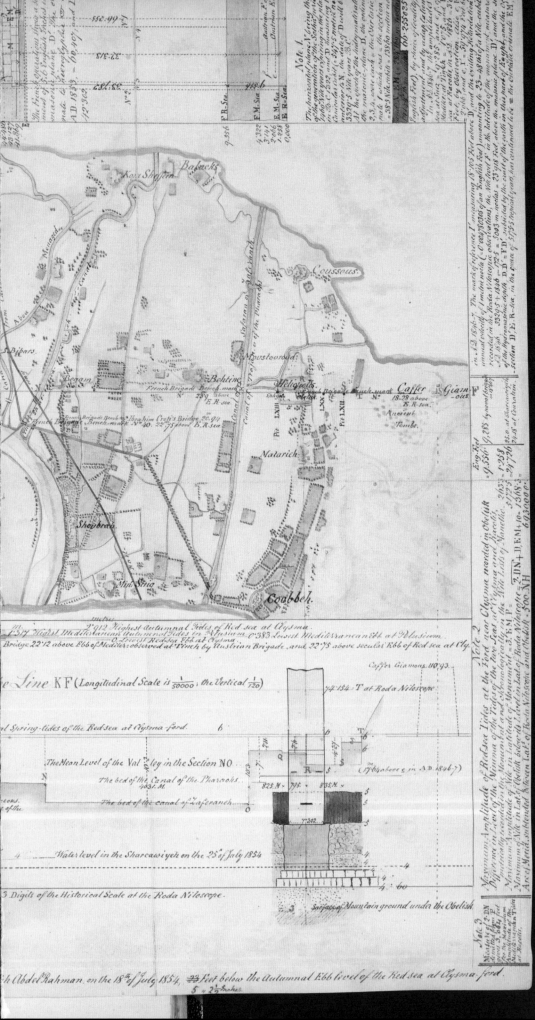

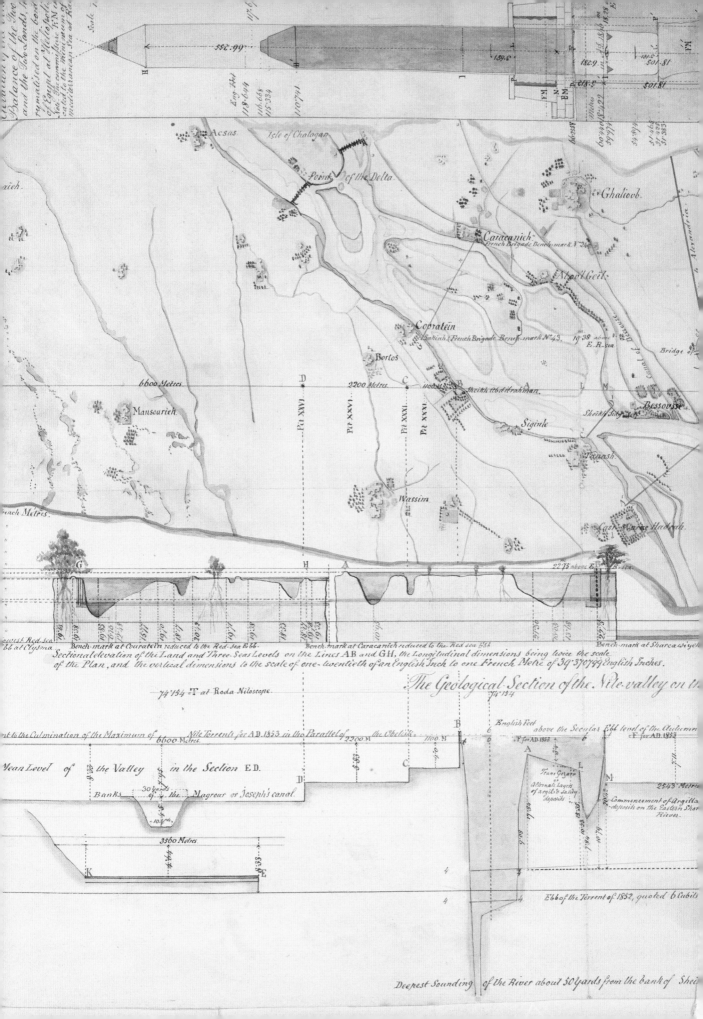

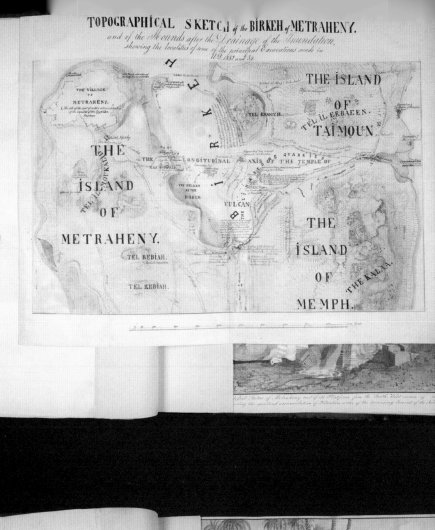

TOPOGRAPHICAL SKETCH of the BIRKEH of METRAHENY.
and of the Mounds after the Drainage of the Inundation,
showing the localities of some of the principal Excavations made in
A.D. 1852 and 54.

THE ISLAND
OF
TAÏMOUN.

TEL IL ERBAEEN.

TEL KHANZÎR.

THE VILLAGE
OF
METRAHENY.

THE LONGITUDINAL AXIS OF THE TEMPLE OF

THE

RAS TCHAUD

THE MELIAH OF THE BIRKEH

VULCAN

THE

ISLAND

OF

METRAHENY.

TEL IL ZOUKAUR

TEL REBIAH.

TEL REBIAH.

THE ISLAND

OF

MEMPH.

THE KALAA.

QUARRIE

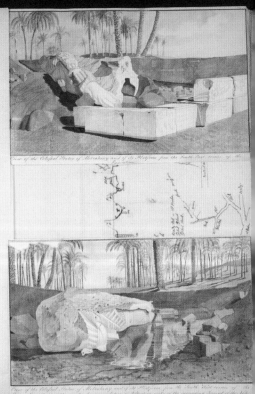

He took measurements of the heights of natural and man-made features to work up the geographical framework with which he would plan and describe his excavations. These maps are a vitally important record of the landscapes of Memphis and Heliopolis in the middle of the 19th century – but they are only the beginning. Hekekyan also created section drawings of his test-pits; views of the landscapes around them; and detailed drawings of the archaeological pieces he found, either *in situ* or alongside graphic representations of the strata they were buried in. These technical drawings are a masterclass in the art of representing information in graphic form. Hekekyan often set multiple drawings onto single, very large, sheets, leaving only tiny slivers of paper unused so that as much information as possible could be displayed.

Hekekyan moved to Memphis in order to study the area around the colossus of Ramesses II that had been excavated in 1821. He took a series of samples at strategic points along a line at the approximate latitude of the colossus, from the western edge of the ruin field eastwards across the site of the city and beyond to Helwan, an ancient quarry, on the other side of the river. He chose low-lying ground that would allow him to penetrate to the greatest possible depths, measuring the height of the land and the quantity of alluvial deposits at each point. At some, he dug conventional test-pits; at others he used a rudimentary auger, a drill-like device used to extract a core of soil. He opened over 400 test-pits in the area of the great temple of Ptah. As the main temple at what was the capital city of ancient Egypt for most of pharaonic history, this must have been a vast construction in its heyday, but it had all but disappeared by Hekekyan's time. However, well-executed though Hekekyan's work was, the choice to use man-made structures to date natural processes meant that man-made interferences in the landscape complicated the picture. Horner concluded, based on Hekekyan's data, that 9 centimetres (3.5 inches) of alluvium were deposited on average every century, and thus that the earliest occupation of Memphis could be dated to 11517 BCE – some 8,500 years earlier than today's best estimates. The problems were severalfold: the collapse of mudbrick buildings over the centuries of settlement deposited far more sediment onto the ground than would have been the case had the landscape been unoccupied; phases of occupation did not simply lie one on top of another – the city's ancient inhabitants sometimes cleared older buildings and dug beneath them to lay new foundations; and pottery sherds, which Hekekyan diligently recorded to assist with dating, were sometimes present in mudbricks made much later than the pots from which the sherds came, and were perhaps even swept downwards through the layers by his own excavations and drilling.

The work was criticized upon publication, and the inaccuracy of the interpretations blamed on Horner's having observed the results only from a distance – there is no evidence that he ever visited Egypt or met Hekekyan. In fact, the latter's records are so good that this criticism is invalid; indeed, his recording of the basic data is so clear and accurate as to allow modern archaeologists to assess the situation and apply their own interpretations.

While Hekekyan's work failed in its intended mission to reconstruct the geological processes that formulated the Nile floodplain, it reveals archaeology that was never seen again, rendered in such detail that modern scholars have been able to correct various misunderstandings about the ancient city. In the area of the Ptah temple enclosure, Hekekyan found numerous fragments of statues and elements of temple architecture, some still in their original positions, overturning the generally accepted view that the stonework from the temple was entirely removed (except for the west gate) in the 12th century CE to be used in the construction of the Citadel in Cairo. His records also showed that the temple comprised a series of covered buildings with numerous sculptures throughout and a main entrance to the east, as was conventional in Egyptian temple architecture, rather than a series of open courts approached from the west, as some scholars had proposed.

Hekekyan found a remarkable number of statues in various finestones, including travertine, granite and quartzite, many of them inscribed with the names of pharaohs. Many of these have since been lost, but among those that can be traced is one of the best-known, or at least most prominently displayed, examples of colossal royal sculpture. It was, in fact, Hekekyan's first significant discovery, and he made a characteristically careful recording of its condition:

This colossus, which measured 15 cubits in height, originally stood facing the east. It fell on its right side, and the body occupied a north and south position, the head being toward the south. In its fall

↓ The excavation of a statue of Amenemhat III of the 12th Dynasty, reused by Merneptah of the 19th Dynasty.

↘ Sketch of the same statue showing the accumulation layers from which it was excavated, with Hekekyan's annotations on each. The inscriptions on the various stone blocks were transcribed by Hekekyan and include the names of Psamtek and Hakoris of the 29th Dynasty, and fragments of the later form of the name for the Aten.

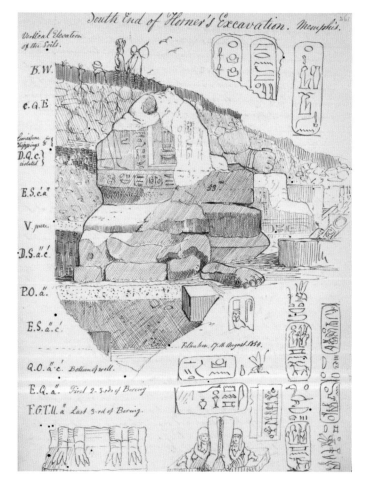

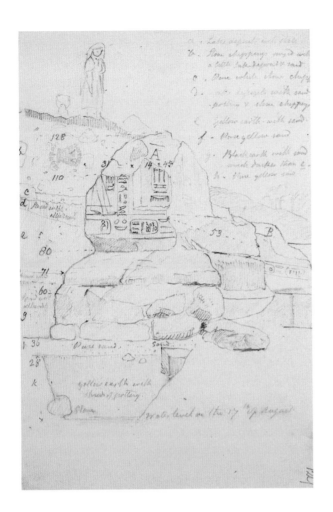

↑ A third drawing of the excavation, with further descriptions of the deposits in which the statue of Amenemhat III was buried.

↗ The excavation of a statue, accompanied by a cross section of the ground and a cartouche containing the name of the king in question, in this case 'Ramesses-Meryamun' (Ramesses II). This statue can be identified as the one that stood for many years in Ramsis Square in front of the main railway station in Cairo. It is now in the entrance hall of the Grand Egyptian Museum.

both of the legs were broken a little above the ankles. The pedestal, which was the continuation of the dorsal bracket, appears to have been removed, [the] squareness of its form and thickness rendering it well adapted for conversion into a millstone for grinding cement or a trough for watering cattle.

The statue represented the great king Ramesses II. It was eventually moved to the large plaza in front of Cairo's main railway station, which consequently came to be known as 'Ramsis Square'. It was moved again in 2006 to the site of the new Grand Egyptian Museum at Giza, where it will greet visitors arriving in the entrance hall.

Hekekyan and Horner would not have considered themselves Egyptologists, or even archaeologists, but by excavating two of ancient Egypt's most important sites so methodically and documenting the process so comprehensively Hekekyan achieved probably the most scientific archaeological work undertaken in Egypt in his time. His work would not be superseded in this regard for another fifty years, though, because it was geological rather than strictly Egyptological, it was largely ignored by Egyptologists and all but forgotten until, in 2010, David Jeffreys, director of the Egypt Exploration Society's Survey of Memphis, rediscovered his papers in the British Library and published them. We must be thankful that he worked at such important places, but it is difficult not to regret that he did not also work elsewhere.

Luigi Vassalli

1812–1887 Italian Egyptologist and curator

Vassalli helped organize Egypt's national collection of antiquities in its earliest days. His sketches have preserved many important artefacts, particularly coffins excavated by Auguste Mariette, which are now lost.

→ The lid of a coffin discovered by Vassalli in Tomb 104 at Dra Abu el-Naga. A date, 12 December 1862, is given at bottom left, perhaps the date of discovery. The owner was a lector-priest named Ibes. The hieroglyphs at far left come from a different coffin discovered in the same tomb.

Luigi Vassalli was born in Milan. In his teenage years, he studied painting at the city's Academy of Fine Arts, where he fell into the circle of the political activist Giuseppe Mazzini. This meeting kindled a lifelong patriotism that would get Vassalli into a good deal of trouble, but also ultimately led him to Egypt, where he would make his name.

Mazzini was a leading advocate for the reunification of Italy, which had been divided at various times between the Spanish, Austrian and French empires. Vassalli became embroiled in a revolutionary plot and was sentenced to death by the Austrian government, but this was subsequently commuted and he was instead sent into exile. He earned a living selling paintings and teaching Italian in Switzerland, France and England before travelling to Egypt in 1841, where he painted portraits and showed wealthy tourists around Cairo's historic sites.

In 1848 he returned to Italy to join a nationalist uprising against French rule, but when this was suppressed he was forced to return to Egypt. Now he began dealing in antiquities. By 1860 he had come to the attention of Auguste Mariette, who had recently inaugurated Egypt's Antiquities Service to protect its sites and monuments and established a staggeringly broad programme of excavations throughout the country. Vassalli became his assistant, joining him in excavations at Giza and Saqqara. He was a brave man to do so: Mariette's first assistant, Bonfoi, had died of heatstroke while excavating in the scorching heat of late summer in Thebes. Nonetheless, Vassalli enjoyed a productive first season, during which he discovered the tomb of Khafra-ankh, recorded the decoration in the tombs of two individuals named Seshemnefer, and transported the sarcophagus of Khufu-ankh from Giza to the Boulaq Museum. Soon, however, Vassalli was again feeling the call of his home country, and left to join Giuseppe Garibaldi's *mille* ('the thousand'), an army of redshirts, in a campaign against the Neapolitan monarchy. This time he had backed a winner, and became curator of Egyptian antiquities in the National Archaeological Museum of Naples. But yet another shift in the political situation led to the position becoming suppressed after only a few months, and Vassalli again returned to Egypt.

Between 1861 and 1868, Vassalli participated in important excavations under Mariette's direction at sites around the country, including Tanis, Faiyum, Thebes, Saqqara, Abydos, Dendera and Edfu. He made numerous drawings of the objects revealed during Mariette's excavations, many of which remain unpublished. Some document objects now lost, which are of inestimable value to Egyptologists in their attempts to reconstruct two crucial periods of Egyptian history. The first was that of the 17th Dynasty kings, a line of pharaohs based in Thebes during an era of political turmoil that saw the country divided between north and south. They struggled against, and eventually overthrew, their rivals, the hated 'Hyksos', a group of foreigners who had come to control the northern part of the country. Their victory

Mumia di
Drah abou Negah.
Tebe 12 dic 1862

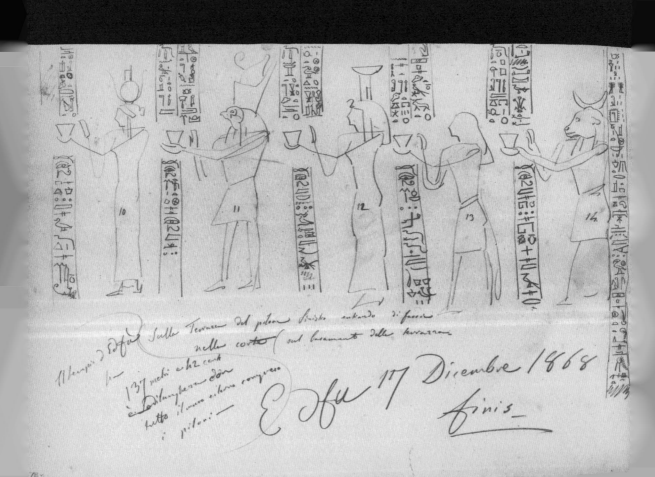

Edfu 17 Dicembre 1868

finis

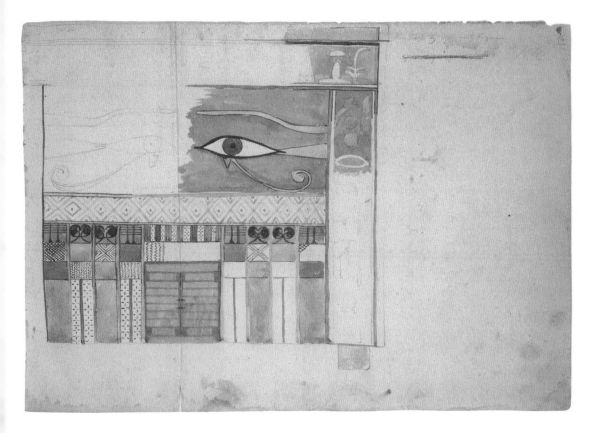

↑ Drawing from December 1862 showing the 'palace façade' decoration on the long side of the coffin belonging to a 'corn-measurer' named Sehetepibra, from Tomb 104 at Dra Abu el-Naga.

↖ Vassalli's transcription of two donation texts by Nectanebo I of the 30th Dynasty. Both were copied from the eastern boundary wall of the temple of Horus at Edfu. The two small pieces of paper glued to the main sheet show a pyramid-topped tomb-chapel at Abydos and a pair of cartouches from Dendera.

← A rough sketch of a procession of deities led by Hathor, Harsiesi and Nepthys, from the temple of Horus at Edfu. Vassalli's florid inscription suggests the copy was made on 17 December 1868.

reunified the country and ushered in the great New Kingdom, to which some of the most spectacular treasures of Egyptian history belong. The second was another time of transition, the Third Intermediate Period. During this time Thebes had come under the influence of rulers descended from Libyan tribal chiefs, but was subsequently liberated by another foreign group, the wingdom of Kush, which was from northern Sudan but culturally Egyptian. Mariette and Vassalli found numerous coffins from both periods, which Vassalli meticulously documented. His drawings are notable for several reasons: they are beautiful sketches in their own right; they convey the form and decoration of the ancient objects well; and most distinctively of all, they are covered with his scrawled notes, in which he recorded a brief description of each coffin, the date on which it was discovered and its exact findspot. He also carefully transcribed the inscriptions upon them in clear handwritten hieroglyphs. These drawings have been crucial in helping scholars to reconstruct these murky but important periods.

In 1865 Vassalli became keeper of the Boulaq Museum, the national collection established in 1858 by Mariette, which was held in a former warehouse in the Boulaq suburb of Cairo. The collections were growing rapidly at this time, thanks in large part to the excavations Vassalli was helping Mariette to conduct. When Mariette died in 1881, Vassalli was temporarily put in charge of the Antiquities Service, prior to Gaston Maspero's appointment to the office.

Vassalli died in Rome in 1887, his beloved Italy having finally gained its independence as a reunified kingdom in 1870. He risked his life for his country, but it was his time in Egypt that would make his name.

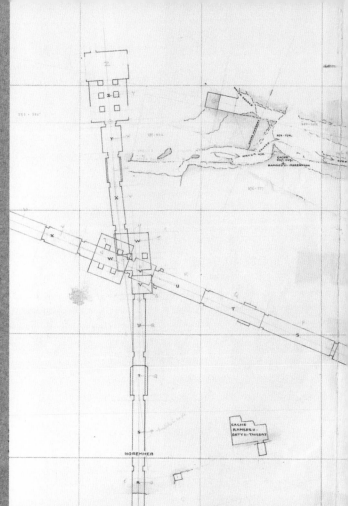

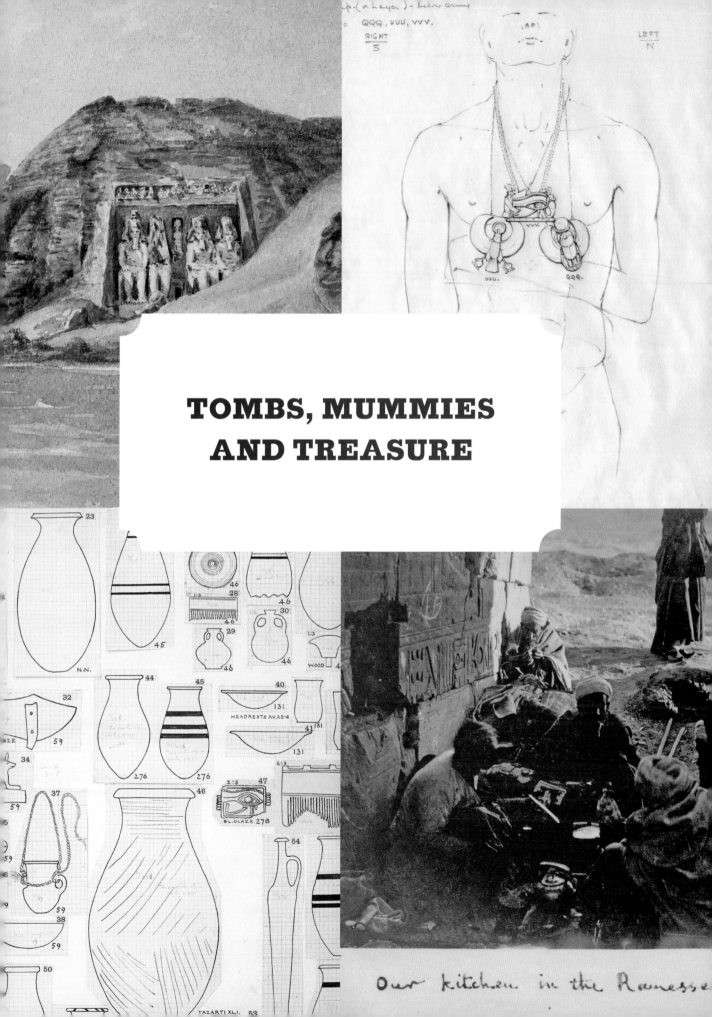

TOMBS, MUMMIES AND TREASURE

Our kitchen in the Ramesse

'The long-desired Society for the Promotion of Excavation in the Delta of the Nile has at last been constituted under very favourable auspices.'

THE TIMES, 30 MARCH 1882

Auguste Mariette, founder of Egypt's national Antiquities Service, was succeeded after his death in 1881 by another Frenchman, Gaston Maspero. Maspero, a professor of Egyptology, had arrived in Egypt in 1880 as the head of a newly established French archaeological mission that would later become the still active Institut Français d'Archéologie Orientale (IFAO). He served as director of the Antiquities Service between 1881 and 1886, and then again after an interlude in France from 1899 to 1914. His tenure is characterized by the proliferation of foreign expeditions to Egypt, motivated by the acquisition of knowledge – rather than objects that could be removed to museums – and organized according to more rigorous scientific principles than their predecessors.

Mariette's arrival in post coincided with two important developments. A grandson of Mohamed Ali, Ismail Pasha, had been granted permission by the Ottomans to take the title of 'Khedive' ('viceroy') rather than 'wali' ('governor') in 1867, finally recognizing the autonomy that Mohamed Ali had established. Ismail invested heavily in modernization and infrastructure, building canals, railroads, telegraph lines, bridges and harbours, and opening the Suez Canal in 1869, but this came at great cost, exacerbated by an expensive and only partially successful war with Ethiopia. By the late 1870s Egypt was deeply indebted to European banks and their governments, and in 1878 control of the country's revenues and administration was passed to Britain and France. The following year the two European powers persuaded the Ottoman government to depose Ismail in favour of his son, Tewfik. The new Khedive recognized that his country was now under European control. His European masters imposed austerity measures, resulting in widespread hardship and resentment of his ineffectiveness. One of his colonels, Ahmed 'Urabi, led an uprising against him in September 1881. Britain and France responded with a show of force, gathering ships off the Mediterranean coast, but a parliamentary crisis in Paris caused the French to withdraw. When a naval bombardment of Alexandria succeeded only in strengthening support for 'Urabi's revolt, the British invaded, restored Tewfik as Khedive and occupied the country.

During the same year, 1882, the traveller and writer Amelia Edwards (pp. 172–77) established an 'Egypt Exploration Fund', an idea she had conceived during her visit to the country nearly a decade earlier to help prevent the destruction of its monuments. Edwards had approached Mariette for permission to excavate, but at that time Mariette was seriously ill, paralysing the Service's ability to issue new permits. She had corresponded with Maspero when he was still a professor in France, and so it was fortuitous that he should be appointed to succeed Mariette. Initially he advised Reginald Stuart

Poole, a nephew of Edward William Lane (pp. 82–87) who worked closely with Edwards in the founding of the Fund, that the time was not yet ripe for the proposed expedition, but when Edouard Naville, a Swiss Egyptologist, visited Egypt in the winter of 1881–82 he asked again on behalf of the Fund and this time was told there would be no objection. Naville would himself become the Fund's first explorer. In 1883 he undertook a short season at Tell el-Maskhuta in the Eastern Delta, identifying the site with the biblical 'store city' of Pithom. This hypothesis was eventually proven incorrect but was well received by the Fund's subscribers, who hoped future missions would help uncover evidence for the Old Testament narrative. The next year, when Naville was unavailable to direct the season, the Fund turned to the young William Flinders Petrie (pp. 178–83), who had just published the results of his two seasons' work at Giza and was generally regarded as a careful and meticulous worker. Maspero granted permission for the dig on the condition that any objects excavated by Petrie would pass into the possession of the Egyptian Museum – except duplicates, which the excavator was free to take home.

This principle would prove hugely important in shaping the fieldwork taking place across the country. Foreign excavators were obliged to maintain certain standards in their work, but were also incentivized to work within the new system. While this allowed the long-established process of the removal of objects from the country to continue with renewed legitimacy, the desire on the part of those in the West to acquire objects was so strong, and the recognition of Egypt's claim over its own heritage still so new, that the policy represented a pragmatic way forward. Maspero's new system was undoubtedly a compromise, but to have restricted the export of artefacts entirely would only have encouraged the illicit trade (which remained a problem, albeit reduced in scale), and it was an important step on the road towards the retention of a greater proportion of antiquities in Egypt.

The more rigorous, regulated excavations of the late 19th century led to the spectacular discovery of tombs even at sites that had been the subject of much activity in the past, such as the Valleys of the Kings and Queens. Though some damaging investigations continued to take place, an awareness of the importance of excavating sites responsibly and creating accurate records of standing monuments began to take hold. Scholars' ability to read hieroglyphs was by this time much improved, aiding copyists in identifying and reconstructing damaged inscriptions. Photography was becoming a useful tool in the recording process, and would become indispensable by the beginning of the 20th century. Moreover, the institutions that were beginning to establish an ongoing presence in Egypt were able to support multiple initiatives simultaneously; the Egypt Exploration Fund launched its ambitious Archaeological Survey, and other organizations followed suit. While the discovery of new material remained a preoccupation for Egyptologists, there was a rapidly growing awareness that measures must be taken to preserve as much as possible and to use documentation – the accurate capture of the present state of the monuments – as a means of minimizing any loss that might occur. Egyptology was heading in the right direction.

Amelia Edwards

1831–1892 Artist, writer, traveller and founder
of the Egypt Exploration Fund

*Edwards began her epic journey
through Egypt in 1873. Her travelogue,*
A Thousand Miles Up the Nile, *was
hugely popular upon publication and
remains a classic of the genre. After
witnessing first hand the destruction
of the ancient monuments she founded
the Egypt Exploration Fund, hoping to
preserve the history of Egypt for future
generations of visitors and scholars.*

↗ Edwards's watercolour of the double temple
of Sobek and Haroeris at Kom Ombo. The site, on
the banks of the Nile, is picturesque, but its location
had also caused much of the temple complex to
be washed away. Edwards was concerned about
one of the pylons: 'A day must soon come when
it will collapse with a crash, and thunder down
like its fellow.'

→ 'Native boat, Derr, Nubia.' Although today it
is quite possible to get from Cairo to Aswan and
beyond by land, or even by air, in Edwards's day
– as in ancient times – the only way to travel was
along the river.

Amelia Edwards was already an established writer when she arrived
in Egypt for the first time in 1873. The previous year she had visited the
Dolomites in Italy, then virtually unknown in England, and published
her account of her travels, *Untrodden Peaks and Infrequent Valleys*.
After leaving Italy she and her travelling companion, Lucy Renshawe,
embarked on a walking tour of France, but it was spoiled by rain.
They decided to visit Egypt not so much out of a passion to explore its
ancient sites but, to use Amelia's own phrase, due to 'stress of weather'.
Despite this inauspicious start, the country would define her work for
the rest of her life.

Edwards and Renshawe arrived in Alexandria on 27 November 1873
after a rough passage from Italy and endured two days of quarantine
before being allowed to proceed to Cairo. On their first night of freedom
they dined at the Shepheard's Hotel, among the most famous in the
world until it burned down in 1952. Edwards quickly found much
that appealed to her artistic eye: 'In order thoroughly to enjoy an
overwhelming, ineffaceable first impression of Oriental out-of-doors
life, one should begin in Cairo with a day in the native bazaars …. Every
shop-front, every street corner, every turbaned group is a ready-made
picture. The old Turk who sets up his cake-stall in the recess of a
sculptured doorway; the donkey-boy with his gaily caparisoned ass,
waiting for customers; the beggar asleep on the steps of the mosque;
the veiled woman filling her water jar at the public fountain – they all
look as if they had been put there expressly to be painted.'

A few days' exploring the city and its surrounds rewarded Edwards
with her first glimpse of the Great Pyramid: 'The effect is as sudden as
it is overwhelming. It shuts out the sky and the horizon. It shuts out
all the other pyramids. It shuts out everything but the sense of awe
and wonder.' In between their visits to the city's ancient sites, Edwards
and her companions set about the difficult business of finding a boat
and crew to take them on an excursion up the Nile:

> *Our first business was to look at dahabeeyahs; and the looking
> at dahabeeyahs compelled us constantly to turn our steps and our
> thoughts in the direction of Boulak – a desolate place by the river,
> where some two or three hundred Nile-boats lay moored for hire ….
> Each Reis, or captain, displays the certificates given to him by
> former travellers; and these certificates, being apparently in active
> circulation, have a mysterious way of turning up again and again
> on board different boats and in the hands of different claimants.*

> *Nor is this all. Dahabeeyahs are given to changing their places,
> which houses do not do; so that the boat which lay yesterday
> alongside the eastern bank may be over at the western bank today, or
> hidden in the midst of a dozen others half a mile lower down the river
> … their prices … vary from day to day, according to the state of the*

Kom Ombos. Upper Egypt
March 1874

Native boat. Derr Nubia.

market as shown by the returns of arrivals at the principal hotels .... Thus it came to pass that, for the first ten days or so, some three or four hours had to be devoted every morning to the business of the boats; ... deliberating, haggling, comparing, hesitating.

On Saturday 13 December Edwards and Renshawe set sail on a boat named *Philae*, one of the largest on the river. Edwards would immortalize their journey in her published account, *A Thousand Miles Up the Nile*, an instant bestseller. The book was illustrated with her own paintings and drawings, reproduced in the form of engravings. The original delicate and charming watercolours came to light only recently, enlivening this most compelling of journeys still further.

A Thousand Miles Up the Nile is a veritable gazetteer of the ancient sites the traveller would encounter along the river. Edwards's colourful descriptions reveal her great sense of wonder at the sites, as well as her developing understanding of them:

Here at Sakkarah the whole plateau is thickly strewn with scraps of broken pottery, limestone, marble, and alabaster; flakes of green and blue glaze; bleached bones; shreds of yellow linen; and lumps of some odd-looking dark brown substance, like dried-up sponge. Presently some one picks up a little noseless head of one of the common blue-ware funereal statuettes, and immediately we all fall to work...one finds a fragment of iridescent glass – another, a morsel of shattered vase – a third, an opaque bead of some kind of yellow paste. And then, with a shock which the present writer, at all events, will not soon forget, we suddenly discover that these scattered bones are human – that those linen shreds are shreds of cerement cloths – that yonder odd-looking brown lumps are rent fragments of what

↓ The temples of Abu Simbel: the great temple of Ramesses II at left, and the smaller temple, dedicated to his Great Royal Wife Nefertari, at right. It was in the cliffs to the south (left) of the great temple that Edwards and her party discovered a small rock-cut chapel of Ramesses II.

TOMBS, MUMMIES AND TREASURE

once was living flesh! And now for the first time we realize that every inch of this ground on which we are standing, and all these hillocks and hollows and pits in the sand, are violated graves.

We soon became quite hardened to such sights, and learned to rummage among dusty sepulchres with no more compunction than would have befitted a gang of professional body-snatchers. These are experiences upon which one looks back afterwards with wonder, and something like remorse; but so infectious is the universal callousness, and so overmastering is the passion for relic-hunting, that I do not doubt we should again do the same things under the same circumstances. Most Egyptian travellers, if questioned, would have to make a similar confession. Shocked at first, they denounce with horror the whole system of sepulchral excavation, legal as well as predatory; acquiring, however, a taste for scarabs and funerary statuettes, they soon begin to buy with eagerness the spoils of the dead; finally they forget all their former scruples, and ask no better fortune than to discover and confiscate a tomb for themselves.

At Saqqara Edwards and her party visited the Step Pyramid, the Old Kingdom cemetery and the Serapeum, before finding a building with an interesting but more recent history: 'How pleasant it was, after being suffocated in the Serapeum and broiled in the tomb of Ti, to return to Mariette's deserted house, and eat our luncheon on the cool stone terrace that looks northward over the desert!' Leaving the deserts of Saqqara behind, they visited the great colossus of Ramesses II in Mit Rahina, but were disappointed not to see more of the ancient city of Memphis: 'Where, however, is the companion colossus? Where is the Temple itself? Where are the pylons, the obelisks, the avenues of sphinxes? Where, in short, is Memphis?'

Edwards seems also to have been underwhelmed by what she saw in Luxor: 'The temple has here formed the nucleus of the village, the older part of which has grown up in and about the ruins ... these half-buried pylons, this solitary obelisk, those giant heads rising in ghastly resurrection before the gates of the Temple, were magnificent still. But it was as the magnificence of a splendid prologue to a poem of which only garbled fragments remain. Beyond that entrance lay a smoky, filthy, intricate labyrinth of lanes and passages. Mud hovels, mud pigeon-towers, mud yards, and a mud mosque, clustered like wasps' nests in and about the ruins.' However, she had cause to rejoice some time after she had returned to England: 'The ruins of the Great Temple of Luxor have undergone a complete transformation since the above description was written .... After twelve months of negotiation, the fellaheen were at last bought out on fair terms, each proprietor receiving a stated price for his dwelling and a piece of land elsewhere, upon which to build another .... In 1886, the few families yet lingering in the ruins followed the example of the rest; and in the course of that season the Temple was cleared from end to end, only the little native mosque being left standing within the precincts, and Mustapha Aga's house on the side next the landing-place.'

Edwards's itinerary took her beyond the ancient southern frontier of Egypt into Nubia, as far as the temple of Abu Simbel, where her

↑ 'Digging for Mummies': the excavation by
the Antiquities Service of a tomb in Thebes. It was
located 'in the rear of the Ramesseum' and yielded
a coffin and other items from the Third Intermediate
Period. The drawing is otherwise notable for the
attire of the excavators, who appear almost naked.

→ The two northern colossi of the great temple
of Abu Simbel. This sketch, along with those on
pp. 173–74, belongs to a recently discovered album
that formed the basis for illustrations in *A Thousand
Miles Up the Nile* and two of Edwards's other books.

party discovered a rock-cut shrine. 'The Painter' of Edwards's account, Mr Andrew McCallum, had begun clearing the sand from an intriguing fissure in the rock close to two stelae of Ramesses II to the south of the main temple. He revealed figures in relief, and began to suspect they had been carved above a doorway in the rock. Edwards and her companions were taking lunch when they received a pencilled note: '"Pray come immediately – I have found the entrance to a tomb. Please send some sandwiches – A. M'C."' He had in fact found a small chapel, part of Ramesses II's great temple. The party laid claim to the discovery in a manner by this time long established: 'The Painter wrote his name and ours, with the date (February 16th, 1874), on a space of blank wall over the inside of the doorway; and this was the only occasion upon which any of us left our names upon an Egyptian monument.'

Ironically, it was not long after this defacement that Amelia gave voice to the growing frustration at the vandalism and destruction of the ancient monuments that would guide her work for the rest of her life:

> I am told that our names are partially effaced, and that the wall-paintings which we had the happiness of admiring in all their beauty and freshness, are already much injured. Such is the fate of every Egyptian monument, great or small. The tourist carves it all over with names and dates, and in some instances with caricatures. The student of Egyptology, by taking wet paper 'squeezes,' sponges away every vestige of the original colour. The 'collector' buys and carries off everything of value that he can get; and the Arab steals for him. The work of destruction, meanwhile, goes on apace. There is no one to prevent it; there is no one to discourage it .... The Louvre contains a full-length portrait of Seti I, cut out bodily from the walls of his sepulchre in the Valley of the Tombs of the Kings. The Museums of Berlin, of Turin, of Florence, are rich in spoils which tell their own lamentable tale. When science leads the way, is it wonderful that ignorance should follow?

In the years following her return to England, Edwards devoted herself to her efforts to arrest the decay of the monuments, eventually founding the Egypt Exploration Fund in London. Through the Fund, ordinary members of the public could contribute to the conservation of Egyptian monuments, their subscription fees sending an 'explorer' to excavate a site in Egypt. These explorers would be tasked with uncovering new monuments and objects not for their removal to foreign museums, but so that they could be recorded scientifically and then passed the Egyptian museum authorities. Edwards recruited some of the finest excavators of the era, including Flinders Petrie (pp. 178–83), who would help set new standards for archaeology in Egypt. More than 130 years later, the EEF – now the Egypt Exploration Society – continues to support field research in the country. Edwards would also endow the first chair in Egyptian Archaeology in Britain, awarded to Petrie and guaranteeing him an income. This post established Egyptology in the country as a scientific subject in its own right. Her legacy is as great as that of any other British Egyptologist – not bad for a woman who was sneered at by Samuel Birch, keeper of Oriental Antiquities at the British Museum, for her interest in 'sentimental archaeology'.

William Matthew Flinders Petrie

1853–1942 British archaeologist and Egyptologist

One of the great pioneers of modern archaeology, Petrie surveyed and excavated dozens of archaeological sites in Egypt and Palestine in a career spanning seven decades. He was among the first to apply serious scientific techniques in his excavations, and invented new methods to deal with material that had never been properly studied before, laying the groundwork for future archaeological investigation in Egypt.

→ Petrie's photograph of a female statue of the Middle Kingdom discovered at the Osiris temple at Abydos in 1901–3. Petrie was not the first to use photography to document the archaeological process, but he helped to raise the standard. His photographs, taken on site using a pin-hole camera, were generally of extremely high quality.

William Matthew Flinders Petrie was born in Charlton, Kent. His grandfather, Captain Matthew Flinders, had circumnavigated Australia, and William was to inherit this taste for adventure. He was home-schooled in a variety of subjects, the lack of formal tuition perhaps encouraging his latent intellectual curiosity and instilling in him both the ability to acquire knowledge by himself and an inventive approach to problem-solving – attributes that would characterize his archaeological practice. Frequent visits to the British Museum, whose displays he came to know intimately, inspired a fascination with the past. He surveyed Stonehenge with his father in 1872, and went on to map a number of archaeological sites in the south of England, depositing plans of forty monuments in the British Museum.

In 1880 he travelled to Egypt for the first time, to make a survey of the pyramids at Giza. The astronomer Charles Piazzi Smyth had argued that the dimensions of the pyramids contained divine messages for mankind, and Petrie had written in support of the theory in his first book, *Researches on the Great Pyramid*, published when he was just twenty-two years old. This had caused some controversy among scholars, prompting Petrie to visit Egypt to take his own measurements of the monuments over the course of two seasons, during which he lived on meagre rations in a rock-cut tomb leading off the causeway to the Great Pyramid. He maintained throughout his career that tombs made the best dwellings for archaeologists on campaign – 'no better lodgings are to be had anywhere for solidity and equable temperature' – though admitted that 'the minor advantages may be a question of taste, such as the gratis supply of ancient bones or mummy cloth in the dust and sand of your floor.' Famously, he stripped to his underwear while undertaking his survey – partly to keep cool in the heat, and partly to deter tourists from disturbing his work. Over the course of these two seasons he made the most accurate survey of the Giza plateau to date, taking triangulations of all three main pyramids and disproving Piazzi Smyth's theories in the process.

Whilst working at the pyramids Petrie also visited a number of ancient sites beyond Giza. He was both enthralled by the ruins and appalled by their ongoing destruction. Realizing that the excavation techniques being practised by his contemporaries were not sufficient to preserve the remains of the ancient past, he resolved to devise a methodology that might arrest the decline of the sites, or at least yield greater knowledge of them before they were lost. Fortuitously, these personal ambitions formed just as Amelia Edwards (pp. 172–77) established the Egypt Exploration Fund (EEF) for the same purpose. She had the contacts and genius to generate support for the cause, and the Fund became the focal point for the necessary finance of rescue missions. The next task was the recruitment of a suitable explorer. The Fund's first expedition was undertaken by the Swiss Egyptologist Edouard Naville at the site of Tell el-Maskhuta, which he believed

TOMBS, MUMMIES AND TREASURE

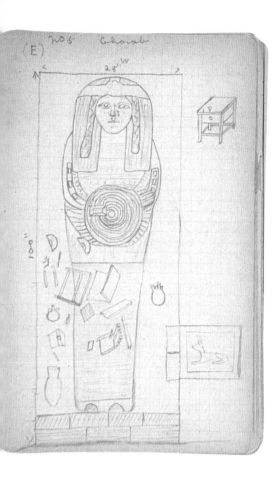

↑ Drawing from an unpublished notebook of an *in situ* burial, grave no. 705, discovered by Petrie's team at Gurob in 1889–90. The drawing shows an anthropoid coffin, oriented with the head towards the west, which the Egyptians associated with death and the afterlife, in a simple, brick-lined chamber, accompanied by a small quantity of funerary objects.

he had identified as the biblical 'store city' of Pithom. The idea that the excavations might bring to light evidence of the Exodus narrative helped the Fund to recruit supporters, and it was decided that the second season would investigate San el-Hagar, thought by some to have been the city of Zoan where, according to the Bible, Moses performed miracles before pharaoh. Naville was unavailable for this second season, and Edwards therefore turned to the enthusiastic author of *Researches on the Great Pyramid*, who had by now become well known in antiquarian circles.

Petrie's first season for the EEF represented a radical departure from the traditional ways of doing things. Previously, excavations had focused on the recovery of architecture and objects that were either inscribed with hieroglyphic texts or were worthy of display in museums. Such objects were so abundantly forthcoming from the Egyptian sands that antiquarians had neither the need nor the capacity to consider other kinds of archaeological evidence that were being lost in their slipshod excavations. One of Petrie's greatest contributions to the discipline was his far broader, indeed comprehensive, focus. He recognized that huge amounts could be learned about the ancient Egyptians by excavating not only temples and tombs, but also more modest houses, towns and cities, and by studying all ancient materials, including the remains of plants and animals, alongside striking man-made objects. As such, it was vitally important that his workforce were trained to recognize previously ignored materials. There persisted as well the age-old concern that labourers would be tempted to sell any of the more choice pieces they found to unscrupulous antiquities dealers. Petrie dealt with this by paying his workmen for the objects they found at a fair rate:

> *When sunset comes near, it is time to go round to all the workings where things are likely to have been found, and take in the spoils. One man hands up, perhaps, a perfect red jar, and some little scraps of figures, and I book in, say, threepence to Sidahmed Abdun; for owing to the scarcity of small change, and the quantity I should need, all the small payments are worked on paper, and settled when they have accumulated. Then at another hole there will be a small bronze figure and a few nails, and fivepence goes down to Mohammed Dafani.*

Would-be purchasers remained a threat, however:

> *There were sometimes sharp steeplechases after Arab dealers. They know their coming to the work is morally indefensible, and they have an indefinite dread of being identified or caught. As however nothing whatever could be done to them, the object is not to catch them, but only to act on their feelings so as to make them flee before you. The way is to walk straight at any suspicious character, openly and ostentatiously; he moves off; you follow; he quickens; you quicken; he doubles; you cross to cut him off; then he fairly bolts; and off you go, with perhaps a furlong between, across the fields, jumping canals, doubling, hiding behind bushes, and so forth; if he once gains a village it is useless to look for him in the house, so the way is to keep*

TOMBS, MUMMIES AND TREASURE

him out in the open for as much time as you can spare for the game; two to four miles is a fair run. This exercise is valuable both morally and physically; the rascals are always laughed at by my diggers for running away.

Petrie's methods allowed him to gather vast quantities of material of all kinds, which he documented meticulously. His next task was to render his records suitable for publication. In this, his arrangement with the Egypt Exploration Fund was ideal. The Fund encouraged supporters to become 'subscribers' by contributing £1 per year, for which they would receive a copy of the report produced at the end of the season. The Fund thus required its explorers to produce thorough reports, and to do so in a timely fashion. This suited Petrie's personal philosophy perfectly, as the preface to his first report on the excavations at Naukratis (1884–85) makes clear: 'It is a golden principle to let each year see the publication of the year's work, in any research; but a writer places himself thus at the disadvantage of showing how his information may have been defective, or his views requiring change, as year after year goes on. Such a course, however, is the most honest, and the most useful, as half a loaf is better than no bread.' It was his and archaeology's good fortune that Petrie was ready to begin excavating at almost the exact moment of the founding of the EEF – an institution with the motivation and means to publish rapidly and regularly. He needed the EEF and vice versa. This arrangement would define not only his career, but also much of all archaeological fieldwork carried out in Egypt since.

↓ 'Our kitchen in the Ramesseum.' The brewing of tea is just as important at archaeological sites in Egypt today as it was when Petrie worked at the great mortuary temple of Ramesses II in 1895–96.

265

Our kitchen in the Ramesseum.

↑ A tall jar of the Naqada 1c Period (*c.* 3,700 BCE) decorated with images of barbary sheep, discovered by Petrie at the site of Naqada in 1894–95. It is now kept in the Ashmolean Museum, Oxford. The material he found at this and several other sites in Upper Egypt revolutionized understanding of the development of Egypt's material culture in the Predynastic era.

Petrie's track record is tantamount to a gazetteer of important archaeological sites in Egypt. He began by working in the Delta, which was then the least well-known part of the country. His account paints a bleak picture of the landscape:

> *Beyond the civilized regions of modern Egypt, past even the country palm groves, where a stranger is rarely seen, there stretches out to the Mediterranean a desolation of mud and swamp, impassable in winter, and only dried into an impalpable salt dust by the heat of midsummer. To tell land from water, to say where the mud ends and the lakes begin, requires a long experience; the flat expanse, as level as the sea, covered with slowly drying salt pools, may be crossed for miles, with only the dreary changes of dust, black mud, water, and black mud again which it is impossible to define as more land than water, or more water than land. The only objects which break the horizon are the low mounds of the cities of the dead; these alone remain to show that this region was once a living land, whose people prospered on the earth.*

Over the course of five decades he proceed to work throughout all regions of Egypt, until in 1926 a change to the antiquities law prompted him to change the focus of his research to ancient Egyptian activity in Palestine. He generally published at least one monograph to accompany each mission, usually under the name of the relevant site, so that a library of his excavation reports looks like an A–Z of ancient Egyptian towns and cities. Research on many such sites still starts with reference to Petrie's efforts, which were very often the first thorough, genuinely scientific archaeological excavations undertaken in such places.

Petrie was astonishingly energetic, covering huge amounts of ground in each location and walking vast distances to prospect for sites. He lived a practically spartan lifestyle: T. E. Lawrence, who worked with Petrie at Tarkhan in 1912, wrote that 'a Petrie dig is a thing with a flavour of its own: tinned kidneys mingle with mummy corpses and amulets in the soup: my bed is all gritty with prehistoric alabaster jars of unique types – and my feet at night keep the bread-box from the rats.' This frugality extended to his work at home, causing a rift with the EEF when he accused the committee of wasting funds on poorly produced publications. Lawrence observed that he was a man who believed there was a correct way to do everything, 'from the right way to dig a temple to the only way to clean one's teeth'. The correct way to publish, according to Petrie, involved arranging great numbers of individual drawings – of pots, inscribed material and anything else he found – on the page so as to maximize the amount of information conveyed on the paper available. His volumes were published with a frequency that is unheard of today: one site per year, the monograph completed prior to the commencement of the next year's work. With hindsight this was an astonishing achievement, and avoided the typical backlog that is the blight of many an archaeological project or institution today.

Unable to work for anyone else for very long – he resigned from the EEF in 1886, though returned in 1896 for a decade before going his own way for good after a final season in 1905 – Petrie eventually founded his own organizations, first the Egyptian Research Account and then

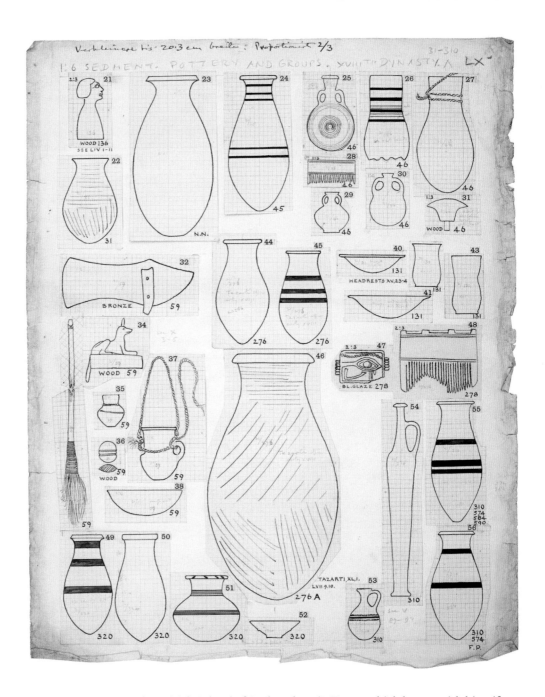

↗ One of Petrie's 'paste-ups': a series of drawings arranged on a page in preparation for publication. They represent 18th Dynasty ceramic vessels discovered by Petrie at the site of Sedment, a cemetery a few kilometres to the west of the ancient provincial capital of Herakleopolis, during the 1920–21 season. Petrie had a genius for making the best use of the resources available to him, including space on the printed page.

the British School of Archaeology in Egypt, which he ran with his wife, Hilda. Like the EEF, he generated the financial support he needed to sustain his excavations from members of the public and institutions, through exhibitions, lectures and a steady stream of publications. His autobiography, published in 1932, was entitled *Seventy Years in Archaeology*. That he worked so productively almost throughout those seventy years has earned him the title of 'Father' – whether of Egyptian archaeology, archaeology in Palestine, or archaeology in general. It is well deserved.

Marianne Brocklehurst

1832–1898 British traveller, antiquarian and collector

Brocklehurst visited Egypt several times in the late 19th century. She met and became great friends with Amelia Edwards in the course of her travels, and would later support the Egypt Exploration Fund as well as displaying her own collection of antiquities to the public, raising awareness of ancient Egypt in England.

↗ 'Donkey boys on the West Bank at Thebes'.

→ Osirid pillars from the second court of the Ramesseum, with the colossus that inspired Shelley's poem 'Ozymandias' at right. Brocklehurst had lunch here on Wednesday 25 March, the same day that Amelia Edwards witnessed the excavation of some coffins nearby (see p. 176).

Marianne Brocklehurst was born in Macclesfield, England, in 1832. Her father, John Brocklehurst, was an MP for Macclesfield and a wealthy silk manufacturer, enabling the family to travel abroad. Brocklehurst set off to Egypt in 1873 with her lifelong partner, Mary Booth. They met Amelia Edwards (pp. 172–77) en route to Egypt and subsequently sailed up the Nile with her in a flotilla of sight-seers. Edwards refers to the pair fondly as 'the two MBs' in her popular account of her own travels. Brocklehurst exemplifies a certain sort of traveller to Egypt in the second half of the 19th century: wealthy enough to indulge their interest in ancient culture by purchasing 'antikas', and well placed to observe important developments that were taking place in the country's archaeological landscape. This was a time when numerous artefacts were being found and monuments being cleared. Brocklehurst, like many of her fellow travellers, was motivated to generate interest in Egyptology back home, which she achieved not by publishing her diaries, as Edwards did, but by collecting antiquities for public exhibition and funding archaeological expeditions to the country.

Along with Mary Booth, Brocklehurst's party on her first visit to Egypt included her sixteen-year-old nephew Alfred and a footman named George, who took to the customs of the country so naturally that she remarked 'one would have sworn that he and Egypt were friends of old, and that he had been brought up on pyramids from his earliest childhood'. The group landed at Alexandria on 27 November 1873, and travelled by train to Cairo three days later. They settled into Shepheard's Hotel – the traditional waystation for wealthy European travellers – and took the opportunity to explore the city while negotiations over the choice of *dahabiyeh* and crew commenced. At Giza, Alfred 'made the ascent' of the Great Pyramid, while the MBs 'were content to visit the Tombs and ramble about the Sphinx with an attendant train of Arabs and do occasional bazaar'. They named their boat *Bagstones*, after the house in Cheshire in which they lived, and set off with Amelia Edwards, who chartered the *Philae*.

Brocklehurst's diary opens a window onto the day-to-day experiences of a Victorian traveller touring a route that was becoming well trod (or sailed). There are frequent references to the difficulties of navigating the river in convoy – 'We are unkindly bumped by the Philae and left on a sandbank' – but there were some advantages: 'Still racing and chasing with the Philae and Fostat into Assouan but just at the last we stick on a sand bank in a high wind and cannot get off till the Philae sends some natives for assistance.' Brocklehurst's diary entries were often little more than short summaries of the day's activities ('Good wind to Keneh. We have to stop to buy charcoal and dates .... Ride donkeys to tour town') but full of interesting details that vividly convey a sense of the journey and her companions. Alfred's constant attempts to gun down the local wildlife was a frequent distraction: 'We spend the afternoon among Karnac's immense halls and gorgeous ruins. It is very

TOMBS, MUMMIES AND TREASURE

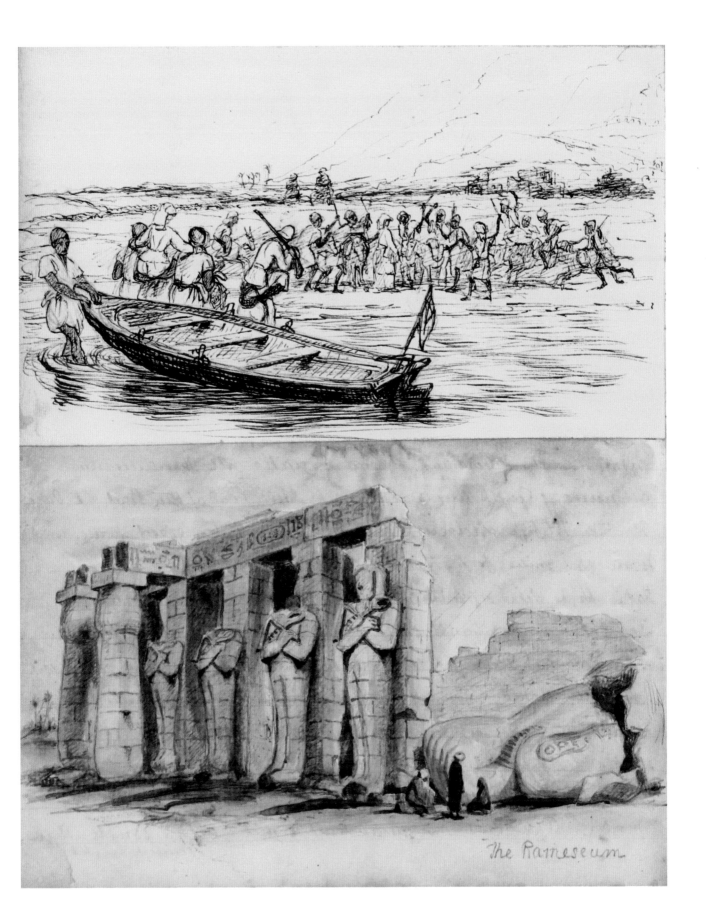

The Rameseum

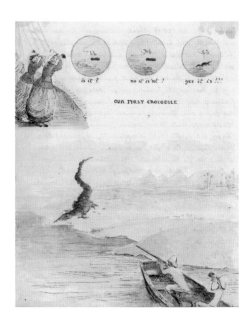

↑ Brocklehurst's record of her party's first sighting of a crocodile – 'is it?', 'no it isn't!', 'yes it is!!!' – and her nephew's attempt to shoot it.

splendid. Alfred shoots a fox and thinks more of it than the temples, naturally.' Sometimes, this pastime had disastrous consequences: 'A. shoots a native instead of his quail – he quails! But the native recovers and the village is satisfied with three shillings backsheesh, which seems cheap for a man.' Certainly, the tour was not uneventful. Brocklehurst reported a number of incidents that demonstrate the risk to a travelling flotilla, though they never came to any real harm: 'At night, an alarm of robbers. A man swims round both boats, but is well shouted at before he can get on either, after which they make great demonstrations of catching him, in the felucca, which is a safe course. Presently I see the guard subside again into his little hole on the bank and all is over.'

In Luxor they visited the house of the consular agent and antiquities dealer Mostafa Agha, 'a very old gentleman, very polite and pleasant for an old Turk'. Brocklehurst seems to have been very eager to purchase antiquities from Agha, recording in her diary a dinner attended by the Consul and his son that involved 'Much secret conference over antiquities'. Such dealings were the basis for her most important and lasting contribution to Egyptology: the substantial collection that she displayed to the British public. She travelled to Egypt three more times, in 1882–83, 1890–91 and 1895–96, but several of her most important acquisitions were made on this first trip. She actively sought out information on unofficially discovered tombs from Egyptians she met, including the Abd er-Rassoul family, who would later become infamous for finding – and then concealing – the cache of New Kingdom pharaohs hidden away in the cliffs at Deir el-Bahri (TT 320). In fact, a silver ring with faience bezel inscribed for Ramesses II and five shabtis of the high priest Pinudjem I in her collection may have come from this cache, though the discovery was still a carefully guarded secret.

It is also possible that Brocklehurst bought the star piece in her collection from the Abd er-Rassouls: a brightly coloured cartonnage mummy case belonging to a chantress named Shebmut. Not content merely to purchase pillaged pieces from local looters, Brocklehurst and her companions set out to recover it from the tomb directly:

> We stole off together on foot … and scrambled in the dark up the rocky hill above those noble ruins which stand upon the desert to the house – or rather tomb, for rock cut tomb it was – where the Arab family in question resided. A series of chambers cut in the solid rock and running deep into the hill, where the old hieroglyphics showed in places through the modern plaster of mud, was the rendezvous …. Here we had Kalam and coffee of a horrid description …. We then proceeded underground through several rooms, each hotter and hotter like a Turkish bath, to an upper den, to which we were hoisted perhaps twelve or fifteen feet high by the strong arms of our black friends …. Here we found the mummy in its very prettily painted case (white ground and coloured figures) and all enclosed in a wooden sarcophagus more than an inch in thickness, which from its size and weight was necessarily out of all question in a smuggling point of view. The case did not appear to belong to a mummy of great importance, having no gold on the outside, it was about five feet long. We liked its looks, however, and we liked the idea of smuggling on a large scale under the nose of the Pasha's guards who, as excavations

TOMBS, MUMMIES AND TREASURE

were then going on near at hand, were pretty thick on the ground and on the alert.

We returned alone with our friendly Arabs, a four miles ride in the dark to the Dahabeeiah, leaving Mr Maguilp R.A. to do the bargaining for us .... If successful he was to bring the Mummy to us in the night and land it through our cabin window. Thus we sat up the first night watching, but in vain, nothing came of it .... Afterwards we were left to our own devices and had many secret interviews with the proprieters. Again we visited their den, this time to see a fine papyrus which finally was included in the bargain – first price asked was a hundred pounds for the two! But now we got entangled with another Arab who wished to act as a go between and have a finger in the profits and whom we had reason afterward to suspect of treachery, informing against us to a man in authority, but I think we propitiated both by a present of champagne and cognac and by purchasing some doubtful antiquities at a good price.

At last it was all arranged. Alfred and George were to steal off in the felucca after the moon had set and receive the mummy on the opposite shore, the Arabs bringing it there, carrying it at least four miles and running the gauntlet of all M. Mariette's guards, and then, as it was of the utmost consequence that our sailors should know nothing about it, we were to receive it in at the window of our cabin. Thus we waited and watched the second night, all lights out, A. and G. asleep in their clothes but ready for action.

↓ On Saturday 13 December 1873, Brocklehurst and her party set sail from Cairo for Bedrashein, in the region of ancient Memphis, where they moored for the night. She wrote in *Journey up the Nile* how 'The views on each side have been beautiful, first passing picturesque old Cairo with its little mosks and date trees .... On the other hand, the pyramids of Giza and then ... Sakkara ... the river and pretty old boats painted up by the setting sun and afterglow into exquisite pictures.'

The mummy finally arrived on the third night. They opened the case; either the Abd er-Rassouls had already unwrapped the mummy, or they proceeded to do so now. Marianne wrote almost touchingly of the mummy, which she believed to be the body of a young boy: 'The features of his face were really pleasant and happy in expression and there was hair on his woodeny little head ... no ornaments, papyrus,

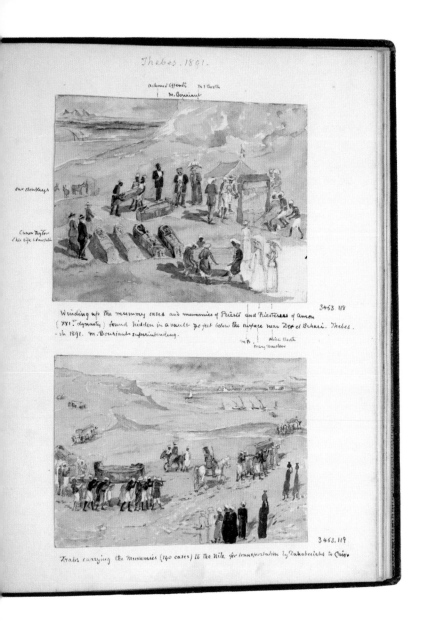

Thebes. 1891.

achmed Effendi   M. Booth
M. Bouriant

our donkeys

Canon Taylor & his life & daughter

Winding up the mummy cases and mummies of Priests and Priestesses of Amon (XXI.st dynasty) found hidden in a vault 40 feet below the surface near Deir el Bahari, Thebes, in 1891. M. Bouriant superintending.

3453. 118

M.B.   Alice Booth
Mary Moulson

Arabs carrying the mummies (140 cases) to the Nile for transportation by Dahabeiahs to Cairo.

3453. 119

↑ Two sketches by Brocklehurst documenting the discovery of the burials of over 150 priests of Amun, now known as the Bab el-Gasus cache. The first is labelled 'Winding up the mummy cases and mummies', while the second shows the coffins being transported to the river for shipment to Cairo.

scarabs, not even a little god or two had been placed on his little person. We supposed they thought him too innocent to need such help on his journey to heaven, from where, I trust, if he looked down upon our proceedings, he felt no bitterness of wrath.' Wishful thinking on Brocklehurst's part, perhaps; the removal of the assemblage from its proper place of burial would, in the ancient Egyptian worldview, have compromised the owner's place in the eternal afterlife. Even worse, it was all for naught: 'The little Mummy was buried by night with great secrecy and left in his native land.' But despite their fear that the suspicious odour would be noticed by their cook – who had worked for Mariette himself – they were able to keep the mummy case concealed. Upon their arrival in Cairo it was transferred directly to the railway station for the journey to Alexandria, where they 'got everything bribed on board the steamer without difficulty'.

Upon her return to England, Brocklehurst helped to set up a branch of the Egypt Exploration Fund in Macclesfield, of which Mary Booth was the secretary. She returned to Egypt several times. In 1891, she witnessed the discovery of a cache of high-ranking priests, the largest ever discovered – even larger than the cache of New Kingdom pharaohs clandestinely discovered by the Abd er-Rassouls, who had been found out a decade earlier. The tomb, which lay to the north-east of the temple of Hatshepsut at Deir el-Bahri, contained a total of 153 coffin assemblages, 101 of which belonged to 21st Dynasty priests of Amun. It was in fact first spotted by Mohamed Abd er-Rassoul who, on this occasion, reported his suspicion to the head of the Antiquities Service, Eugène Grébaut, then excavating the temple of Hatshepsut. Grébaut's excavation revealed a shaft leading to a long corridor, with a second branching off to the left, both almost choked full of coffins. They began the process of removing them almost immediately. Brocklehurst drew two sketches of the coffins laid on the ground and being carried away – a rare visual record of one of the great moments in Egyptian archaeology.

After her fourth visit to Egypt, Brocklehurst decided that her own collection, including the objects from the royal cache, should be put on public display, and with her brother, Peter, she built a museum in Macclesfield to house it. Sadly she was unable to attend the opening of the museum in 1898, having broken her collarbone. While Brocklehurst participated in what nowadays would be regarded as illicit looting rather than respectable archaeology, she made an enormous contribution to Egyptology by raising awareness of the subject on behalf of the Egypt Exploration Fund. The diary account of her first visit in particular

Brocklehurst's drawing of the colossi of Memnon (twin statues of Amenhotep III) at Luxor, and a scarab depicting the pharaoh and his wife, Tiye, which she purchased in Qena 'for 12 shillings, an old railway reading lamp and a small bottle of castor oil. Afterwards Dr Birch wanted to buy it for the British Museum.'

epitomizes the kind of tour that had become commonplace by the later years of the 19th century; her reactions – good and bad – to what she encountered are very much of their time, and her treatment of antiquities often lamentable, but her work in promoting Egyptology in England helped to set the tone for a new, more responsible way of approaching archaeology in Egypt.

Victor Loret

1859–1946 French Egyptologist and discoverer
of numerous tombs in the Valley of the Kings

*Loret was director of Egypt's Antiquities
Service and discovered the tombs
of the pharaohs Tuthmosis III and
Amenhotep II in the Valley of the Kings.
Amenhotep II's tomb contained an
extraordinary cache of the mummified
bodies of a series of New Kingdom
pharaohs, deliberately hidden during a
spate of robberies in the royal cemetery.*

→ Watercolour by Loret of decoration in the tomb
of Ramesses IX (KV 6) in the Valley of the Kings.

Loret arrived in Egypt in 1881 barely into his twenties, having studied
Egyptology under Gaston Maspero in Paris and then followed him to
Cairo as one of the first members of the new École Française du Caire,
which would become the Institut Français d'Archéologie Orientale
(IFAO), still one of the major archaeological research institutes in Egypt
today. By the time he died, aged eighty-six, in 1946, Loret had published
well over a hundred books and articles on a wide range of Egyptological
themes, and had founded a school of Egyptology in Lyons, where
he had a long career as a teacher. He contributed particularly to the
decipherment of the ancient Egyptian language, publishing his *Manuel
de langue égyptienne: Grammaire, tableau des hiéroglyphes, textes et
glossaire* in 1889, although his ambitous *Dictionnaire hiéroglyphique*
and accompanying thesaurus were never fully realized. He is perhaps
best known, however, for an astonishing streak of discoveries he made
in the late 1890s in the Valley of the Kings.

The Antiquities Service's first survey of the known tombs
in the valley, which at that time numbered approximately thirty
(there are now sixty-two), was undertaken by Eugène Lefébure in
1883. Loret joined the project. In just a few months, Lefébure's team
copied all of the texts in the tombs of Sety I and Ramesses IV, and
created plans and copied the principal texts and scenes in all of the
remaining accessible tombs. This short but heroic burst of activity led
to the publication, in two volumes, of *Les Hypogées royaux de Thèbes*,
which contains the first published plans of half a dozen of the tombs.
Very few of Lefébure's assistants in this endeavour lasted the whole
season, but Loret survived, and it seems likely that he imagined that
further tombs might be found.

Loret was to nurture this idea for a decade and a half. In 1897,
he became director of the Antiquities Service, and the very next year
he began excavating in the valley. Over the course of two years he made
a breathtaking series of discoveries to rival Belzoni's (see pp. 136–43),
increasing the number of known tombs to forty-one. Sadly his records
do not reveal precisely how the sequence of discoveries unfolded, but
it seems that under his direction tombs KV 26 to 31 were investigated,
and 32 to 41 revealed for the very first time.

One of these, KV 34, which belonged to the 18th Dynasty
pharaoh Tuthmosis III, is almost unique in its style and decoration
and was found in extremely good condition, making it one of the finest
and most interesting tombs in the valley. A cartouche-shaped burial
chamber's curving walls are decorated with curious images relating to
the 'Book of What is in the Netherworld', a religious text that narrates
the journey of the sun-god through the night to be reborn again at the
start of the next day. The tomb's discovery should perhaps properly
be credited to Hassan Hosni (see pp. 238–41), the Antiquities Service
inspector who was supervising the excavations, as Loret was away
on business.

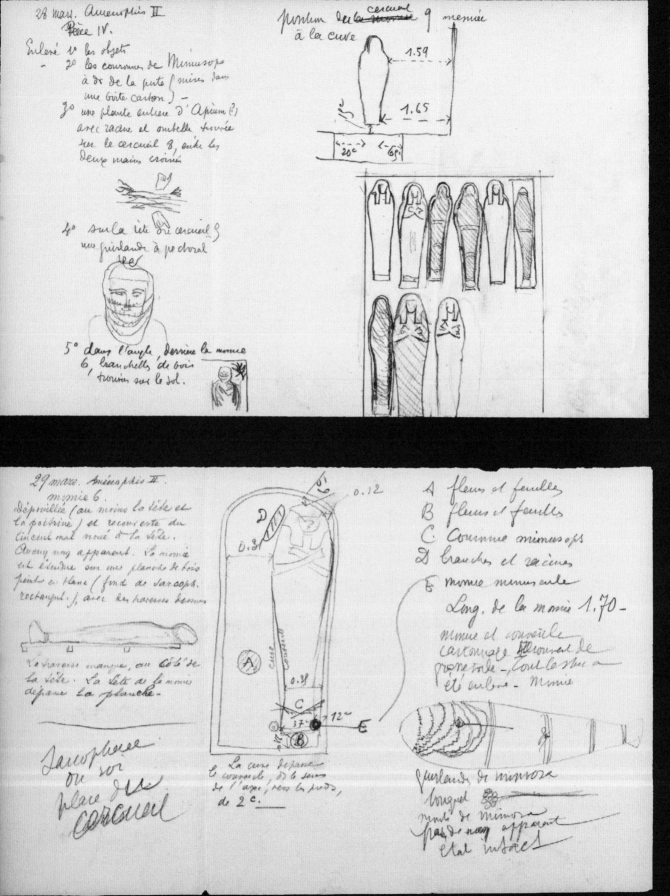

28 mars. Aménophis II
Pièce IV.

Enlevé 1° les objets
- 2° les couronnes de Mimusops
  à dr de la porte (mises dans
  une boîte carton) -
- 3° une plante entière d'Apium (?)
  avec racine et ombelle trouvée
  sur le cercueil 8, entre les
  deux mains croisées

4° sur la tête du cercueil 9
une guirlande à pectoral

5° dans l'angle, derrière la momie
6, branchelles de bois
trouvées sur le sol.

position de la [~~momie~~ cercueil] 9 momie
à la cuve
1.59
1.65
20c   65c

29 mars. Aménophis II
momie 6.
Dépouillée (au moins la tête et
la poitrine) et recouverte du
cercueil mal noué à la tête.
Aucun nom apparent. La momie
est étendue sur une planche de bois
peint en blanc (fond de Sarcoph.
rectangul.), avec les traverses dessous

La traverse manque, au côté de
la tête. La tête de la momie
dépasse la planche.

Sarcophage
ou sol
place de
cercueil

La cuve dépasse
le couvercle, du côté
de l'axe, vers les pieds,
de 2c.

0.12
0.31
0.38
37
12c
A
B
C
D
E

A fleurs et feuilles
B fleurs et feuilles
C couronne mimusops
D branches et racines
E momie minuscule

Long. de la momie 1.70 -
momie et couvercle
cartonnage recouvert de
propre toile -, Tout le rite a
été enlevé - momie

guirlande de mimosa
longueur
ronds de mimosa
pas de nom apparent
état intact

← Loret's record, dated 28 March 1898, of the side chamber of a tomb he had recently found in the Valley of the Kings. The tomb belonged to the 18th Dynasty pharaoh Amenhotep II, and the cache proved to contain the mummies of nine other pharaohs.

✓ Loret found the mummy of Amenhotep II still in its sarcophagus, the first in the Valley of the Kings to be discovered *in situ*. He did not realize that it had been placed in a new coffin as part of the same reburial process that introduced other mummies into the tomb. This sketch records his initial observations.

The most important of the discoveries made during Loret's campaign is one of the finest tombs in the valley, that of Amenhotep II, another 18th Dynasty king. Richly decorated and complex architecturally, this one, too, was found to be in good condition, and unusually for this period, which was blighted by a spate of tomb robberies the king's mummy was still in place in the sarcophagus. It was not simply remarkable in that the tomb had never been robbed, however: in the side rooms leading off the main burial chamber, Loret found two caches of mummies. In the first were three unwrapped bodies lying side by side: in the centre, a young male; to his right, a young woman, now known as the 'Younger Lady'; and to his left an 'Elder Lady'. In the absence of any coffins or other inscribed grave goods, Loret was unable to identify them. A combination of evidence

→ A notebook kept by Loret, with a sketch of a 'poorly preserved' mummy of the 21st Dynasty.

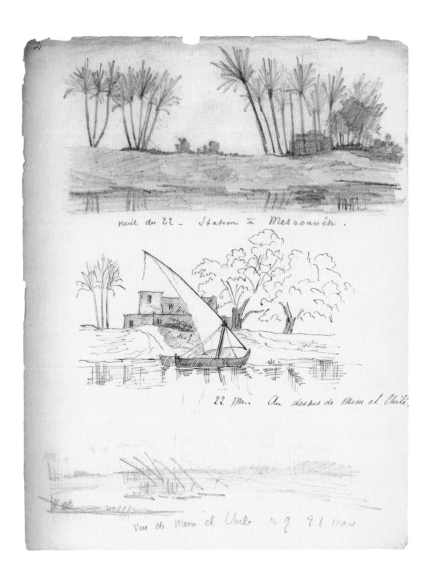

↑ A page from Loret's travel journal of May 1881, with sketches of scenes on the Nile.

gathered since and DNA testing has now revealed that the 'Elder Lady' was the famous Queen Tiye, wife of Amenhotep III and grandmother of Tutankhamun. It has even been suggested that the 'Younger Lady' may be Nefertiti. In the second room, Loret found another cache of mummies, though these were wrapped and contained within coffins. Loret had discovered the bodies of nine New Kingdom pharaohs, in addition to that of Amenhotep II himself, which had also been reburied as part of the caching process – although, as he was the original owner of the tomb, he had rightly been returned to his sarcophagus. They had all been moved into the tomb on a single occasion during the reign of the 21st Dynasty king Smendes I to protect them from desecration by robbers.

Loret's excavations in the valley ceased when he left his post as director of the Antiquities Service, but his discoveries in those two seasons assured him of his place among the giants of Egyptology. His notes and drawings are all the more valuable since he never published his discoveries as fully as Egyptologists would have liked; rich and beautiful, they are the only records remaining of some aspects of these crucially important seasons in one of Egypt's most celebrated sites.

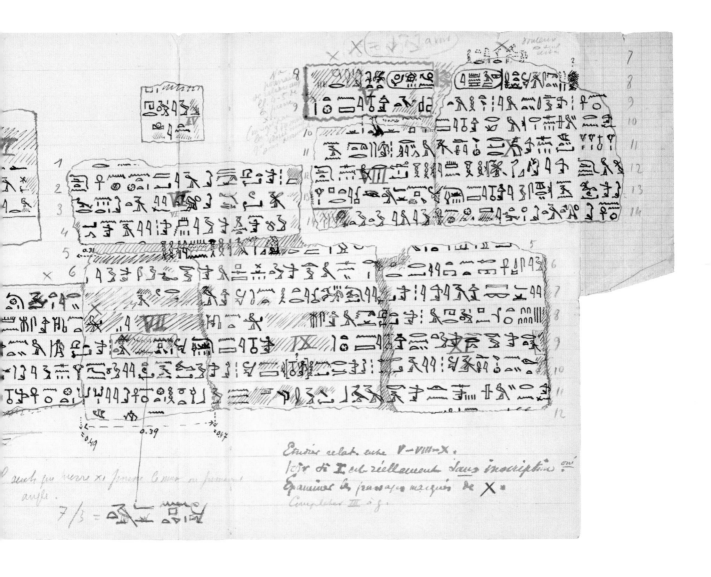

↑ An inscription found on some blocks near the tomb of a scribe of the Treasury of Ptah under Ramesses II. Loret uncovered this official's tomb at Saqqara in 1898.

→ A cigar box used by Loret to hold lexicographical cards.

Percy Newberry

1868–1949 British Egyptologist

Newberry was the first field director of the Egypt Exploration Fund's Archaeological Survey of Egypt, which helped set a benchmark for the epigraphic recording and publication of standing monuments in Egypt.

→ Detail of a watercolour by Rosalind Paget showing a group of bulls, part of a much larger scene of the 'exotica' encountered during Hatshepsut's expedition to the land of Punt, as recorded on the walls of her temple at Deir el-Bahri. The EEF's practice at this time was to make a complete record of the decoration in pencil and to reproduce certain details in watercolour to give readers of the published reports a greater sense of the reliefs' finesse and bright colours.

Percy Newberry was born in Islington, London, and educated at the prestigious King's College School and King's College London. As a teenager he assisted the archaeologist Reginald Stuart Poole with his work for the Egypt Exploration Fund (EEF), where Poole was joint honorary secretary with Amelia Edwards (pp. 172–77). Newberry had a particular interest in botany, contributing chapters on this subject to volumes by William Flinders Petrie (pp. 178–83) on Hawara (1889) and Kahun (1890). His hard work and dedication would pay off with his first opportunity to work in the field when in 1890 he was invited to lead a new branch of the EEF's activities: the Archaeological Survey of Egypt.

The Survey was established at the suggestion of Francis Llewellyn Griffith, who had trained in archaeology under Flinders Petrie as the Fund's first apprentice. He had, unlike his mentor, gained a deep understanding of the ancient Egyptian language. The EEF's modus operandi was to send, each year, an 'explorer' to a particular site that was considered either to be under particular threat or especially likely to yield valuable new archaeological material and information. The focus was on the excavation of sites that had previously received little or no attention, and therefore the much-better known standing monuments, which were felt to be safe somehow, were passed over as potential sites of work. Griffith, like many others, however, had witnessed the rapid destruction of these better-known monuments and saw a pressing need for the Fund to create a second branch of activities, to focus on recording the architectures and decoration at these sites before they were lost. In 1889, he proposed at the Fund's Annual General Meeting that they launch a 'rapid sketch-survey', which 'might in a few years sweep the whole surface of the country'. Two years later, at the next AGM, he remarked:

> *It is not difficult for one who has studied Egyptian archaeology in the country for some years to see what is required in order that the archaeological inheritance of so many centuries may not be swept away at the very moment when the world appears ready to receive and appreciate it. What can be done to stem the torrent of absolute destruction? ... The Nile valley contains a multitude of monuments and ruins, some partly described, some as yet almost unknown, but all alike exposed to the attacks of the dealer in antiquities, the quarryman and the wanton iconoclast.*

The aim of the Survey was thus to preserve the salient features of Egypt's standing monuments – what Griffith described as 'the harvest that hastens to ruin with every day that passes' – through careful recording of the ancient architecture, reliefs and inscriptions throughout the country. It was quickly realized that the scope of the project might be too ambitious, however; thus Newberry, whom Griffith had appointed following the General Meeting in 1889 to direct the work

TOMBS, MUMMIES AND TREASURE

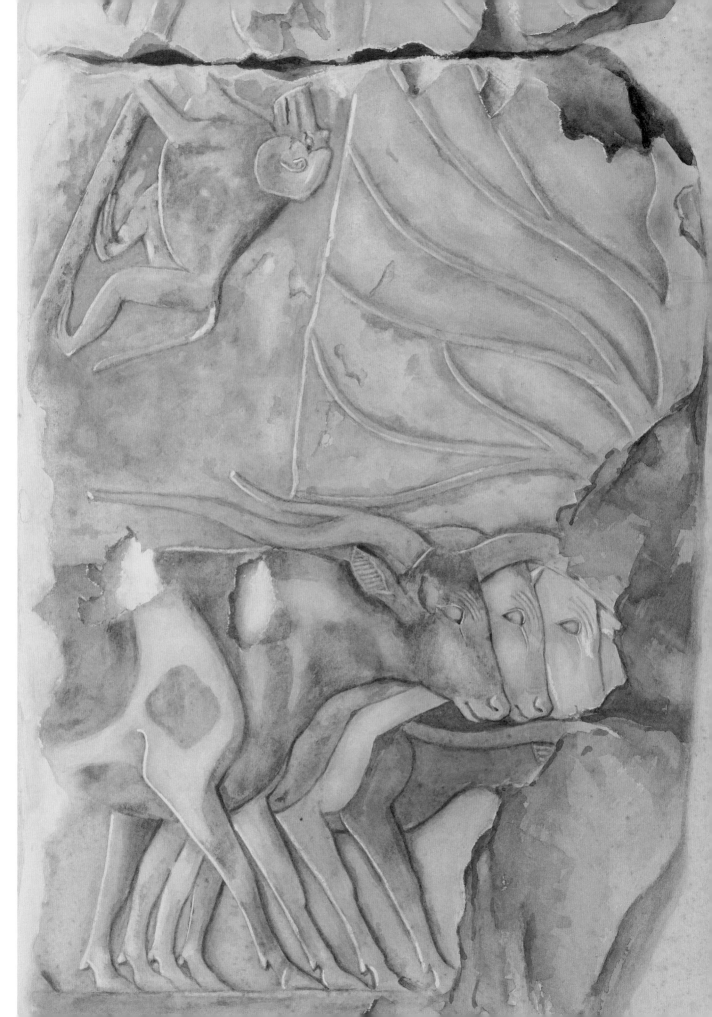

↑ Tracing by Newberry of a copy made by Winifred Firth of decoration in the tomb of Akhmerutnesut (G 2184) at Giza. This scene shows a group of goats eating leaves from two trees.

in the field, recommended that the Survey instead select single sites that could then be the focus of thorough study. The Fund chose to begin work along a 25-kilometre (15-mile) stretch of the Nile within which were found several groups of tombs including those at Beni Hasan, cemetery of the Middle Kingdom governors and administrators of the sixteenth Upper Egyptian nome. These tombs were well known but, in the view of the Fund, had never been adequately documented. The sheer quantity and quality of the decoration would provide rich pickings for the commencement of the Survey's activities. Griffith set out the task awaiting the team: 'All these twelve thousand square feet have to be puzzled out and the colours identified, while a faithful transcript, of which every details is as of as much importance as the *ensemble*, must be made by means of tracing paper.' During the first season (1890–91), Newberry was accompanied by G. W. Fraser, a surveyor who would record accurately the location and architecture of each of the tombs, and M. W. Blackden, an artist who would assist Newberry with the copying of the decoration and produce colour facsimiles of the most important details.

Over the course of the next two seasons, during which the Survey also visited the tombs at Deir el-Bersha, Deir el-Gebrawi, Sheikh Said and el-Amarna (although the work at the latter site was curtailed when the team was refused permission to operate there by the Antiquities Service), the team was joined by Newberry's brother John, as surveyor, and two more artists, Percy Buckman and a seventeen-year-old named Howard Carter (pp. 202–11) on his first assignment in Egypt. One of the main aims of the project was to capture the basic information recorded in the tombs' decoration, and in particular the hieroglyphic texts. Carter would later criticize the Survey's adopted method of recording the figures and inscriptions, objecting that it failed to capture anything of the sense of the artistry of the painters responsible, treating the walls instead merely as media for conveying information. The Fund, mindful of the cost of publishing plates in colour, favoured tracing the ancient imagery, although a number of coloured drawings were made that capture the finer details of the decoration inside the tombs. In these, Blackden, Buckman and Carter could make much fuller use of their talents, and the drawings reflect their artistic abilities as well as their observational skills. Percy Buckman also painted a landscape at each of the major stops made during the expedition, and these were reproduced at the beginning of the published volumes and in the EEF's *Archaeological Report* as a means of setting the scene for the reader.

The drawings made during the first three intensive seasons at Deir el-Bersha, Sheikh Said and Deir el-Gebrawi were exhibited in London and Manchester during 1893. The Survey was suspended thereafter for several years owing to a lack of resources and the pressing need to complete the publication of the work already undertaken. By this time the intensity of working so closely together in such lonely landscapes over so long a period had taken its toll on the relationships between certain members of the team. By the middle of the 1891–92 season, a rift had opened between Newberry and Carter on the one hand and Fraser and Blackden on the other. Matters came to a head when, on Christmas Eve 1891, while the party was working at Deir el-Bersha, Carter and Newberry were guided by a group of Bedouin to a spot rumoured to be the location of the tomb of the pharaoh Akhenaten. This proved not to be the case, but Newberry and Carter immediately recognized the site as being something else of great importance – the alabaster quarries of Hatnub, which were known from ancient texts but had never been found. On returning to camp, Newberry and Carter related the discovery to their colleagues, who seemed

↓ Coloured facsimile by Marcus Blackden of a bush containing several types of bird, from the tomb of Khnumhotep II at Beni Hasan. Blackden's drawing reflects the attention to detail that artists invested in every part, however small, of the decoration of tombs such as this.

M.W.Blackden

One of a group of foreigners entering Egypt. (the Aamu,
a northern tribe); they wear handsome coloured garments
with fringe; have brown skin not red - black hair &
a short beard. The face is Semitic in type. Many
of the group wear boots.

Catalogue
10

↑ Painting by Newberry of a glass chalice bearing the coronation name of Tuthmosis II, 'Menkheperre'. It was purchased by an English antiquarian, Edward Dodwell, in about 1825, before entering into the collections of the State Museum of Egyptian Art, Munich. It is believed to be the oldest surviving glass vessel in the world.

not entirely pleased at the news. A day or so later, Fraser and Blackden disappeared in a hurry at the break of dawn without explanation. Newberry and Carter learned from the Bedouin that they had gone to Hatnub. After five days they returned, announcing that they had made a thorough survey and copied all the major inscriptions, effectively stealing any claim their colleagues might have made to the discovery and right of publication. 'Dirty Dogs!' was Carter's reaction. Newberry was, understandably, incensed and left shortly afterwards for London, although he would return to the expedition for a third season and retained the allegiance of the Fund. Blackden and Fraser, conversely, would not be recommissioned. While deprived of the find, Carter would in the end benefit from Blackden and Fraser's duplicity. Blackden was due to be seconded to Amarna to train under Petrie, but following the Hatnub episode it was Carter instead who was sent to join the great master. Thus he gained his first experience of archaeology alongside the best tutor he could have hoped for.

The Survey's work would be continued by the main Exploration Fund. When Edouard Naville took on the job of clearing and documenting the great temple of Hatshepsut at Deir el-Bahri, the EEF insisted that Carter join the team, in part to help supervise the archaeological work, but Naville also gave the young man free reign to determine the best way of capturing the exquisite painted reliefs. Carter rose to the challenge superbly, and the records, assisted by several other artists including Rosalind Paget and Percy Brown, made over the course of several seasons and published in six lavish volumes, are among the finest made of such reliefs. The Survey proper would be revived at the end of the century under the direction of Norman de Garis Davies (pp. 212–29), and would continue for many decades thereafter.

In many ways the great triumph of Newberry's Archaeological Survey was to accomplish, at least for the sites that it visited, what the great British copyists of the early 19th century had, for the greater part, not been able to do. Robert Hay (pp. 88–97), James Burton (pp. 74–81), Edward William Lane (pp. 82–87) and even to some extent John Gardner Wilkinson (pp. 110–19) had amassed vast corpora of drawings and notes with a view to creating and publishing a comprehensive record of Egypt's ancient sites and monuments, but often lacked the financial backing to bring their projects to fruition. Newberry, along with Carter, Blackden, Buckman, Paget and others, did likewise, but benefited from the backing of the Egypt Exploration Fund, a publisher in its own right with a ready base of hundreds of supporters eager to pay to read about every season's activities. The Survey's publications have in many cases never been superseded, and remain indispensable tools for the study of a series of important sites throughout the Nile Valley.

← Watercolour by Blackden showing one of a group of foreigners identified by a hieroglyphic label (not fully copied here) as 'Ibsha', who was a 'ruler of foreign lands'. The original Egyptian term for this – *heka khasut* – was given to foreigners who settled in the Delta shortly after this tomb was built, in the Second Intermediate Period.

Howard Carter

1874–1939 British artist, archaeologist and Egyptologist

Carter first travelled to Egypt in 1891 as a teenager, already with an enthusiasm for the country's antiquities. He trained with Flinders Petrie and became one of the finest archaeologists of his era, working for many years in and around the Valley of the Kings before making, in 1922, the discovery that would ensure his legacy as perhaps the most famous archaeologist of all: the tomb of Tutankhamun.

→ Coloured facsimile by Carter of a scene showing Tuthmosis I and his mother, Seniseneb, making offerings to Anubis. It comes from a small chapel to the god on the upper terrace of the temple of Hatshepsut at Deir el-Bahri. After the death of Tuthmosis II, Hatshepsut claimed the kingship for herself, basing her legitimacy on her descent from Tuthmosis I.

Howard Carter was born in Kensington, London, and grew up in Swaffham, Norfolk. He was trained in painting from an early age by his father, the artist and illustrator Samuel John Carter. His interest in ancient Egypt was prompted by the collection of antiquities at nearby Didlington Hall, one of the most significant in the country at the time. This was the home of the 1st Baron Amherst of Hackney, a notable sponsor of excavations in Egypt, including the first of the Egypt Exploration Fund's (EEF) Archaeological Survey expeditions under the direction of Percy Newberry (pp. 196–201). The Survey's first season at Beni Hasan had yielded extraordinary results, but progress was slower than Newberry had hoped. Any expansion of the project was contingent on the Survey receiving additional funds. Newberry succeeded in persuading Mrs Thyssen Amherst, wife of the baron and an important supporter of Egyptology in her own right, to make a contribution. This seems directly to have led to the appointment of Carter, though he was just sixteen years old, as one of the additional artists, very likely with Mrs Amherst's encouragement, if not at her instigation.

The undecorated rock-tomb that the Survey team chose for their lodgings at Beni Hasan must have felt a far cry from Carter's family home: 'I lay somewhat bewildered in my new surroundings, endeavouring to sleep upon a roughly made palm-branch bedstead. That first night I watched from my bed the brilliant starry heavens visible through the open doorway. I listened to the faint flutterings of the bats that flitted around our rock chamber and, in imagination I called up strange spirits from ancient dead until the first gleam of dawn when, from sheer fatigue I fell asleep.'

Carter was employed to make simple black-and-white tracings of the scenes painted on the walls of these ancient tombs. The Survey's mission was to record as much basic information from the tombs as possible in their limited season, and the young artist was deeply frustrated by their elected methods:

The moment I first saw Egyptian art I was struck by its immense dignity and restraint. Indeed from the moment I began to study that art, I was struck by the beauty of its line, and above all its deep understanding in interpreting character. It was for that reason, and for no other reason, that I was disappointed with the method I was obliged to employ to copy the art so dependent upon its purity of line.

To my horror I found the modus operandi in force was to hang large sheets of tracing paper upon the walls, and with a soft pencil trace the scenes upon them, no matter whether those scenes were painted on the flat, or sculptured in relief, and no matter the wall surfaces were smooth or granular. These completed paintings were then to be rolled up, transported to England, where they could be inked in with a brush, and all inside the outlines of the figure filled in black like a

TOMBS, MUMMIES AND TREASURE

Howard Carter.
March -

↑ Letter from Howard Carter to Mrs Kingsmill Marrs, dated 25 October 1908. Mrs Marrs had recently come to know Carter and would purchase six paintings from him, of a kind he often sold as a way of generating income. In this letter Carter includes a sketch of an image of Nefertari, Great Royal Wife of Ramesses II, from her tomb, and reports that he has finished a painting of her.

↗ Detail of Tuthmosis I's mother from the scene illustrated on p. 203, signed 'Howard Carter, 1899'. Whereas the complete scene was prepared in part for a report for the Egypt Exploration Fund, the detail was probably made for private sale.

silhouette, as it proved afterwards, often by persons without any real knowledge of drawing …. Needless to say, from the point of view of Egyptian art, the results were far from being satisfactory.

In addition to these shallow tracings, Carter made 'careful coloured drawings' in watercolour of the finer details. These were objects of beauty in their own right; the originals were displayed at an exhibition in Manchester in 1893 but have rarely seen the light of day since.

Thanks to the ignominious departure of M. W. Blackden from the EEF (see p. 201), Carter found himself the only remaining candidate to join William Flinders Petrie (pp. 178–83) as his apprentice on a dig at the 18th Dynasty capital city of el-Amarna at the close of the Survey work. The young artist thereby gained his first training in archaeology entirely by accident, and moreover with the great master of what was then still a very young discipline.

Carter learned quickly, and after his second season with the Survey was seconded by the EEF to another of its projects, the excavation of the great temple of Hatshepsut at Deir el-Bahri in Thebes, a short distance from the Valley of the Kings. Here he was given full charge of the epigraphy, allowing him to make best use of his artist's eye and superior ability in capturing all the subtleties of ancient Egypt artwork. At Deir el-Bahri this involved three dimensions, not two, as the figures and hieroglyphs had been carved in fine raised relief before being painted, which presented Carter with an intellectual challenge: 'I felt that if I attempted to copy the scenes sculptured upon the walls of Hat.shep.sut's mortuary temple by the prevailing system of tracing, the essential charm of those beautiful reliefs would have vanished in my copy .... The temple setting, the delicate sculptured reliefs upon its walls, were always a feast for the mind. In those six years, although full of hard work, I learnt more of Egyptian art, its serene simplicity, than in any other time or place.' It was here that Carter produced some of his most iconic work, perhaps most notably the sensitive rendering of the head and shoulders of Queen Ahmes, Hatshepsut's mother. In this he proved himself the equal of the greatest of copyists.

Despite his evident love of, and great talent for, this kind of work, Carter was contemplating taking his career in a new direction, and in 1899 a new appointment and an important introduction allowed him to do just that. First, the returning director of the Antiquities Service, Gaston Maspero, reorganized its structure so that there would from then on be two chief inspectors, one for Lower Egypt and one for Upper Egypt. James Quibell, one of Petrie's 'pups', was appointed to the former, and Howard Carter to the latter. Secondly, he was introduced by Percy Newberry to Theodor Davis, a wealthy American lawyer who regularly visited Egypt and would shortly begin excavations in the Valley of the Kings, the site where Carter was to make his name.

In early 1900, within a month of taking up his new post as chief inspector, Carter had commenced investigations of a site just in front of the temple of Hatshepsut where in 1898 his horse had stumbled into a depression that, his brief investigations suggested, was perhaps

↓ Watercolour of the temple of Hatshepsut at Deir el-Bahri and surrounds. Carter's first work in Thebes had been for the Egypt Exploration Fund expedition. He would later carry out much important archaeological work in this part of the necropolis.

a tomb. As it lay outside the area of the EEF's concession, he was at that time unable to investigate any further, but as chief inspector he lost no time in returning to the spot. The 'Bab el-Hosan' ('Tomb of the Horse') proved to be a substantial cutting into the bedrock, which took two months to clear before a sealed – and apparently intact – entranceway was discovered. The chamber beyond contained a very well-preserved and striking seated statue of Mentuhotep II Nebhepetra (now in the Egyptian Museum, Cairo), founder of the Middle Kingdom. Unfortunately, the wooden coffin that accompanied it was empty. The assemblage was probably a ritual deposit associated with the nearby temple-tomb of the same king, which was to be fully revealed by the same EEF expedition under Naville by which Carter had previously been employed. Carter's discovery was significant, and the statue spectacular, yet he was probably disappointed, having hoped to find a royal tomb. His watercolour of the scene in the chamber is the only visual record of the contents as found.

Carter continued to work in the valley, clearing and restoring tombs and installing electric lighting, though he was still yet to break new ground when in 1902 Theodor Davis accepted his proposal that they should look for the tomb of Tuthmosis IV. This pharaoh's reign fell after those of Tuthmosis III and Amenhotep II, and before that of Amenhotep III, all of whose spectacular tombs had been found elsewhere in the valley. Davis would provide the funds, and Carter the expertise. They were quickly rewarded: in the minor wadis around KV 20, Carter found glazed fragments from Tuthmosis IV's burial, the distribution of which seemed to point in a particular direction: 'What was even more pleasing, at a point where the small valley forked, where there might have been a doubt as to which of the two tributaries should next be taken, at the beginning of the right hand tributary a portion of fine alabaster vase bearing an engraved cartouche of the king was found.'

→ Carter's copy, made for the Egypt Exploration Fund's Archaeological Survey, of tomb decoration at Beni Hasan. It shows a hoopoe, from the same scene as the image on p. 199. Comparison of the two paintings reveals a difference in approach. The expedition's leader, Percy Newberry, noted how 'Mr. Blackden aimed at ascertaining the original design in a somewhat diagrammatic style: Mr. Carter and Mr. Brown copy faithfully what they see, and render it in its present condition.'

TOMBS, MUMMIES AND TREASURE

While exploring this part of the valley, Carter discovered another tomb, KV 60, which contained two mummies including a wet-nurse of Hatshepsut. Just above this tomb was a ledge that Carter thought was a likely point of entrance for another. He set his men to work, and indeed they uncovered two holes cut into the rock, found to contain a number of objects inscribed for Tuthmosis IV. Further digging revealed a much larger cutting in the rock: the entrance to a tomb. On 18 January Carter entered with the American Robb de Peyster Tytus:

> A few eroded steps led us down to the entrance doorway partially blocked with stones. We crept under its lintel into a steep descending corridor that penetrated into the heart of the rock. As we slithered down the mass of debris that encumbered this corridor the stones under our feet rolled with a hollow rumbling sound, echoed, re-echoed, in the depths of the tomb. At the end of this corridor we came to a steep flight of steps with a shallow recess on either side. These steps, sixteen in number, led down to another descending corridor which brought us to the brink of a large gaping well .... At the edge of this abyss we waited until our eyes became more accustomed to the dim light of our candles, and then we realised in the gloom that the upper part of the walls of this well were elaborately sculptured and painted. The scenes represented the pharaoh Tuthmosis IV standing before various gods and goddesses of the Netherworld .... Here was final proof that I had found the tomb of Tuthmosis IV, which, as you may conceive, gave me a considerable degree of satisfaction.

On the other side of the well, Carter could see a rope that had been used by robbers to continue their passage into the chambers beyond. The tomb had been thoroughly ransacked; the only objects that were not smashed or stolen by the plunderers were the massive granite sarcophagus and the remains of a ceremonial chariot.

When Carter was appointed chief inspector it had been agreed that he would transfer, after a pre-agreed period, to the northern inspectorate, with Quibell taking his place in the south. This had been postponed while Carter continued his excavations, but it could not be put off for ever. In 1905 Carter's time in Luxor came to a temporary end. The north of the country was not to his liking, however, and his attitude towards his new posting further soured by an incident involving a group of French tourists at Saqqara (Carter had complained of their behaviour and demanded that action be taken, but refused to acknowledge any culpability on his part in bringing about a difficult situation within diplomatic circles). Carter resigned before the year was out.

Returning to Luxor in 1906, Carter abandoned archaeology for a time, instead acting as a guide for tourists and selling watercolour views of the local monuments. He also contributed drawings to several important publications for archaeologists working in the region. It was not until 1909 that he would resume his own excavations. He was engaged by the earl of Carnarvon, an English aristocrat who had holidayed in Egypt since 1903 in the hope that the warmer climes would help him to recover from the ill-effects of a serious motoring accident. Together they would uncover a number of important tombs in the Theban necropolis – most famously, of course, that of Tutankhamun.

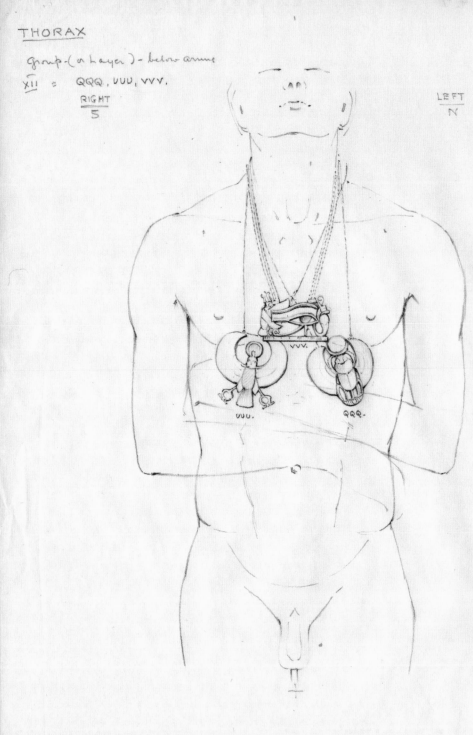

THORAX

Group (or Layer) — below arms

XII = QQQ, UUU, VVV,

RIGHT
5

LEFT
N

VVV.

UUU.

QQQ.

↑ One of a series of detailed drawings made by Carter during the examination of the mummy of Tutankhamun between 11 and 19 November 1925. Carter made over a dozen such drawings, each illustrating separate groups of jewelry found on the mummy.

→ A page from an album of photographs taken by Harry Burton showing the contents of three painted wooden boxes, including several pairs of ornate sandals and a headrest.

NEG. 86.

21.

21.

NEG. 87.

21.

21.

NEG. 85.

21.

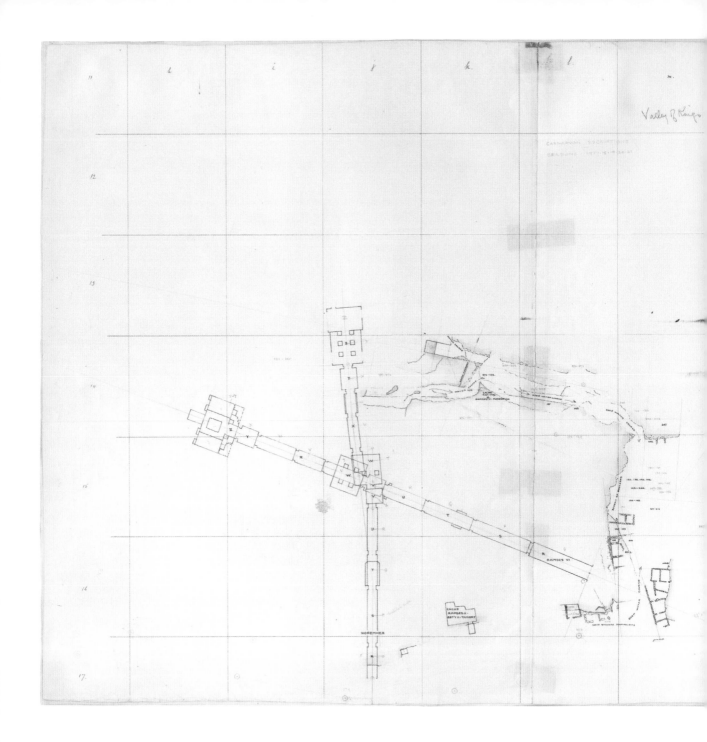

Valley of Kings

↑ Carter's map of the Valley of the Kings, made prior to his discovery of the tomb of Tutankhamun. It shows the exact area in which the tomb would be found, then still occupied by huts that Carter would later dig through. The tombs of Ramesses VI, Horemheb, Ramesses IX and the 'Cache Akhenaten' (KV 55) surround the site.

The First World War interrupted Carter's archaeological activities; the precise nature of his involvement in the war is unknown, but he later complained of having been 'tired of war work and secret ciphers'. He was nevertheless able to undertake some archaeological prospection, locating one and perhaps two royal tombs, thanks in no small part to his local connections. In 1916 Carter was holidaying in Luxor when he was notified that a tomb had been found by a group of locals, whose discovery had then caused a confrontation with a second group. Carter was summoned to try to prevent any further conflict and made the journey into the mountains by moonlight: 'It was midnight when we arrived on the scene, and the guide pointed out to me the

TOMBS, MUMMIES AND TREASURE

end of a rope which dangled sheer down the face of a cliff. Listening, we could hear the robbers actually at work, so I first severed their rope, thereby cutting their means of escape, and then, making secure a good stout rope of my own, I lowered myself down the cliff. Shinning down a rope at midnight, into a nestful of industrious tomb-robbers, is a pastime which at least does not lack excitement.' Within, Carter found a sarcophagus of yellow crystalline sandstone bearing the name of Hatshepsut, a pharaoh Carter had been following around Thebes for many years, but made at a time before she became king.

Although he was by now well established as an excavator, Carter's talents as a draughtsman and copyist were still in demand. In the same year as the discovery of Hatshepsut's earlier tomb, he was commissioned by Sir Alan Gardiner, the great philologist and patron of British Egyptological work, to produce copies of the decoration on the walls surrounding the colonnade of Tutankhamun and Horemheb at the Luxor temple. These beautiful, delicate scenes are full of fascinating details of the passage of the sacred barks of Amun, Mut and Khonsu, containing the holy statues of these gods, from Karnak to Luxor during the annual festival of Opet. Gardiner envisaged a lavish publication of the scenes and Carter produced drawings of extremely high quality, but he never completed the work and the book never appeared. The drawings, believed by some to be Carter's finest, have only rarely been seen.

Carter was acutely aware that his responsibility was primarily to Carnarvon, who had finally secured a permit to undertake excavations in the Valley of the Kings. Previously the concession had been held by Davis, but he had relinquished it, believing that there were no more tombs to find. Carter and Carnarvon began work in 1917, guided by Carter's hunch that, contrary to Davis's belief, the tomb of the obscure pharaoh Tutankhamun had not yet been found and might still be hidden beneath the valley floor. Several seasons passed before Carter was proven right, when at last in November 1922 he discovered a staircase leading to a sealed doorway bearing the name of Tutankhamun, though perhaps even he could not have imagined that beyond the blocking lay treasures that would come to define archaeology at its most spectacular:

> At first I could see nothing, the hot air escaping from the chamber causing the candle flame to flicker, but presently, as my eyes grew accustomed to the light, details of the room within emerged slowly from the mist, strange animals, statues, and gold – everywhere the glint of gold. For the moment – and eternity it must have seemed to the others standing by – I was struck dumb with amazement, and when Lord Carnarvon, unable to stand the suspense any longer, inquired anxiously, 'Can you see anything?' It was all I could do to get out the words, 'Yes, wonderful things.' Then, widening the hole a little further, so that we could both see, we inserted an electric torch.

The considerable legacy Carter left Egyptology rests not just on Tutankhamun, but on many years of lesser-known but equally important achievements in the field prior to 1922. Accurate record-keeping is a fundamentally important part of archaeology, and in this, and especially in capturing the artistry of the Egyptian sculptors and painters of thousands of years ago, Carter was unmatched.

Norman & Nina de Garis Davies

1865–1941 & 1881–1965 British husband-and-wife
Egyptologists and illustrators

*Norman and Nina de Garis Davies
were a married couple who raised
the standards of the reproduction
of Egyptian tomb decoration to new
heights, working prolifically at Amarna
and in the cemeteries of Thebes. They
often published their work together as
'N. de Garis Davies'.*

→ Reconstruction by Norman de Garis Davies of the
doorway leading to the north chapel in the tomb of
Puimra (TT 39), second priest of Amun in the time
of Tuthmosis III, with the chapel visible beyond.

Norman de Garis Davies was born in Lancashire. He became, like his
father, a congregational minister. At his posting in Ashton-under-Lyme,
Greater Manchester, he met Kate Bradbury (who would later marry
the eminent British Egyptologist Francis Llewellyn Griffith); their
friendship sparked Davies's interest in Egyptology, which he began
to study earnestly. It was on the strength of her recommendation that
in 1897 he was invited to travel to Egypt by the great William Flinders
Petrie (pp. 178–83), to join his expedition to Dendera.

In 1898, the Egypt Exploration Fund's (EEF) Archaeological
Survey launched a mission at Saqqara. As part of the Survey's earlier
work in the cemeteries at Beni Hasan and Deir el-Bersha, directed
by Percy Newberry (pp. 196–201), the Fund had published *A Collection
of Hieroglyphs* (1898), showing not only the shapes of the signs as they
appeared on tomb walls but also a great wealth of internal detail –
not just the outline of an owl, but its feathers, claws, eyes and beak.
The Fund wanted to expand this work to include a selection of signs of
the Old Kingdom, when the Egyptian language was in an earlier phase,
and so they chose to investigate the 5th Dynasty tomb of Ptahhotep
at Saqqara. Davies was the ideal candidate to lead the expedition: he
saw himself primarily as a draughtsman and copyist, and preferred to
work alone, which suited the long seasons – sometimes as long as six
months – in which he was isolated from almost all of his peers. This
also meant the Fund could avoid squabbles of the kind had troubled
Newberry's team in the Survey's early years.

Davies's careful work always began with the study of earlier
publications, enabling him to avoid repetition where no improvements
could be made, but also to make them where he could (as he did,
frequently). He also recorded any damage that the monuments had
sustained between surveys. He quickly found that a description of
the tomb of Ptahhotep provided by Auguste Mariette was inaccurate
and misleading, omitting entire chambers that appeared to have
been dedicated to a second individual, Akhethotep (probably a son of
Ptahhotep). Davies thus spent much longer at the site than had been
anticipated, from December 1898 to May 1899. In the introduction to
the first of two volumes he published on the monument, Davies made
clear his own deep appreciation of the ancient art:

> *Outline drawings, even the most accurate, are but a poor substitute
> for the beauty of the surfaces in relief; and some of the work in
> this exhibits that astonishing accuracy, vivacity and freedom
> which Egyptian art affords when at its oldest and best. We must
> also picture the chapel as affording, when its glories were fresh,
> a most brilliant blaze of colour. The bright blue, red, green, black
> of the hieroglyphs, the ruddy-brown flesh-tints, the yellow animals,
> and the vivid blue of the water and the wine-vat would be subdued
> a little, no doubt, by the dull grey of the ground colour. But taken*

TOMBS, MUMMIES AND TREASURE

↓ A feast in the home of Nakht, the scribe and astronomer of Amun, from his tomb (TT 52). In this famous scene, bouquets of flowers are offered to the deceased and his wife, who are seated at right (figures partially destroyed), while in front of them a group of musicians entertains the guests.

together with the deep red of the ceiling, and the magnificent scheme of variegated colour on the false door, they would have an effect which it is difficult for the imagination to approach.

In 1902, Davies commenced a new project for the Archaeological Survey: the creation of a comprehensive record of the decoration on the walls of the tombs at the heretic pharaoh Akhenaten's capital city, el-Amarna. It would continue to occupy him in the field until 1908. At the outset he noted that the tombs had been visited by several past expeditions, including those headed by Robert Hay (pp. 88–97),

Nestor l'Hôte (pp. 104–9) and Karl Richard Lepsius (pp. 126–31), but of these only l'Hôte attempted to copy the texts, and only Lepsius published the result of his work. Davies started his survey by examining the tomb of the high priest of the Aten, Meryra (i). He was saddened to find that 'lamentable injury was wrought to the texts of the tomb ... for the purposes of plunder', and grateful to the earlier copyists in whose work the original scenes were to an extent preserved: 'Fortunately the whole can be restored from L'Hôte and Lepsius.' This was a persistent problem that plagued his campaign at Amarna; Davies even observed damage that had been inflicted since his work started: 'I must add that since last year violence has been done to the fine tomb of Ay, the most exquisite relief and the invaluable Hymn to the Aten only escaping demolition by the caprice of the malefactor. This is the second injury to *locked* tombs in the group during my stay.'

The six volumes arising from Davies's work at the site, *The Rock Tombs of El Amarna*, published between 1903 and 1908, set a new standard for publications of this kind. Davies's drawings were excellent, and his careful study of the copies made by earlier visitors allowed him not only to fill in the blanks where elements of the decoration had subsequently disappeared, but also to provide new readings and interpretations and to correct earlier mistakes. No attempt has ever been made to supersede his meticulous investigations of the tombs, for which he was awarded the Leibnitz Medal of the Prussian Academy in 1912. As his work at Amarna came to an end, he was recruited by Albert Lythgoe on behalf of the New York Metropolitan Museum of Art's new Department of Egyptian Art to join the museum's Egyptian Expedition to Thebes. Davies was looking for something more settled than the EEF, which had always operated on a shoestring, could offer. This was a defining moment for his career: he would remain director of the Graphic Section of the Expedition for the next three decades. In the same year, a second great defining event in Davies's life would take place.

Anna (Nina) Macpherson Cummings had trained as an artist at the Slade School of Fine Art and Royal College of Art. In 1906 she travelled to Egypt to visit friends, and there met Norman; she fell in love not only with the country but also with the man. She was sixteen years younger than Davies, but they would marry in October 1907, and moreover would become one of the great double acts in the history of Egyptology.

While initially Nina had no official role beyond providing assistance to her husband, she took to the work of the Graphic Section immediately, and the Metropolitan Museum soon engaged her on a half-time basis. She spent the rest of her time making copies for private collectors. By the end of their first season together, which began only weeks after their wedding, Davies wrote to Griffith: 'Her coloured work is at least as good as mine, better in technique.' The project that would occupy them both for the rest of their working lives was outlined, along with a sense of their place among illustrious predecessors, in the introduction to the first of the Graphic Section's great publications:

> *With this volume the Metropolitan Museum of Art commences an enterprise which, though far from being pioneer work, has the merit and privilege of renewing a task long neglected – that, namely, of*

using the fullest mechanical resources of the time to present the sepulchral art of Thebes in faithful reproduction for the benefit of those who must perforce study the wonders of the world in books. The heroic age of Egyptology lies nearly a century behind us when gentlemen of France and England, following the first gleams of inward light thrown by the genius of Champollion on the sun-bathed monuments of Egypt, were kindled to an enthusiastic quest, and happily for us, employed their pencils even more than their pens through long years of toil. The determination, industry, and public spirit required to carry such enterprises on to the printing point are, however, rarer gifts, and not all reached this promised land of research. Thebes by its extent, its associations, the comparative accessibility of its monuments, and their brilliant coloring, naturally attracted special devotion, and more than one worker became a well-known resident on the sacred hill of burial. Some of their names still cling about the ruins of the houses they built for shelter there – ruins which retain potent memories of international comradeship in a romantic pursuit.

Norman and Nina lived in the house that had been built for Sir Robert Mond during his own Theban work between 1903 and 1905 (see p. 248). It lay just off a pathway leading behind the grand 'Metropolitan House' – built by the museum as the main base of its operations in 1911 – and was the Davies' home until 1939. It remains standing to this day and is used by the Ministry of Antiquities as a resthouse. They were assisted each season by an additional artist and the Egyptian Expedition's photographer, Harry Burton, whom they found to be most amiable even under stress. When, one Christmas, their Egyptian cook served a Christmas pudding set ablaze with kerosene (there being no brandy available), it was Burton who ate it to avoid causing offence. Photography had always been an important part of Norman Davies's

↓ Nina Davies's copy of part of a scene showing provisions from Nubia with monkeys being transported to storehouses. From the tomb of Rekhmira (TT 100).

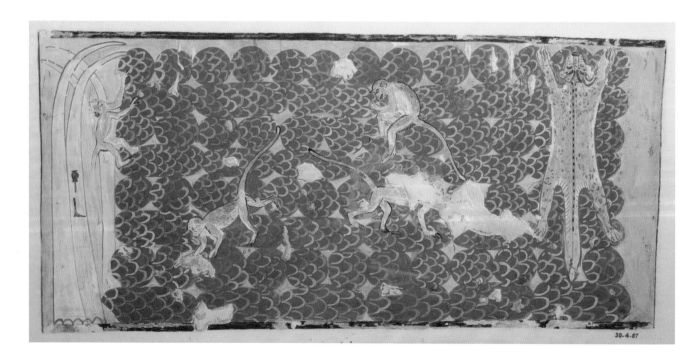

TOMBS, MUMMIES AND TREASURE

↑ A female figure kneeling on a funeral bark with her arms raised to her head in the traditional gesture of mourning. She is flanked by two goddesses. Painting by Norman de Garis Davies, from the tomb of the scribe of divine offerings of Amun, Horemheb (TT 207).

working practice, and the quality of photographs – particularly of the dark interiors of tombs, and, importantly, their reproduction in the published volumes – had steadily improved. And yet there was no danger of it replacing the work of the copyist: what the Davies were able to capture in their finished drawings and paintings was the result of their having scrutinized the tombs' walls in the minutest detail, from all angles, and with the benefit of their immense knowledge and experience. They could see much more than the camera could – not only what was there on the walls, but also the elements now damaged or lost that *should* have been there.

↑ A scene of fishing and fowling from
the tomb of Ipuy (TT 217), from the reign
of Ramesses II. A woman in a boat with
a prow in the shape of a duck's head
approaches a cluster of papyrus reeds in
which several birds are scattering before
a very animated cat.

Incredibly, the Davies found time outside their work for the Graphic Section to continue recording other tombs (as Norman wrote, 'Set in the midst of paintings threatened with disaster or calling loudly for speedy publication, I gradually found myself also with a certain amount of material on hand, the fruit of leisure hours'), and offered the results of their labours to the EEF for its Archaeological Survey. A first publication, *Five Theban Tombs*, concentrated on tombs that had been discovered in relatively recent times, at least one of which had nonetheless been badly damaged by unscrupulous types attempting to remove sections of the wall paintings for sale. The illustrations in this volume were all Nina's and confirmed her as an epigrapher of equal standing to her husband. Shortly after this, the eminent Egyptologist Sir Alan Gardiner – a brilliant philologist as well as a generous sponsor of the campaigns and projects of other scholars – initiated a new series on the Theban tombs, to be published by the EEF. Gardiner had previously been involved with the work begun by Howard Carter (pp. 202–11) of clearing, recording and protecting the tombs of Thebes, and he had also been Nina's patron since 1909, purchasing all of her paintings and paying her an annual sum for some twenty years. By the time Gardiner's 'Theban Tombs Series' was begun, over 250 tombs in the area had been catalogued and numbered, providing, for the first time, a framework for the management and further investigation of the site. The five volumes in the series published nine of these tombs, almost all of the line drawings and fine coloured copies being Nina's work. Among the highlights were the beautiful scenes of tribute being brought from Nubia to Tutankhamun that adorn the walls of the tomb belonging to his 'Viceroy of Nubia', Huy.

The Davies would also assist Gardiner with his *Egyptian Grammar*, a landmark work that has formed the core basis of learning the ancient language for generations of Egyptologists (including the present writer); it is known to students simply as 'the Gardiner'. Gardiner arranged for a new hieroglyphic font, based on standardized 18th Dynasty forms, to be created for the Oxford University Press. Norman and Nina Davies helped select examples of the 750 signs required and drew each in outline. The Gardiner sign list based on their drawings remains the standard point of reference for Egyptologists.

Norman died in 1941, two years after the couple had returned to England. Nina continued her work for some years afterwards. In 1936 she published two folio volumes of coloured facsimiles of the very finest examples of Egyptian art, entitled *Ancient Egyptian Paintings*, followed by a miniature Penguin edition with reduced versions of the paintings and a text by the author in 1956. Her paintings, either acquired by Gardiner or made for the Graphic Section, survive in various institutions around the world, but most of them are at the Metropolitan Museum, where a gallery is devoted to the finest – a fitting tribute to her achievements not merely as a copyist but as an artist in her own right. Together, the Davies were perhaps the finest copyists to document the ancient Egyptian tomb paintings. The published record they left behind constitutes one of the greatest services rendered to Egyptology – one that will only increase in value, as Gardiner himself suggested: 'Whereas pure scholarship dates rapidly, faithful copies grow in value according as destruction exacts its relentless toll.'

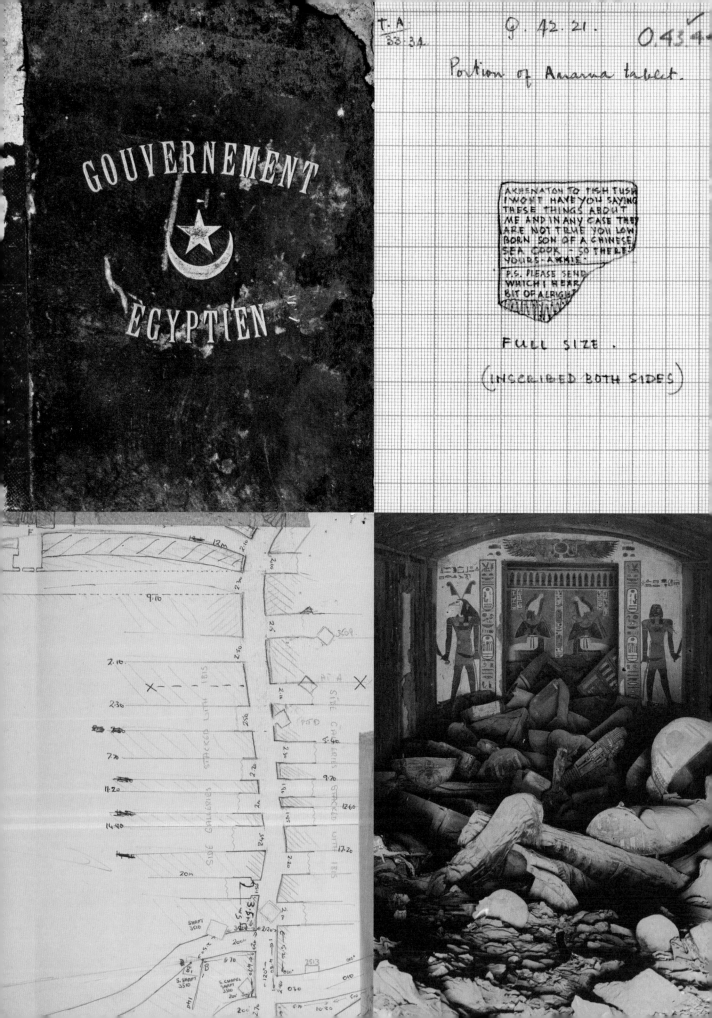

Top right (graph paper):

T.A
33.34.   Q. 42. 21.   O. 43.4

Portion of Amarna tablet.

AKHENATON TO TISH TUSH
I WON'T HAVE YOU SAYING
THESE THINGS ABOUT
ME AND IN ANY CASE THEY
ARE NOT TRUE YOU LOW
BORN SON OF A CHINESE
SEA COOK - SO THERE!
YOURS AMMIE.

P.S. PLEASE SEND
WHICH I HEAR
BIT OF ALRIGHT

FULL SIZE.

(INSCRIBED BOTH SIDES)

Top left (book cover):

GOUVERNEMENT ÉGYPTIEN

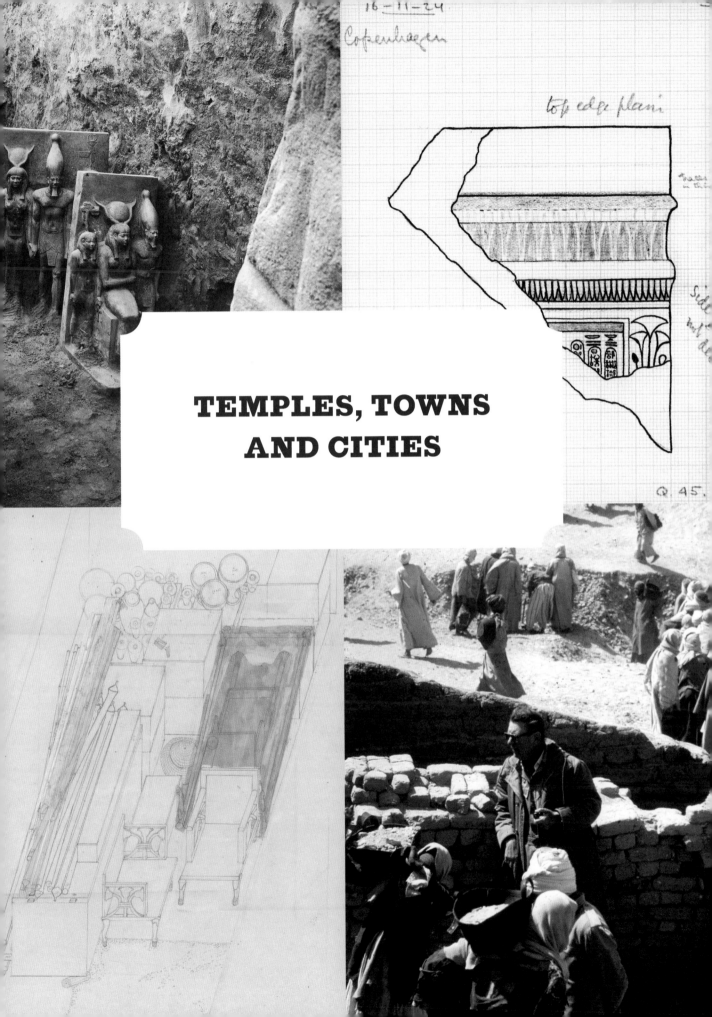

TEMPLES, TOWNS AND CITIES

16 - 11 - 24.

Copenhagen

top edge plain

Q. 45.

'All excavations destroy historical material, and should only be permitted to trained archaeologists competent to observe and record this material. The historical material of Egypt is legally the national property of Egypt, but morally a legitimate concern of the civilized world.'

GEORGE REISNER

By the dawn of the 20th century, concerns surrounding the safety of archaeological sites and the dangers of an uncontrolled antiquities trade were driving Egyptology. There was a growing realization that earlier explorers had ignored – and thus destroyed – a huge range of archaeological evidence at the sites they mined for novel treasures. New methods had been developed not only to recover such evidence – aided by technological innovations in electrical lighting and photography – but also to document the archaeological process. The study of Egypt's ancient past was becoming a true science.

The American archaeologist George Reisner (pp. 224–31) believed firmly in the importance of recording an excavation so thoroughly that it could be reconstructed by any scholar who read the site report. By now, various Western institutions had established a permanent presence in Egypt and could provide excavators with a guarantee that their work would be published. The downside to Reisner's meticulous documentation was that the information gathered from his excavations took longer to process, and much of his work remained unpublished at his death. Balancing thoroughness with timely publication has been a challenge for archaeologists ever since, and Reisner would certainly not be the last archaeologist working in Egypt to leave behind vast quantities of unpublished documentation.

Reisner excavated vast sites, including great swathes of the Giza plateau, and such ambitious projects could proceed only with the involvement of lots of excavators. Generally speaking, the lead Egyptologists on such missions were supervisors, rarely directly involved in the digging itself; their role was to supervise and observe, intervening only when necessary. Reisner's exacting standards meant that he needed to be able to trust his workmen to undertake the delicate work of trowelling back centuries of ancient detritus with great care and skill. To this end, he was equally meticulous in his selection of staff, following in the footsteps of Petrie (pp. 178–83) in engaging the men of a town called Quft (who called themselves Quftis), known to be skilled in archaeological work. Petrie first worked with the Quftis in 1893 when excavating the ancient city of Coptos, and would continue to work with them for many years, even employing some to travel with him to Palestine much later in his career. The Quftis became an integral part of Reisner's work, and his insistence on thorough documentation extended to his most senior Egyptian team members; their diaries, in Arabic, reveal just indispensable they were to his operations. There are excavation projects operating in Egypt – and beyond – today that employ the descendants of Petrie and Reisner's skilled excavators, still referred to as Quftis. Slowly, archaeology in Egypt came to be less and less the preserve of foreigners. Yet the essential contributions made by these men remain largely unacknowledged.

But developments on the world political stage in the years leading up to and during the First World War were changing the balance of power in Egypt. After the Ottomans declared their allegiance to Germany, Britain declared Egypt an official protectorate, abandoning the fiction that they were governing in the Ottomans' interest. Hundreds of thousands of British troops arrived in the region to ensure that control of the country – and most crucially, the Suez Canal – could be maintained, along with civilians to staff the civil service. The most senior British official remained the consul-general, a role held by Evelyn Baring (1st Earl of Cromer), Sir Eldon Gorst and then Lord Kitchener. The Egyptian royal family was retained, but the monarch (now the 'sultan') was chosen by the British. To assist in the war effort, the British raised taxes, reclaimed land and buildings, and conscripted the population as auxiliary troops. These policies were, unsurprisingly, deeply unpopular and led to the creation of the national Wafd Party, whose leader, Saad Zaghloul, visited Britain in 1919 to demand that Egypt be granted independence. The British had no intention of allowing this to happen, but in the years that followed nationalist sentiment continued to grow in Egypt, and it became clear that the protectorate could not continue. In February 1922 it was declared 'terminated', and Egypt declared an independent sovereign state. While for a time Britain retained much of its control over the country, Egypt was heading inexorably towards true independence. A new constitution was promulgated in 1923, and Zaghloul was elected Prime Minister in 1924.

It was against this backdrop, in November 1922, that Howard Carter (pp. 202–11) made the most famous discovery in the history of archaeology: that of the tomb of Tutankhamun in the Valley of the Kings. Although Carter had received his training in field archaeology from Petrie, his expedition was somewhat old-fashioned, being sponsored by an English aristocrat, Lord Carnarvon. Any expectation Carnarvon might have had of claiming objects from the tomb fell foul of the new nationalist mood and government. In February 1924, following a series of slights and insults on both sides, Carter went on strike, and the concession, held in Lady Carnarvon's name following the earl's death, was withdrawn. It was eventually reinstated – Carter returned to work in January 1925 – but only on condition that the Carnarvons renounced any claim to the objects discovered. It established an important precedent, reinforcing the government's authority over the country's archaeology.

At the time that Carter was making his great discovery, Walter Bryan Emery (pp. 248–53) was just beginning a career that would last until the 1970s. He would work for the British government during the Second World War, have his excavations at Saqqara interrupted by the Suez Crisis, and campaign to rescue the monuments of Nubia during the construction of the High Dam at Aswan. By the time he resumed his work at Saqqara, the Free Officers Movement had overthrown the monarchy and declared Egypt an independent state. The Antiquities Service had been run by Egyptian directors since the revolution; ancient Egypt was finally back in Egyptian hands.

George Andrew Reisner

1867–1942 American archaeologist and pioneer
of Nubian studies

Reisner was the first great American archaeologist to work in Egypt. Backed by wealthy individuals and institutions, he excavated on a vast scale and introduced new standards of excavation and documentation.

→ Two of the famous triad statues of Menkaura at the moment of their discovery at the Valley Temple of the king at Giza.

George Andrew Reisner was born in Indianapolis in 1867. He studied Semitic languages at Harvard University, gaining his PhD in 1893. That year he travelled to Berlin to examine texts from Assyria, Babylonia and ancient Egypt under the renowned linguists Adolf Erman and Kurt Sethe, and took up a post as a temporary assistant at the Berlin Museum. On his return to America in 1896 he became a teacher of Semitics at Harvard, but Egyptology had become his true passion, and in 1897 he travelled to Cairo to catalogue amulets and model boats in the collection of the Egyptian Museum.

Two years later, it was Reisner's good fortune to be recommended to Phoebe Apperson Hearst, an American philanthropist who was visiting Egypt. Hearst had a particular interest in archaeology and would found the University of California's Museum of Anthropology in 1901, financing fieldwork across the globe. Reisner was appointed director of her first sponsored campaign in Egypt, the Hearst Expedition, which surveyed Deir el-Ballas, site of a late Second Intermediate Period palace, before moving on to Naga ed-Deir, a cemetery spanning the Predynastic Period to the Middle Kingdom. At Deir el-Ballas Reisner built a good relationship with the local community, allowing farmers to take the remains of ancient mudbricks (*sebakh*) from his spoil dumps to fertilize their fields. In return they presented to him a papyrus that had been found in the area two years earlier. Although damaged, most of the text was legible. It proved to be a medical papyrus of the 18th Dynasty that offered treatments for such ailments as hair loss and animal bites. Reisner published the papyrus, with a nod to his patron, as the 'Hearst Medical Papyrus'. When the Hearst Expedition concluded its mission, Reisner became professor of Egyptology at Harvard and director of a newly established Harvard–Boston expedition to the Giza plateau.

Reisner had no field experience when he joined the Hearst Expedition but was assisted by the British archaeologist Arthur Mace, who had trained with William Flinders Petrie (pp. 178–83). He admired Petrie's rigorous methods, quickly recognizing that excavation is an inherently destructive science – an unrepeatable experiment – since exposing archaeological remains through digging inevitably means destroying their context, as well as removing artefacts from the spaces they have occupied for thousands of years. He thus kept meticulous records of his excavations, believing firmly that the archaeological process must be documented so thoroughly that the site's original condition could be mentally reconstructed by any archaeologist reading the reports. He lamented the destruction had been wrought by unscrupulous plunderers and early, untrained excavators: 'The foreign consuls began gathering antiquities, and a horde of adventurers sprang into activity as agents for the consuls and other collectors. From about 1815 nearly to 1880, this second great period of plundering continued – a mad search for salable curiosities. Some of these looters made a

TEMPLES, TOWNS AND CITIES

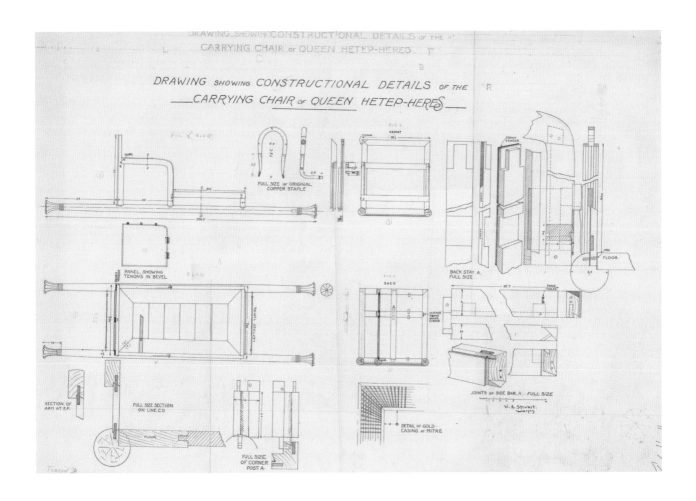

↑ The furniture that once belonged to Hetepheres remains among the finest ever found in Egypt.

pretense of interest in historical research; but the naked truth was that they knew nothing of scientific methods and cared nothing for any object whose market value was beyond their recognition.'

In an effort to regulate the excavation work taking place in Egypt and prevent the illicit plundering of archaeological sites, the director of the Antiquities Service, Gaston Maspero, had begun awarding concessions to foreign missions. In 1902 he issued permits to excavate at Giza to three such missions: the Italians, led by Ernesto Schiaparelli (pp. 232–37); the Germans, led by Ludwig Borchardt; and the Americans, led by Reisner and financed by his patron, Hearst. The three expedition leaders met on the veranda of the nearby Mena House Hotel in December to decide how the vast site should be fairly divided between them. The cemetery to the west of the Great Pyramid would be divided into three parts from north to south; as the largest and richest tombs were built along the western side of the pyramid, and those further west belonged to individuals of lower status, this system ensured that each team would be granted the opportunity to excavate tombs belonging to an equal cross-section of Old Kingdom society. Lots were drawn by Reisner's wife to determine how the strips would be allocated. In addition, the pyramids were divided between the three, the Italians taking the Great Pyramid, the Germans the second, that of Khafra. Reisner declared himself 'perfectly willing' to take the third: that of Menkaura. The mission would operate at the site under his direction for twenty-three years.

→ Isometric drawing of the distribution of objects in the tomb of Hetepheres. The poles and beams from the canopy were on top of the sarcophagus, with furniture arranged all around.

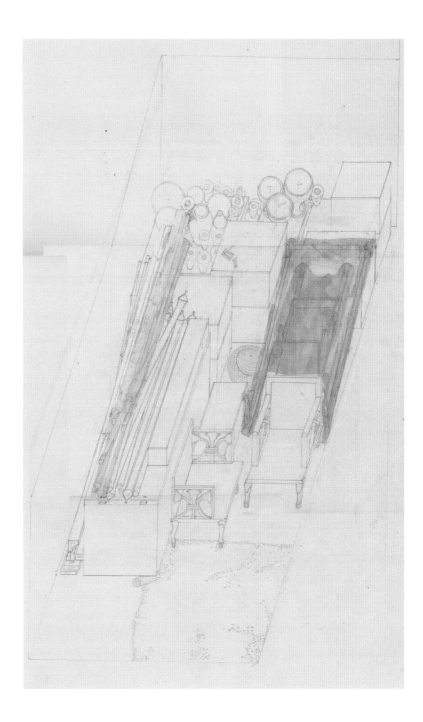

Reisner's interest lay not in the pyramid itself, but in the peripheral buildings associated with it. Such buildings were a fundamental part of the funerary complex of the king, but archaeologists had generally focused their attentions on the pyramids, and so they remained poorly understood. Reisner first investigated the 'pyramid temple' that lies in front of the east face of Menkaura's pyramid, where he found numerous alabaster fragments from a colossal statue of the king that probably formed the centrepiece of the temple's courtyard. It has since been reconstructed and is now on view in the Museum of Fine Arts, Boston. Reisner suspected, based on the evidence from later pyramid complexes, that a second temple connected to the pyramid must exist. The so-called 'valley temples' lay some way from the pyramids

↑ Plan view of some of the objects discovered in the tomb of Hetepheres as found, densely packed together.

themselves, near the banks of the Nile. The Germans' work on the 6th Dynasty pyramid field at Abusir had led them to the conclusion that the granite temple at the end of the causeway of the pyramid of Khafra was the corresponding monument of that king. Although there were no visible traces of any such temple built in association with the pyramid of Menkaura, Reisner believed there was a strong chance it would be found at the end of its causeway. But the visible remnants of the causeway extended only a short distance down the plateau, to the level of the pyramid of Khafra, before it was interrupted by a water course. Reisner began his investigations by digging a trench some 100 metres (330 feet) further along the same axis. This revealed a continuation of the causeway, and so Reisner opened further trenches at regular intervals along the same line, closer and closer to the valley. Five days later he found what he was looking for: a weathered surface that appeared to be the remains of a decayed mudbrick building. Over the course of the next week his team discovered some of the finest statues ever to have been found in Egypt, including the now famous 'nome triads' – statues of Menkaura accompanied by the goddess Hathor and a goddess representing one of the administrative districts (nomes) of Egypt.

Reisner's concession at Giza also included the area to the east of Menkaura's pyramid as far south as the Great Sphinx, containing the pyramid temple of Khufu and the three pyramids belonging to his

TEMPLES, TOWNS AND CITIES

wives, and a broad street to the east of the queens' pyramids nicknamed 'Queens Street'. It was at the north end of this street, thirteen years after Menkaura's valley temple was located, that the mission made perhaps its greatest discovery: the intact tomb of Queen Hetepheres. Reisner was in fact in the United States at the time the discovery was made, and it would be some months before he returned to Giza to see it for himself. On 9 February 1925 the team's photographer, Mohammedani Ibrahim, was repositioning his tripod when one of the legs sank into the ground, exposing a patch of plaster. On 20 February the plaster was removed, revealing a cutting into the rock; four days of digging later, the team had cleared a stairway of twelve steps leading to a short passageway which then broke into a vertical shaft, also blocked with masonry, extending both above and below the point of entry. The excavators found its opening on the surface, cunningly concealed beneath a layer of undressed limestone blocks fitted together to look like natural rock.

The clearance of the shaft, supervised by Reisner's chief *reis* (foreman), Ahmed Said, took twelve days. About a third of the way along they encountered a niche containing parts of an ox and two beer jars. This discovery – apparently of provisions for the afterlife – convinced them that they were excavating a tomb. At a depth of 26 metres (85 feet) they finally reached the bottom of the shaft and were confronted with a masonry wall – the blocked entranceway to the burial chamber. Late in the afternoon of 7 March, Rowe removed a single block from the top of the doorway. Reisner's report conveys little of the excitement and frustration that his team must have felt at having to wait until the next day to gain a better understanding of what they had found, true to his characteristic privileging of scientific facts over emotional reactions:

> *By the light of a candle he saw only dimly a chamber, a sarcophagus, and a glitter of gold. The block was replaced for the night to keep out the dust, and the next morning the three upper courses opposite the doorway were taken out. The doorway was not blocked as usual with a separate wall, but the packing of the pit went on down to the bottom and thus closed the doorway. Thus it was on March 8 that the closed alabaster sarcophagus was recognized, the canopy, the gold-cased furniture, and other objects. Photographs were taken by reflected light.*

Lying on top of the sarcophagus were several sheets of gold inlaid with hieroglyphic signs in faience. The excavators could read the name of pharaoh Sneferu, the first king of the 4th Dynasty. The tomb belonged to a wife of that king named Hetepheres: the mother of Khufu, builder of the Great Pyramid. The objects in the tomb were among the finest ever discovered in Egypt. Although the tomb itself was intact, its alabaster sarcophagus showed signs of having been forced open with a chisel and was empty, prompting Reisner to hypothesize that the queen had originally been buried elsewhere – perhaps alongside her husband at Dahshur – and reburied at Giza by her son, explaining the relative modesty and secret location of the tomb.

In addition to his work in pioneering rigorous excavation methods at Giza, Reisner was a key figure in the emergence of the study of Nubia, the territory to the south of ancient Egypt's borders. In 1899, the British had begun construction of the Aswan Low Dam at the First Cataract of the Nile, designed to store water to allow the irrigation of the lower Nile Valley even at times of year when the river was low. It quickly proved incapable of storing enough water to meet the demands of the proposed development, and was raised between 1907 and 1912. This would flood the lands to the south of the cataract, resulting in the loss of any archaeological remains, so Reisner was engaged to gather as much information and material as possible before it was too late. His survey helped to establish a chronological framework for the region's ancient cultures that remains in use to this day, albeit with modifications. Reisner subsequently moved further south into Sudan, where he investigated the richest and most important sites of the kingdoms that existed alongside that of Egypt from the period equivalent to the Egyptian Middle Kingdom down to Christian times. Among these were Kerma, capital of Egypt's rival during the Middle Kingdom; Napata, capital of the 1st millennium BCE kingdom of Kush; the nearby holy

↓ The tomb of Hetepheres was found to contain large quantities of beadwork, which had been lain over other items inside a large inlaid box. The beadwork had decayed, scattering the beads around the tomb, but some had adhered together in clusters, allowing the intricate pattern to be reconstructed.

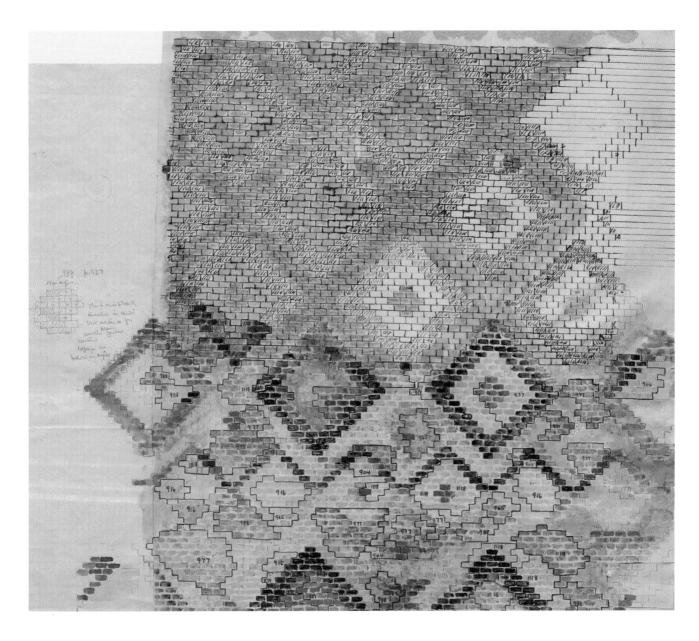

TEMPLES, TOWNS AND CITIES

mountain of Gebel Barkal, and the associated cemeteries at el-Kurru and Nuri; and finally Napata's successor as the Kushite capital, Meroë.

While Reisner was, more than any other archaeologist, responsible for uncovering the material remains of the ancient civilizations that occupied the Nile Valley to the south of Egypt, many of his interpretations were heavily influenced by the prevailing Egyptocentrism and have now been shown to have been misguided at best. For instance, in 1918 he wrote that 'The native negroid [Nubian] race had never developed either its trade or any industry worthy of mention, and owed their cultural position to the Egyptian immigrants and to the imported Egyptian civilization.' More recent excavations at Kerma have instead revealed a city with its own distinct material culture, architectural styles and funerary tradition. This civilization flourished over many centuries, and while it may at times have been subjugated by Egypt it was unquestionably independent for much of its history, and occasionally even gained the upper hand over its northern rival.

Thorough though his excavation records are, Reisner's publication record arguably fell short of the standards set by his contemporaries. Reisner might have argued that the publications of, for example, Petrie were not as detailed as they should have been; Petrie, in response, might have countered that the speed with which he published allowed his findings to circulate more quickly, enriching scholarly discourse and guiding future fieldwork more effectively. In any case, both were preoccupied with method and rigour and perhaps less with some of the other reasons why a person might become interested in ancient Egypt. Reisner seems to have been suspicious of the popular fascination with the subject:

> *It is the habit of most of us to condemn the public for its great interest in 'mummies.' To the experienced eye, a mummy is only a bundle of human bones and skin trussed up as a sorry remnant of a living man. But to the layman who imagines that he is gazing on the lineaments of a person who lived thousands of years ago, preserved by some miraculous secret, not dead in the common sense, but in some way still existing – to him the mummy makes an appeal which is obviously not one of mere morbid curiosity. To me a mummy is a loathsome thing, but I feel that to others it is the gathering point for dreams. In like manner, the task of excavating ancient tombs appears to the layman as fraught with thrilling and romantic moments – the descent through passages and stairways which no foot has trod for thousands of years, the first glance into a chamber just as it was when the last priest passed out and his assistants blocked the doorway with masonry, or the opening of the sarcophagus of a king, undisturbed through the passing of dynasties and empires. The recent great publicity campaign surrounding concerning the tomb of Tutankhamun was based largely on this appeal to the imagination of the layman.*

Reisner ushered in a new era of rigorous, scientific archaeology in Egypt, of a kind that still obtains to this day. But did his focus on the cold, hard science sacrifice something of the excitement of exploration and discovery? Perhaps.

Ernesto Schiaparelli

1856–1928 Italian Egyptologist, archaeologist and curator

Schiaparelli was a curator at the great museums of Egyptian antiquities in Florence and Turin, greatly expanding the collections first through purchasing missions to Egypt and then a series of excavations he directed himself. Among his most important discoveries were the tomb of Ramesses II's principal wife, Nefertari, and the intact tomb of a chief architect at the Valley of the Kings, Kha, and his wife Merit.

→ The jumbled mass of coffins and mummified human remains uncovered by Schiaparelli in the tomb of Prince Khaemwaset in the Valley of the Queens (QV 44).

Ernesto Schiaparelli was the son of historian Luigi Schiaparelli and his wife, Francesca. He studied Egyptology first in Turin and then in Paris under Gaston Maspero, future director of Egypt's Antiquities Service. He became curator of Egyptian antiquities in Florence's Egyptian Museum in 1880 and was subsequently, for more than thirty years, director of Turin's Egyptian Museum. It was in this capacity that he directed twelve astonishingly productive fieldwork seasons between 1903 and 1920. He belonged to the first generation of scholars to apply a rigorous methodological approach to excavation in Egypt, taking care to document all stages of the process so that ancient objects could be understood in their archaeological context. He also displayed artefacts alongside photographs of the places in which they were found, to emphasize the importance of their particular histories.

Schiaparelli first visited Egypt in 1884, on a mission to augment the Egyptian Museum of Florence's collections, which comprised some objects that were housed previously in the Uffizi, along with those collected by Ippolito Rosellini during the great Franco-Tuscan expedition (see pp. 103–9) and those in the collection of Alessandro Ricci, which was acquired in 1832. Seeking a quiet atmosphere that would allow him to focus on the task at hand, he stayed with a group of Franciscan monks in Luxor. He was very taken with the friars and their way of life, but was concerned by the treatment of Italians of various religious persuasions in Egypt and consequently established the Associazione Nazionale per Soccorrere i Missionari Italiani (National Association for the Assistance of Italian Missionaries) in Florence. The association quickly became active not just in Egypt, but elsewhere in Africa and even in China. This aspect of his work is, incredibly, almost unknown, although the association built schools and hospitals under his direction until his death in 1928 and continues its work to this day.

In 1892, during a second visit to Egypt to acquire antiquities for the Florence collection, Schiaparelli made the first of a long sequence of important discoveries. On arriving in Aswan he was alerted to a tomb on the slopes of Qubbet el-Hawa, cemetery of the governors of the ancient province. Inscribed on its walls was a now famous autobiographical text recounting, among other things, four expeditions made by the owner, a 6th Dynasty governor named Harkhuf, into Nubia. This has become one of the classics of Egyptian literature and is often used by teachers of the ancient Egyptian language to train their students. Harkhuf's account is full of useful details about the lands to the south of Egypt and the goods he returned with, which included, most memorably, a pygmy, whom the king, Neferkare, writing to Harkhuf, was anxious to see.

Schiaparelli left Florence to take up a post at the Egyptian Museum of Turin, which held perhaps the finest collection of Egyptian antiquities in the world, founded by Bernardino Drovetti. But the museum was facing competition from rapidly expanding museums elsewhere in Europe and, by the end of the 19th century,

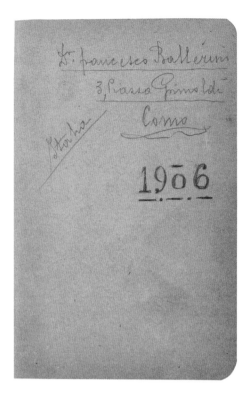

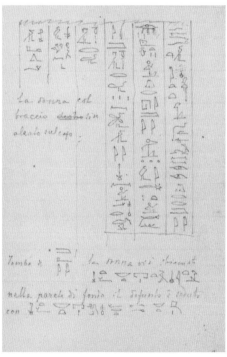

↑ Front cover and a page from the 1906 notebook of Schiaparelli's assistant Francesco Ballerini. On the page reproduced here, we find Ballerini's transcription of a text from the tomb of a man called Maia; later pages describe the discovery of the tomb of Kha and Merit.

the United States. Schiaparelli would continue to actively acquire antiquities to expand the museum's collection, but after an initial purchasing expedition in 1901 changed his tactics. He seems to have been concerned not only by the antiquities' expense, but also by the uncertain provenance of objects available on the market. In 1903 he set up the Missione Archeologica Italiana (Italian Archaeological Mission) with the help of his old teacher, Gaston Maspero. Under Schiaparelli's direction, the mission carried out large-scale excavations at a series of important sites, including Heliopolis, Giza, the Valley of the Queens and nearby Deir el-Medina in Luxor, and Aswan further to the south.

Schiaparelli began his work on the West Bank of Thebes, in the Valley of the Queens, where he uncovered thirteen tombs. Among them was the beautifully decorated tomb of Nefertari, Great Royal Wife of Ramesses II and mother of at least six of his children. But he abandoned work in the Valley in 1905, believing that there was nothing further to be found – perhaps a rash decision, given Egypt's habit of yielding new discoveries even in areas that have been thoroughly excavated, yet subsequent work suggests he was right. He moved to Deir el-Medina, site of the village of workmen who cut and decorated the tombs in the Valley of the Kings. Here, Schiaparelli was to make perhaps his most famous discovery, one that would provide his museum with the centrepiece of its collections: the intact tomb of a husband and wife, Kha and Merit. These individuals were already known to Egyptologists, as a stela bearing their names had arrived in Turin in 1824 as part of Drovetti's collection. Karl Lepsius (pp. 126–31) had even visited their tomb-chapel at Deir el-Medina, unaware that the tomb itself lay concealed beneath.

The workmen's village is now almost entirely revealed, the layout of the houses and the streets in between them clear for all to see. At the time of Schiaparelli's excavations, however, very little was visible other than the remains of some tomb-chapels built onto, or cut into, the slope of the hill above. Schiaparelli began systematically excavating the debris at the bottom of the hill, from north to south:

The work was neither easy nor straightforward because the rubble was piled incredibly high; it took four weeks' strenuous work with over 250 workmen divided into various teams working separately, but the results did not prove encouraging .... Only a few tombs came to light. They were either shaft tombs or chamber tombs, but they had all been plundered .... But then, after almost a month of backbreaking and unrewarding work, in the last days of February, after completing the excavation of over two-thirds of the valley, we came to an area where the rubble seemed to be intact: chips of beautiful white limestone, unaffected by weathering, which were still compact by not having been disturbed for centuries, without any mixture with bones or fragments of grave goods or furnishings, and which had probably been extracted from the depths of the mountain by workmen who had dug a tomb. It was clear that if a tomb was found here it would probably be intact, and it also seemed likely that tomb was not far away. Indeed, by continuing the excavations for another two days, the edges of an irregular opening appeared in the side of the mountain. It was completely blocked by rubble. Once the debris was removed, the entrance rapidly emerged and

TEMPLES, TOWNS AND CITIES

↑ The burial chamber of the tomb of Kha and Merit as found by Schiaparelli, its contents entirely undisturbed since antiquity. The outermost coffin of Kha lies against the back wall, with that of his wife, Merit, to the right; both are draped with a linen pall. Carefully arranged around them are numerous items of furniture and other grave goods.

↓ Pages from a notebook of Ballerini's from the 1903 excavations, recording details of the tomb of Tyti (QV 52), queen of Ramesses III and daughter of Sethnakht, including a plan of the layout, text transcriptions and brief notes.

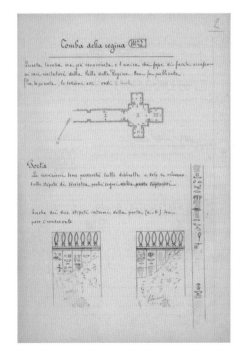

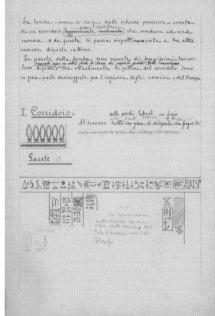

ERNESTO SCHIAPARELLI

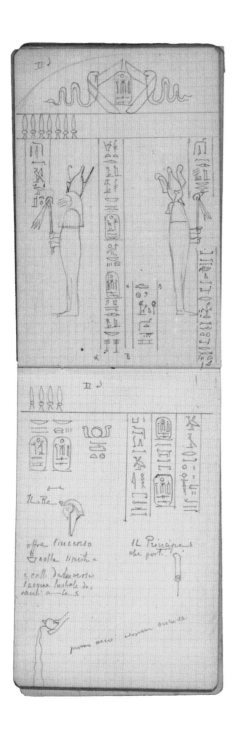

↑ Pages from Ballerini's 1904 notebook with notes on the tomb of Pareherwenemef (QV 42), which had been studied during the 1902–3 season.

provided access to a fairly wide staircase which descended deeply into the bowels of the mountain. As the white chips filling the whole of the staircase were hastily removed and carried away, a beautiful large piece of carefully folded reed matting was discovered below the chips and on the steps of the staircase which had been roughly carved in the cliff. Going further down for several metres, there was a corridor sealed by an intact wall, built with stones and carefully faced with mud.

What they had found was one of the most perfectly preserved Egyptian tombs ever discovered. An entrance shaft descended into the rock to a depth of 4 metres (13 feet) beneath the surface. Beyond this a flight of steps led further downwards to 8.5 metres (28 feet), at which point they encountered the first blocking. Beyond there lay a 13.4-metre (44-foot) long corridor, halfway along which they found a second, intact blocking. At the end of this passage, they were confronted by what in the popular imagination might always be found in Egyptian tombs, but which in reality is almost never present: a locked door. Arthur Weigall, inspector general for the Antiquities Service in Luxor, accompanied Schiaparelli as he entered the tomb and wrote that the door 'looked for all the world as though it had been set up but yesterday .... The whole contrivance seemed so modern that Professor Schiaparelli called to his servant for the key, who quite seriously replied, "I don't know where it is, sir."'

The tomb's owner, Kha, lived during the reigns of Amenhotep II, Tuthmosis IV and Amenhotep III and held a series of important titles, including 'chief' and 'overseer of works' in the Valley of the Kings. Although he was not, therefore, of the highest rank, he was clearly an important individual, and his burial assemblage reflected it. He was buried along with his wife, Merit. Each was interred in a nest of coffins, the two innermost anthropoid in form and beautifully decorated with gold leaf and inlaid crystal. Kha's mummy was adorned with garlands of flowers and accompanied by a papyrus bearing texts and images from the Book of the Dead, measuring 15 metres (50 feet) when unrolled. Their outer, rectangular coffins were covered with linen drapes and surrounded by the most beguiling collection of offerings: a beautiful folding stool of wood, leather and ivory; boxes containing toiletries and linen; a statuette of Kha wearing a floral garland; a miniature coffin containing a shabti figure; a bronze cup and situla; a gilded cubit given to Kha by Amenhotep II – every object evoking the real, day-to-day lives of the tomb owners, and yet also a testimony to the skills of the craftsmen who made them. The objects were almost all taken by Schiaparelli for the Turin Museum, so the assemblage has remained intact and today forms one of the most spectacular displays of ancient material in any museum anywhere in the world. The arrangement of the objects – captured in Schiaparelli's photographs – must have been one of the most haunting sights with which any archaeologist has ever been confronted, from the items left in the entrance corridor, to the sealed doorway, and the undisturbed burial chamber itself. Merit had taken her bed with her, and it still had on it her headrest and sheets. Low tables were piled with the remains of vegetables and loaves of bread. A lamp stand in the shape of a papyrus column supported a copper bowl that still held the ashes produced by a flame at the time of the burial, three and a half thousand

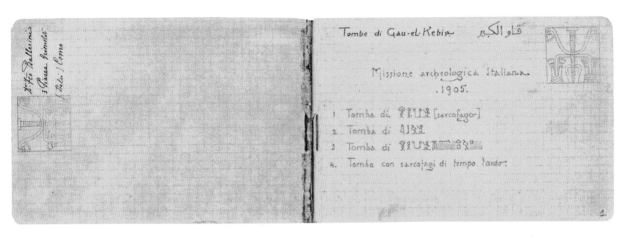

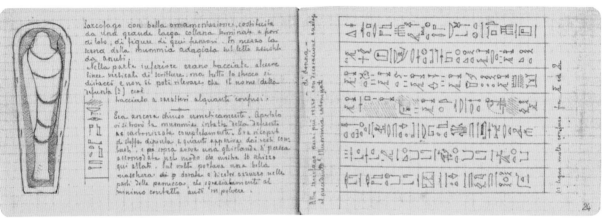

↑ Ballerini's notebook for 1905, with his comments on four tombs discovered in the necropolis of Qau el-Kebir (Wahka I, Ibu, Wahka II, and another of the Late period).

years before. Could any discovery ever leave an archaeologist feeling so close to the ancients themselves? One suspects not.

Schiaparelli directed excavations on behalf of the Turin Egyptian Museum for seventeen years, augmenting the collections with a vast array of provenanced material. It remains arguably the most important collection of Egyptian antiquities outside Egypt to this day. Hundreds of cases were shipped from his excavations to Turin. Their value is indicated by his practice of equipping his teams with cavalry muskets, ostentatiously placed in full view to deter any would-be robbers, and a supply of blanks. Further, because Schiaparelli's archaeological approach was rigorous and forward-looking, and his teams included specialist architects, conservators, geologists, palaeontologists and bioanthropologists, his excavations are of great scientific and historic value. Though Schiaparelli produced only two publications – one on the tomb of Kha and Merit, and another on the tombs in the Valley of the Queens – his unpublished excavations can nonetheless be reconstructed owing to the quality of the field documentation, in particular the records left by his assistant, Francesco Ballerini, whose notebooks contain a wealth of information, sketches and technical drawings that are now proving invaluable in filling in the gaps. Schiaparelli was also something of a pioneer in his use of photography as part of the archaeological process, and his photographs are among the most spectacular ever taken in the history of Egyptian archaeology.

Hassan Effendi Hosni

Life dates unknown. Pioneering Egyptian Egyptologist

Hosni was an Egyptian Egyptologist and Antiquities Service inspector. One of the first graduates of an Egyptian school of Egyptology, he worked during a period of growing nationalism, when Egyptians began to play a more prominent role in archaeology alongside their foreign colleagues.

Egyptology was initially a subject pursued largely by Europeans, first those who visited the ruins and then wider audiences who heard those explorers tell their tales in Britain, France, Italy, Germany and elsewhere. Word of the country's wondrous monuments spread through these travellers' published accounts and the exhibition of objects that they had removed. None of this could have happened without the involvement of Egyptians, but their participation was largely unacknowledged by the Europeans whom they conducted to sites and assisted in excavations, and indeed remained largely undocumented, at least relative to the endeavour of the European actors.

The prevailing attitudes of the European archaeologists two centuries ago not only meant that the Egyptians' participation in excavations was limited, but also ensured that they were not credited for their labours even when they did play more significant roles. The problem has since been compounded: as histories of archaeology in Egypt have been compiled, writers have followed those in the field by failing to recognize the contributions made by Egyptians. Often, of course, scholars are hamstrung by biases in historic documentation, but as the 19th century progressed Egyptians certainly began to assume greater authority over the management of their own cultural heritage. Yet it is only recently that historians have begun to question the established narratives of the development of Egyptology, to interrogate existing sources and to seek new ones that illuminate the experiences and impact of Egyptian archaeologists.

Archival sources remain difficult to access, but an enormous leap forward occurred when a sealed room in the temple of Sety I at Abydos was reopened in 2012. Aside from its important and exquisitely beautiful 19th Dynasty decoration, the temple contained a vast archive of administrative papers – letters, inventories, site maps, plans and account books – relating to the Egyptian Antiquities Service in the 19th and 20th centuries that may prove to be as important for historical research as the more famous and ancient inscriptions of the time of Sety I himself. The collection of papers, known as the Abydos Temple Paper Archive (ATPA), has only just begun to be studied but is already helping us to understand the essential contribution to archaeology made by Egyptians from the late 19th century onwards.

Several figures of interest have emerged from the letters, including one of the first graduates of an Egyptian school of Egyptology, who would make a career as an inspector for the Antiquities Service. His name was Hassan Hosni. Hosni studied at the Egyptology School under Ahmed Kamal, one of the earliest Egyptian Egyptologists, who went on to become assistant curator at the Boulaq Museum in Cairo. This was in fact the second school dedicated to Egyptology in Egypt; Kamal was one of only seven graduates of the first, and the only one to pursue any kind of career within the Antiquities Service. The then director of the Service, Auguste Mariette, did not want to hire Egyptians.

→ A map, recently discovered in the Abydos Temple Archive, of the Girga area in Middle Egypt, showing sites recently acquired by the Antiquities Service (marked in red and green).

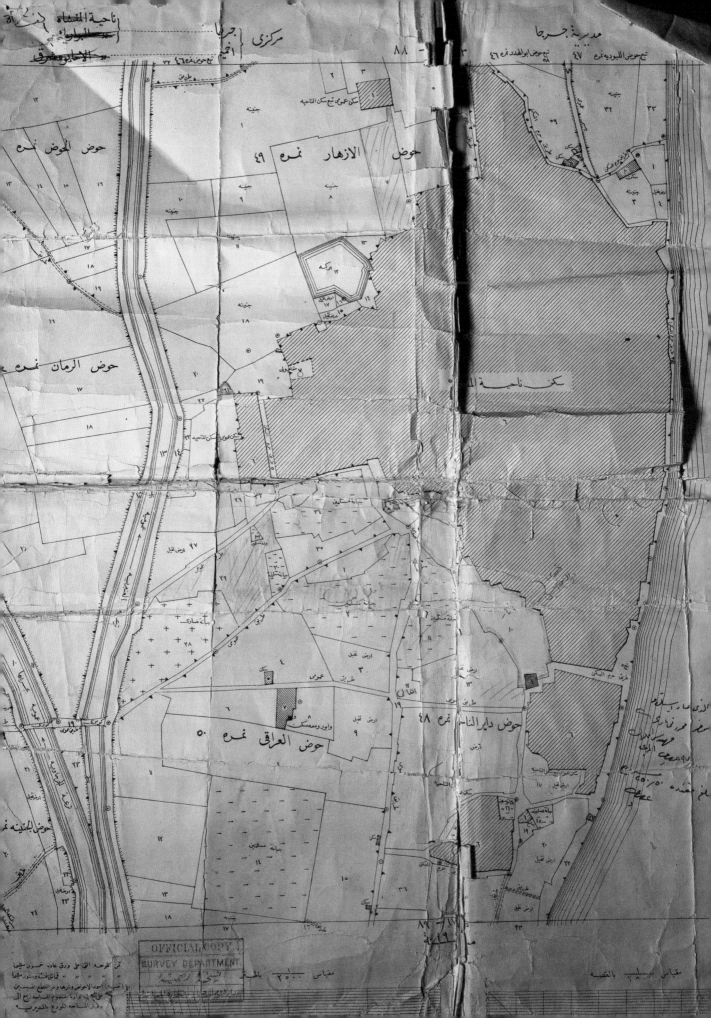

Hosni's class of this second school of Egyptology has been described as a 'lost generation'. He and others from his cohort are represented in the records left by Western archaeologists but often disappear from view. But the ATPA shows that Hosni – and perhaps others – was very active at least until the mid-1920s, and in sometimes surprising ways. In 1922 Hosni instructed Reginald Engelbach, the English chief inspector of antiquities in Upper Egypt, to deputize for Engelbach's counterpart in middle Egypt, Gerald Avery Wainwright, when Wainwright took his annual leave. Similarly, in 1924 Hosni confirmed that Cecil Firth would return to his post as chief inspector at Saqqara following a period of leave. The received wisdom has generally been that positions of authority within the Antiquities Service at this time were held exclusively by foreigners, but the ATPA documents suggest that, at least in these cases, authority lay with the Egyptians.

Hosni was a pioneer in having an education to match that of his Western colleagues, along with the local knowledge that would allow him to deal effectively with the situation 'on the ground' – communities' customs, laws and people, not all of which were aligned with the interests of the Antiquities Service. Crucially, this was a time of great nationalist feeling among the Egyptian people, who sought the right of self-determination and independence from the colonial powers, in particular the British. Hosni was perhaps something of a trailblazer, helping to forge the path to an Antiquities Service that would be more inclusive of trained Egyptian archaeologists and would ultimately be led by them.

The records from the Abydos Temple Paper Archive allow us to see much more clearly how influential Hosni was. Other sources reveal his movements in the barest detail: he was assigned as inspector to the excavations that William Flinders Petrie (pp. 178–83) undertook in the Faiyum region in 1887–88, and worked with George Andrew Reisner (pp. 224–31) at Giza in 1913–14. But these records convey little of the authority he seems to have wielded in his later career. The ATPA records may, in time, help us to understand better the process by which the Antiquities Service developed and reveal that it was under way much earlier than has been recognized in the traditional history of Egyptology.

↓ The cover of a 1914 ledger belonging to the Antiquities Service, marked 'Gouvernement Egyptien', discovered in the Abydos Temple Archive.

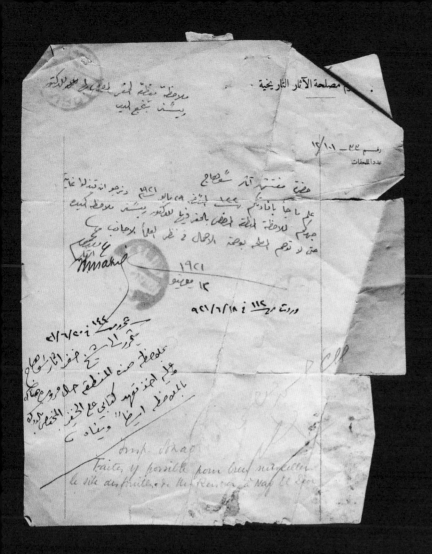

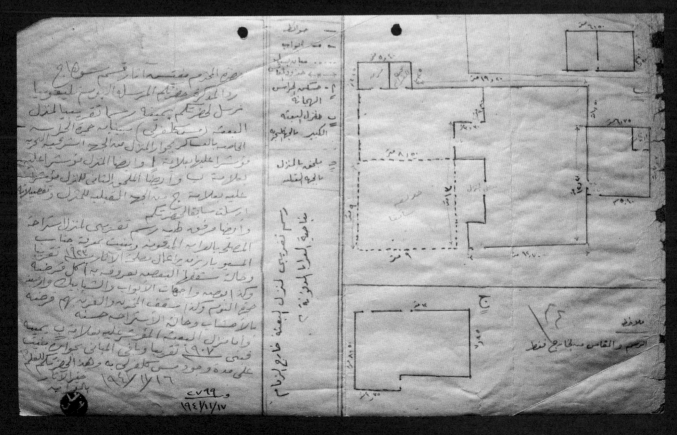

John Pendlebury

1904–1941 British classicist and Egyptologist

Pendlebury was an archaeologist with expertise in the cultures of ancient Crete and Egypt. He was director of the EES excavations at Amarna. An accomplished athlete in his youth, he was also a natural showman and used his talents to promote archaeology to the wider public, helping to generate the funds needed to continue his scientific endeavours.

→ Front of a notebook used by H. W. Fairman during the 1931–32 season at Amarna. Fairman was the team's philologist and was thus in charge of recording any inscriptions that were found.

John Pendlebury was born in London. He studied both classics and Egyptology at the University of Cambridge. Unwilling to drop his interest in either specialism, he joined fieldwork projects in Egypt during the winter months and Crete during the spring. By 1930, aged just twenty-six, he had been appointed both curator of the palace of Minos at Knossos and, after serving for a single season as a field assistant, director of the Egypt Exploration Society's expedition to Tell el-Amarna.

Amarna was well known by this time as the capital city founded by the so-called 'heretic pharaoh' Akhenaten – who had banned the worship of the traditional Egyptian pantheon in favour of a single deity in the form of the sun disc – and his wife, Nefertiti. The Egypt Exploration Society (EES; formerly the Egypt Exploration Fund) had begun their work at the site in 1920, and over the course of a decade revealed much of the architecture of the city. A variety of buildings, including houses, palaces, temples and workshops, were excavated, and thousands of objects recovered in the process. Some of these helped elucidate the story of the city's main protagonists, Akhenaten and Nefertiti, but also other members of the royal family, including Tutankhamun, Akhenaten's son. Others spoke more of the ordinary folk whom Akhenaten had brought to this strangely remote yet beautiful location, isolated from most of the major centres of power in ancient times and modern.

Mary Chubb, assistant secretary of the EES, joined the Amarna expedition during Pendlebury's first two seasons as director. Her account her experiences, *Nefertiti Lived Here* (1998), provides a rare and elegant, non-academic glimpse of life on excavation. Pendlebury played a major role in the story, of course, and she recalls his demeanour on site with affection: 'John had on a bright pink, open-necked shirt and navy shorts with a many-coloured belt of twisted leather. Also his hair was standing up thickly, instead of being slicked down on his head. He looked entirely different from his up-to-Amarna self, and much more approachable.'

In addition to Chubb, whose story as a junior administrator from London joining an expedition to the desert for the first time is fascinating in itself, Pendlebury was joined by a series of other specialists, who become colourful characters thanks to Chubb's account. One such was the architect Hilary Waddington: 'Hilary was our star turn. He came into breakfast last, looking as if he had just discovered Livingstone. He was carrying a brand-new topee, which he laid carefully on the bookcase; and wearing a wonderful khaki tunic with a tight belt which he said was called a bush jumper. It had so many pockets, full of so many useful things, that he could hardly stand up.' Waddington emerges from Chubb's recollections as something of a maverick; he brought a pistol to his first season at Amarna but was prevented from carrying it by Pendlebury ('Not on my dig, my lad').

TEMPLES, TOWNS AND CITIES

H.W.FAIRMAN.   TA.31.32

PATENT

EGYPT EXPLORATION SOCIETY
AMARNA ARCHIVE
Document A8.6
(from File TA.A.6)

1931-2: Inscriptions - H.W.Fairman

PAPER

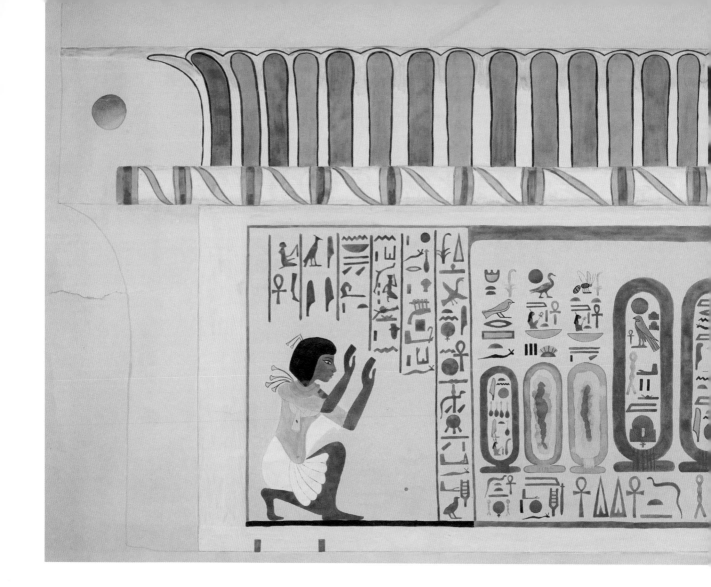

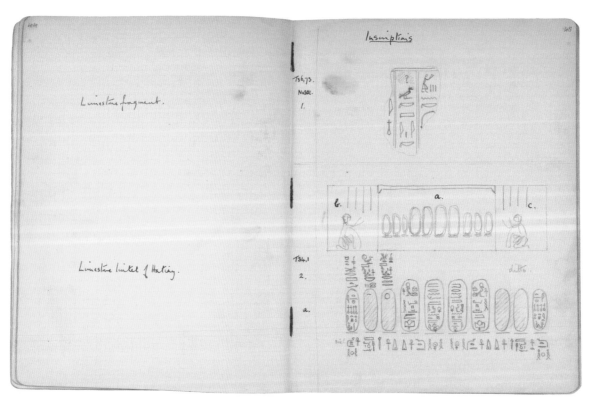

Limestone fragment.

T36,75.
NoSOl.
1.

Limestone lintel of Hatiay.

T34,1
2.

a.

b.

a.

c.

ditto.

↑ Large coloured drawing made by John Pendlebury's wife, Hilda, of the decorated stone lintel discovered in the house of a man called Hatiay in December 1930. Hatiay was an overseer of works in ancient Akhetaten (Amarna), which perhaps explains why his house included stone features in addition to the typical mudbricks. Hatiay is shown twice, adoring the cartouches of the Aten flanked by the names of Akhenaten and Nefertiti.

← A notebook with a hand copy of the inscriptions on the lintel.

He also hid a gold sovereign he carried with him everywhere in a pot of shaving foam to avoid having it confiscated.

The EES's expeditions were funded exclusively through subscriptions of ordinary members of the public and donations made by museums hoping to acquire objects for their collections in return. Consequently, money was constantly in short supply, a consideration that greatly impacted on Pendlebury's recording of the excavations. Yet he wanted to ensure that the recording of the finds was first class, and so every object was photographed, catalogued and given an 'object card' on which a sketch was made and all the appropriate measurements and other details documented. This would help keep the authorities of the Cairo Museum happy, an important consideration at a time when the Egyptian government was exerting greater control over the flow of antiquities out of the country. Demonstrating a thorough and conscientious approach gave Pendlebury the best possible chance of a generous allocation of finds to take home for redistribution to sponsoring museums. The object cards would also provide the team with the opportunity for a little mischief from time to time, perhaps with the encouragement of Pendlebury who, more than any other field director in the EES's history, also wanted to capture all aspects

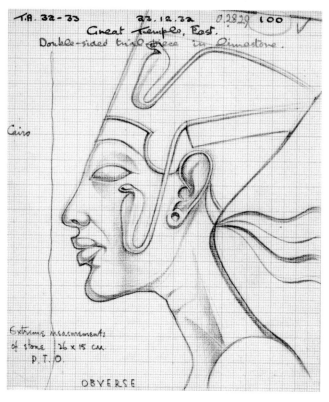

TA. 32-33   33.12.32   0.28.29 100
Great Temple, East.
Double-sided trial piece in limestone.

Cairo

Extreme measurements
of stone   26 x 15 cm
P.T.O.

OBVERSE

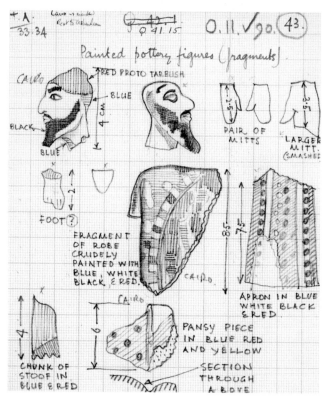

+A.   (lots in circle   Q 42 →
33.34   Rest S.Ashmolen   Q 41.15   0. 11. √90. 43.

Painted pottery figures (fragments).

CAIRO   RED PROTO TARBUSH
                              BLUE
BLACK   4 CM

BLUE   PAIR OF   LARGER
                                  MITTS   MITT.
                                              (SMASHED)

FOOT(?)   FRAGMENT
                 OF ROBE
                 CRUDELY
                 PAINTED WITH
                 BLUE, WHITE   CAIRO
                 BLACK & RED.   APRON IN BLUE
                                              WHITE BLACK
                          CAIRO   & RED

CHUNK OF   PANSY PIECE
STOOL IN   IN BLUE RED
BLUE & RED   AND YELLOW
                                  SECTION
                                  THROUGH
                                  ABOVE

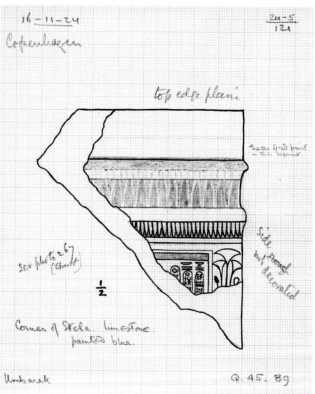

16 - 11 - 24   2u-5
Copenhagen   121

                    top edge plain

see photo 267
(Chult)

      ½

Corner of Stela. limestone
painted blue.

Umbarak   Q. 45. 89

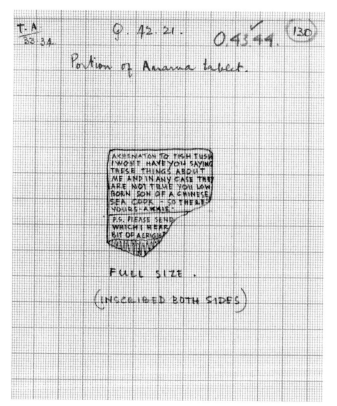

T.A.   Q. 42. 21.   130
33.34   0.43.44.

Portion of Amarna tablet.

AKHENATON TO FISH TUSH
I WON'T HAVE YOU SAYING
THESE THINGS ABOUT
ME AND IN ANY CASE THEY
ARE NOT TRUE YOU LOW
BORN SON OF A CHINESE
SEA COOK - SO THERE!
YOURS - AKHIE.
P.S. PLEASE SEND
WHAT I HEAR
BIT OF ALRIGHT

FULL SIZE.

(INSCRIBED BOTH SIDES)

← Four object cards, from a total of thousands that were used to record every small find made at Amarna by the EES during the 1920s and 1930s. These included descriptions, drawings, publication details and the collections to which each item was sent. At bottom right is a fragment of an Amarna tablet drawn by a mischievous team member. It bears an inscription in English: *'Akhenaten to tish tush i won't have you saying these things about me and in any case they are not true you low born son of a chinese sea cook so there! Yours akhie. P.S. Please send … which i hear … bit of alright.'*

of the adventure, in the hope of igniting a passion for archaeology in the hearts of new potential supporters. He was popular with the locals, arranging a sports day on Christmas Day 1930, in which villagers competed in various races – across an obstacle course, dribbling a ball with hockey sticks, a 'wheelbarrow' race (in which the competitors race in pairs, one holding the feet of the other, who 'walks' on the palms of their hands). Pendlebury was also an enthusiastic participant in the traditional stick-fighting dance, often wore the traditional Cretan costume as a reminder of his expertise in the archaeology of that region, and refused to allow the team the use of a car, which he felt would spoil the atmosphere of the site. He was an enthusiastic athlete, and quickly covered the long distance between the dig house and the excavations each day while his unfortunate companions did their best to keep up.

The archive of the Amarna excavations, particularly in the years during which they were directed by Pendlebury, is the most detailed and varied in the society's collections. The records include drawings, plans, photographs, notebooks, object cards, 'house sheets' (one for every ancient house excavated), letters, telegrams, postcards that were given away to potential subscribers, and even a 'cinematograph' film for which slates were produced as if they were making a Hollywood movie. For Pendlebury, perhaps to the chagrin of some of his academic colleagues, the whole thing was a great adventure, and his memory is kept alive in his vivid and exciting accounts of his exploits. The results of his work, judged a qualified success by today's standards, were scientifically published, but it is perhaps for his personality and particular way of doing things that he is one of the most celebrated Egyptologists.

← Photograph of Hilary Waddington in full expedition gear, manning the cine camera he used to capture the excavations and other aspects of life on expedition. The footage survives in the EES archives and provides a rare and magical glimpse into a long-gone age of exploration.

Walter Bryan Emery

1903–1971 British archaeologist and Egyptologist

Emery was one of the last archaeologists to work on a truly monumental scale, engaging hundreds of workers in a single excavation. He published his many important discoveries in great detail, making excellent use of the technical drawing skills he learned as an apprentice.

→ Emery's sketch map of the North Saqqara plateau, recording the location of numerous mastabas of the 1st, 2nd and 3rd Dynasties. They include no. 3035, in which Emery had found forty-five intact chambers in his first season at the site, and no. 3038, whose stepped mudbrick structure covering the burial chamber Emery believed may have been a precursor to the step pyramid.

Walter Bryan Emery was born in Liverpool. He became fascinated by ancient Egypt after reading the novels of H. Rider Haggard and attending public lectures by John Garstang, who had excavated a series of sites in Egypt and founded the Institute of Archaeology at the University of Liverpool. But Emery's parents feared that there would be few opportunities for him in Egyptology, and so he was briefly apprenticed to a marine engineering firm. There he learned how to make construction drawings, a skill that would serve him well in his subsequent career. He was eventually able to persuade his parents to let him study Egyptology at the University of Liverpool, where he was taught by Percy Newberry (pp. 196–201). After his graduation another of his tutors, Eric Peet, recommended him to the Egypt Exploration Society (EES), and he joined the survey of Akhenaten's capital city at Tell el-Amarna in 1923.

A chance meeting around this time would have a significant impact on Emery's career. Sir Robert Mond, a wealthy chemist and generous patron of archaeology in Egypt, had decided to resume his work in clearing, restoring and protecting tombs in Thebes, which was to be carried out under the auspices of the University of Liverpool. When Mond visited the university one day, it happened that Garstang, Newberry and Peet were all unavailable, leaving Emery to receive him. Mond was impressed by the young man and appointed him director of the project. Emery set up his camp on the Qurna hillside, close to the house occupied a century earlier by John Gardner Wilkinson (pp. xxx–xx). This was an extraordinary time to be working in the area, Howard Carter having discovered the tomb of Tutankhamun only two years earlier; Emery was one of very few who were present at the opening of the sarcophagus. When he was still only twenty-two years old, Emery was put in charge of the clearance of the impressive tomb of the vizier Ramose, supervising 400 labourers.

Emery quickly demonstrated the instinct for discovery that would drive his career. While working on the tomb of Ramose he began exploring the desert behind Armant in the hope of finding the burial place of the sacred Buchis bulls, which had been worshipped as a manifestation of the god Montu. When each bull died, it was buried with great ceremony in a dedicated cemetery called the Bucheum. Emery persuaded Mond to apply for a concession to dig in the area, and in 1927–28 discovered the vast catacombs where the bulls and their mothers – associated with the goddess Hathor – were buried. But Emery was unable to take full credit for the discovery; Mond was concerned that he would be unable to finance the research and publications demanded by a discovery on this scale, and the concession was passed to the EES. Emery subsequently acted as an advisor to the EES expedition and returned to Qurna to continue his work on the tomb of Ramose. However, he was soon recruited by the Antiquities Service to lead a survey of Lower Nubia as the Aswan Low Dam was to be raised

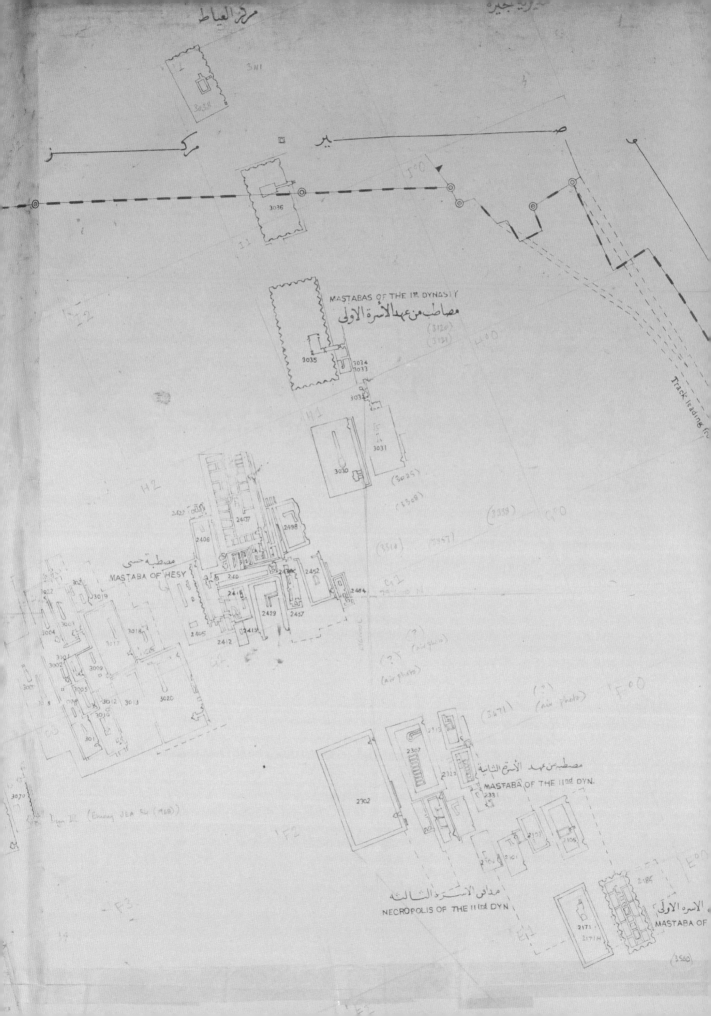

مركز العياط

صير مكز

MASTABAS OF THE 1ᵗʰ DYNASTY

مصاطب من عهد الأسرة الأولى

MASTABA OF HESY

مصطبة حسى

Track leading fro

3036

3035
3034
3033
3032
3031
3030
(3025)
(3308)

(3359)
(3510)   (3357)

2407
2406
2427
2498
240
2416
2452
2464
2429   2457
2412
2405   2419

(?)   (air photo)
(?)   (air photo)
(air photo)

3022
3019
3004
3007
3002
3009
3025
3012   3013   3020
301
3010
3070

Dyn II (Emery JEA 54 (1968))

(3671)   (?)   (air photo)

2713
2307
2323
2302
2331
2153
105
2101
2171
2171/H
2185

مصاطب من عهد الأسرة الثانية
MASTABA OF THE IIⁿᵈ DYN.

مقابر الأسرة الثالثة
NECROPOLIS OF THE IIⁿᵈ DYN.

الأسرة الأولى
MASTABA OF

(3560)

H2   H1   G2   G1

F1   F2   F3   E

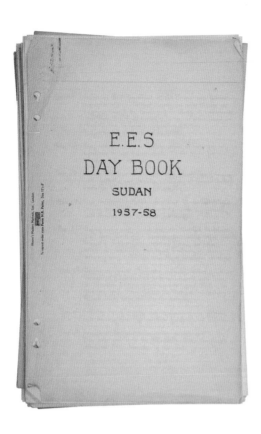

↑ Loose leaves from Emery's daybook for the 1957–58 season in Sudan.

for a second time, causing further flooding of the region. Emery spent five seasons, from 1929 to 1934, prospecting the area, building on the work of George Reisner (pp. 224–31) twenty years previously. The most significant discovery made during the survey arose from Emery's excavations of a group of tumuli at Ballana and Qustul, which lay close to the southern boundary of the flooded area. These had never before been investigated; previous visitors were not even certain whether they were man-made or natural features. It was six weeks before his efforts were rewarded, when one of the elder workmen, Ibrahim, shouted out and brandished a glass bead. Soon, a vaulted burial chamber was revealed. Emery proceeded to excavate the rest of the tumuli, which belonged to the kings, queens and nobility of a pagan group of the 4th to 6th centuries CE. Reisner had designated this culture the 'X-Group', but it was renamed 'Ballana Culture' after these tombs. The burials exhibited a mixture of Meroitic and Byzantine traditions. In the most elaborate, the men were laid out on beds in their full regalia, surrounded by their women and servants; their horses and camels, wearing silver harnesses, lay in the entrance passageway; and a separate storage magazine held the owner's possessions, including fine furniture and weapons.

In 1935 Emery was invited to take over the work of British Egyptologist Cecil Firth, who had just begun investigating the 1st Dynasty mastabas at Saqqara when, during a visit to England in 1931, he was taken ill and died. The appointment set Emery on a path that would define much of the rest of his archaeological career. Over the course of the years leading up to the Second World War, he made a succession of important discoveries in the cemetery, including a massive tomb with forty-five separate storage chambers containing a rich haul of grave goods, and another with a unique steeped mudbrick structure, which Emery believed may have been the architectural precursor to the nearby Step Pyramid. His excavations were interrupted by the war, but he was able to put his skills and knowledge of the landscape to use, joining the Long Range Patrol (later called the Long Range Desert Group) as a specialist in the interpretation of aerial photographs. He was mentioned in dispatches in 1942 and awarded an MBE in 1943, and by the end of the war he had been appointed director of British Military Intelligence and an honorary lieutenant-colonel. He resumed his work at Saqqara, but was unable to continue beyond a single season owing to financial difficulties and entered the diplomatic corps as an attaché at the British Embassy in Cairo.

In 1951 an opportunity to return to Egyptology presented itself: Jaroslav Černý had vacated the Edwards Professorship at University College London, and Emery, with his wealth of experience in the field, was the natural choice as his successor. In 1952 he also became field director of the EES and thus took charge of British archaeological work in Egypt. He returned once more to Saqqara and in four seasons completed the excavation of the large 1st Dynasty mastabas that dominated the escarpment overlooking the Nile Valley and, possibly, the ancient capital of Memphis (though the city in this early phase in Egyptian history has never been securely located). He published the second and third volumes of his *Great Tombs of the First Dynasty* series under the society's imprint. Both contained fine and very distinctive examples of the technical architectural drawings that were his hallmark.

In 1956 the Suez Crisis and attendant breakdown in diplomatic relations between Britain and Egypt forced the postponement of further excavations. The EES transferred its activities to Sudan, where Emery investigated the vast Middle and New Kingdom fortress of Buhen and the fortress of Qasr Ibrim, which, astonishingly, was occupied continuously from the 8th century BCE until 1813 CE, when the last inhabitants were driven away by artillery fire. At around the same time, Egypt began construction of the new High Dam at Aswan. This would flood a much greater part of Lower Nubia than the Low Dam had. Both the Egyptian and Sudanese governments sought Emery's advice for mitigating the inevitable loss of archaeological sites, and he was appointed to the UNESCO committee to consult on the campaign. Emery recommended that two surveys be carried out, one on either side of the Egyptian–Sudanese border, and for a time headed the Egyptian mission himself.

In September 1964, Emery was able to return to Saqqara to resume the investigation that he had begun at the very end of his last season at the site in 1956. He had been interested in a 3rd Dynasty mastaba (no. 3077) first excavated by Firth. Its superstructure looked out over a large area of broken pottery dating from the Ptolemaic and Roman periods. The juxtaposition of the Old Kingdom tomb with this much later pottery was odd. The sherds were probably the remains of votive offerings left by pilgrims, and Emery immediately had in mind why the people of those later times might have travelled to this place to make them. Could it have been the location of the temple of Asklepius, the Greek god of medicine who was identified in the minds of the Egyptians at this late period with the folk hero turned deity Imhotep, who lived at the beginning of the 3rd Dynasty? And might the temple have been located in this place because one of the large mastaba tombs of that period had been Imhotep's? Firth had believed his tomb would be found somewhere on the plateau – indeed, this was why he had chosen to dig there.

Unsurprisingly, given the riches that lay (and still lie) beneath the sands at Saqqara, Emery's excavations quickly yielded spectacular results, but not the prize – the tomb of Imhotep – that he was hoping for. Within a few weeks his team had uncovered a large mudbrick mastaba that had been built during the 3rd Dynasty (no. 3508) but had evidently been the focus of significant

↓ Entries from Emery's daybook for 4, 5 and 6 December during the 1959–60 season at Buhen. Emery was excavating an area just inside the main wall of the fortress. On 5 December he remarks: 'We are not yet down to the lowest levels but already fragments of inscribed stone (NK) [New Kingdom] pieces of cavetto cornice and pillar plinths have been recovered. Vast quantities of pottery, mostly NK are typable.' The following day he notes that 'The President [of the Republic of Sudan] will visit the excavations tomorrow.'

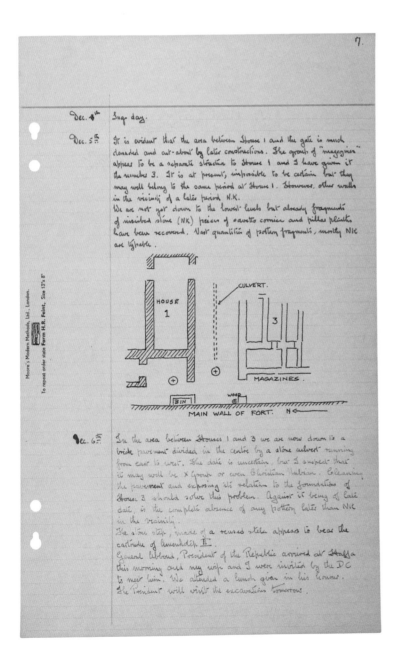

cultic activity in Ptolemaic and Roman times. Sacrificial bulls had been placed outside the north and south chapels, grooves scraped into the brickwork in the fashion observed on temple walls elsewhere in the country – the result of visitors wanting to take for themselves some of the substance of what were considered sacred buildings with magical properties – and votive offerings left behind, including mummified ibises. Extending his excavations, Emery found further mastabas of the period arranged in rows, forming 'streets' of tombs. He could now see that the tops of these tombs had been deliberately cut down to a uniform level and the 'streets' between them filled with rubble to create a vast level platform, on top of which a building might have stood. On top of the platform were huge quantities of mummified ibises, and the burial shaft of one of the largest of the tombs led to a vast labyrinth of catacombs containing thousands more. Reading Emery's preliminary

↓ Plan of the ibis catacombs that Emery's team broke into on 10 December 1964 as they excavated the burial shaft of mastaba no. 3510. Hewn out of the solid bedrock in Late period and Ptolemaic times, the winding corridors gave access to side chambers used to deposit thousands upon thousands of mummified sacred ibis birds – votive offerings made by pilgrims in honour of the gods, in particular Thoth and Imhotep.

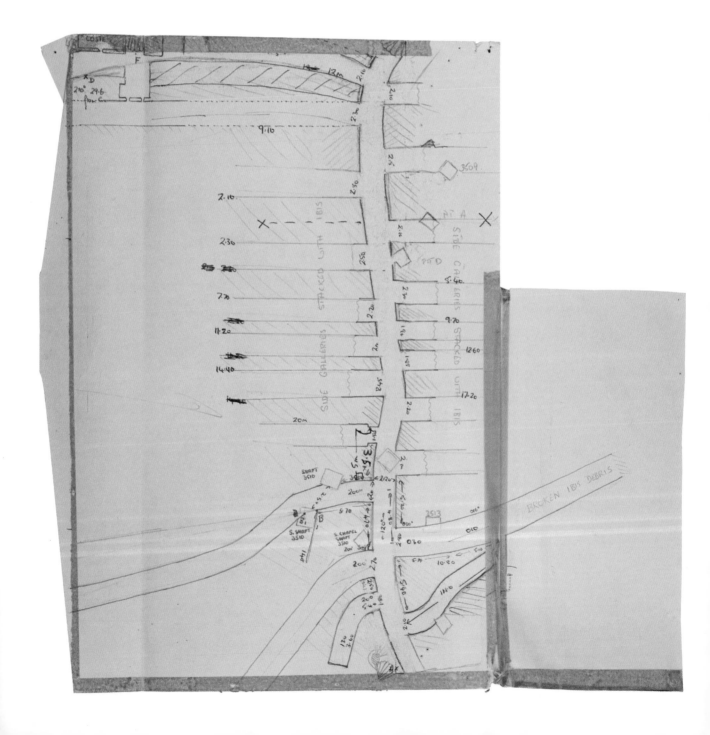

report from the end of the season one gets a sense of the overwhelming magnitude of the discovery:

> *The extent of this labyrinth is still unknown and we are as yet ignorant of the beginning and end of this great underground structure, although we have explored, with some difficulty, hundreds of yards of its passages …. Many of the galleries, which stand 4 m. [13 feet] high and 2.50 m. [8 feet] wide, are packed with mummies of ibis still undisturbed in their pottery jars. There are literally thousands and thousands of these strange deposits of the bird, which at Memphis in Ptolemaic times was sacred to Imhotep; …. Only a preliminary examination and survey has so far been possible, for it is obvious that excavation through the Old Kingdom pits would be impossible, and more over there is in parts the hazard of fragile rock conditions. It is clear that the only solution to this problem is to find the proper entrance and start the clearance of the galleries from there.*

Emery had discovered what is now known as the Sacred Animal Necropolis. Over the course of a further five seasons, his team brought into view a religious landscape that for centuries in the Late, Ptolemaic and Roman Periods would have been bustling with visitors from all over Egypt and beyond. Hundreds of thousands of mummified ibises were found in the catacombs, indicating a major cult of Thoth, another god associated with Imhotep. Emery eventually found the original entrance, around which an entire complex of temple buildings had been built. He also found further catacombs for the burial of baboons (also associated with Thoth), falcons of Horus, and cows sacred to Isis, the mothers of the Apis bulls that were buried a little to the south in the famous Serapeum. The excavations also revealed important texts, including a cache of records, in Demotic and Greek, of the dreams of a man named Hor, which had perhaps been interpreted by the temple's priests. And yet, despite the vast wealth of material suggesting the presence in the area of a temple of Imhotep, the evidence to identify any of the mastabas as his tomb never came to light.

After several years of ill health, through which Emery had continued to work uncomplainingly, he collapsed outside his office on the Saqqara plateau. He had suffered a stroke and died in a hospital in Cairo two days later. He left a vast quantity of material from his last seasons at Saqqara to be published by his successors. His earlier expeditions had been published in numerous excavation reports in which he was thorough and scientific, and dutiful in distinguishing the facts – archaeological data – from his interpretations. Even so, he understood the importance of conveying what he and others had learned to non-specialist audiences, publishing three popular works: *Nubian Treasure*, *Archaic Egypt* and *Egypt in Nubia*. He was also happy for the wider public to regard his last few seasons as a 'search for Imhotep'. Although he had the discovery of that god's tomb in mind as the crowning glory of a long and successful career, it was not to be. He is the last individual in this book to be remembered by anyone still alive – perhaps the last great figure of an age now behind us.

Acknowledgments

This really has been a team effort. First of all, at Thames & Hudson, Ben Hayes deserves the credit for suggesting the idea for this book. Profuse thanks are due to Jen Moore for her willingness to edit me for a second book running, but moreover for conjuring up publishable texts from my scruffy draft chapters. Both have been enormously patient in waiting for text and indulging my harried responses to their gentle enquiries.

For a book like this it's fundamentally important to get the design right, to allow the pictures to speak for themselves, and Ramon Pez and Aman Phull have done a fabulous job in that department.

Sally Nicholls has been instrumental in finding images and suggesting subjects for me to cover in addition to identifying copyright holders and procuring usable versions of everything we wanted to include. Sally generously shared her vast experience of publishing illustrated books, which was enormously useful to a novice like me, not least in the more panicky moments when another deadline went sailing past... She also introduced me to the manuscript collections in the British Library that subsequently became like a second home to me. It has only been possible to include a tiny fraction of the major Egyptological archives in the BL – those relating to Hay, Burton, Lane and Hekekyan in particular. It was an enormous thrill and privilege to go through much – but by no means all – of this material during my research, and I can only hope that some of the joy there is to be had in looking at such things at first hand comes across in this book. It was a great pleasure to work in such a peaceful and stimulating environment, among so many studious-looking people beavering away doing clever things.

Several of the later chapters in the book gave me the very welcome opportunity to return, in my research and in person, to my old stomping ground, the Egypt Exploration Society, where Drs Carl Graves and Stephanie Boonstra were dependably knowledgeable and obliging. The Society's contribution to Egyptology is immense and ongoing, and I hope this book might help contribute in some small way to raising awareness of the importance of its work, past and present.

There are few in the world who know the work of the Society's founder, Amelia Edwards, and the history of Egyptology better than William Joy, who was a constant source of new material and information throughout this project. Frankly, I could not keep up with all his suggestions and can only hope he will forgive me for not including everything. Knowing what riches he has seen, particularly in archives belonging to private collectors, I like to think there might be a follow-up to this book one day.

Numerous colleagues have helped with information and encouragement, including, in particular, Neil Cooke, Dr Jennifer Cromwell, Louise Ellis-Barrett, Dr Paolo del Vesco, Dr Anna Garnett, Simon Guerrier, Marcel Maessen, Prof Patrizia Piacentini and Dr Anna Stevens. I hope those I have failed to mention will forgive me.

Two colleagues in Egypt have been especially helpful. First, Ayman Damarany, of the Ministry of Antiquities, was extremely obliging in providing information about and material from the Abydos Temple Project Archive (https://abydosarchive.org/) for the section on his illustrious predecessor, Hassan Hosni. Relatively little work has been done on the history of Egyptology in Egypt, and the relevant archives have been difficult for scholars to access, to the extent that we don't yet even have a clear picture of what material exists, let alone how it might help us to revise our understanding of the Egyptian contribution to the discipline. In this context, it is impossible to overstate the importance of the Abydos archive. We must all be very grateful that it has come to light thanks to Ayman and his team, and that it is now in their care, and very excited about what will be gained as the material becomes available for study. I had the enormous privilege of visiting the archive in person at the Sety temple in Spring 2019 thanks to Ayman and his colleagues, Mohamed Abuelyazid and Hazem Salah.

Secondly, Medhat Saad will be well known to the thousands he has taken to archaeological sites as a tour guide. He is also an unending source of knowledge about the history of Egypt, from the prehistoric era down to the present day, and was enormously helpful in helping me to translate the permit presented to James Burton by Mohamed Ali's administration. It was a great thrill to see this, the more so once Medhat had helped me to make sense of it, and I'm delighted it appears in this book (see p. 76).

My literary agent, Donald Winchester, has, as always, been unfailingly supportive throughout the writing of this book, wise and calming about the missed deadlines, unflappable when I was really flapping. He made me believe I would get to the finish line eventually, and well, here we are. Thanks Donald!

No one else, though, was as close to this book as Suzanna, who came home, on a daily basis, to updates ranging from 'got nothing done so far' to 'didn't get through as much as I'd hoped'. Suze, this book is for you.

Chris Naunton

Sources of Quotations

Introduction: These Rough Notes (pp. 8–11)

'These were the graves...'
  Sandys, G., *A relation of a journey begun An. Dom. 1610. Fovre bookes. Containing a description of the Turkish Empire, of Ægypt, of the Holy Land, of the remote parts of Italy, and ilands adioyning.* London, 1621, p. 133

An Untouched Antique Land (pp. 14–15)

'With delighted eyes...'
  Sandys, G., *A relation of a journey begun An. Dom. 1610. Fovre bookes. Containing a description of the Turkish Empire, of Ægypt, of the Holy Land, of the remote parts of Italy, and ilands adioyning,* London, 1621, p. 129

'by the immensity of their structures...'
  Diodorus Siculus, translated by C. H. Oldfather, *Library of History, Volume I: Books 1–2.34,* Loeb Classical Library 279, Cambridge, MA: Harvard University Press, 1933, p. 216

'Memphis itself, the royal residence...'
  Strabo, translated by Horace Leonard Jones, *Geography, Volume I: Books 1–2,* Loeb Classical Library 49, Cambridge, MA: Harvard University Press, 1917, p. 87

'This but from the shoulders upwards...'
  Sandys, G., ibid., p. 131

George Sandys (pp. 22–27)

'is said to extend...'
  Sandys, G., *A relation of a journey begun An. Dom. 1610. Fovre bookes. Containing a description of the Turkish Empire, of Ægypt, of the Holy Land, of the remote parts of Italy, and ilands adioyning,* London, 1621, pp. 92–94

'Now having lost the sight of Rhodes'
  Ibid., p. 92

'but Ah how much different...'
  Ibid., p. 114

'those three Pyramides...'
  Ibid., p. 127

'These, as the rest...'
  Ibid., p. 128

'No stone so little...'
  Ibid., p. 128

'By a Sphinx...'
  Ibid., p. 131

'the Fane of Venus...'
  Ibid., p. 132

'The very ruines...'
  Ibid., p. 132

'The most pregnant proofe...'
  Ibid., pp. 132–33

'In that place...'
  Ibid., p. 133

Frederik Ludwig Norden (pp. 28–33)

'The conversations that they had...'
  Norden, F. L., *Travels in Egypt and Nubia,* London: Printed for Lockyer Davis and Charles Reymers, 1757, p. xix

'mixture of antique and modern...'
  Ibid., p. 5

'it is known, that at the time...'
  Ibid., p. 7

'I do not think my supposition...'
  Norden, F. L., *A Compendium of the Travels of F. L. Norden through Egypt and Nubia,* Dublin: Printed for J. Smith on the Blind Quay, 1757, pp. 44–45

'We agreed with a barge-master...'
  Ibid., p. 78

'Janissaries are to be had...'
  Ibid., pp. 272–73

'He then proposed our returning to Cairo...'
  Ibid., p. 146

'Our intrepidity...'
  Ibid., pp. 146–47

'THREE or four crocodiles...'
  Ibid., pp. 148–49

'It was four o' clock...'
  Ibid., pp. 150–51

'more time than I could spare...'
  Ibid., p. 151

'I did not go far...'
  Ibid., p. 152

'During all this walk...'
  Norden, F. L., *Travels in Egypt and Nubia,* London: Printed for Lockyer Davis and Charles Reymers, 1757, pp. 118–19

Richard Pococke (pp. 34–39)

'My observing so nicely...'
  Pococke, R., *A Description of the East and Some Other Countries. VOLUME the First. OBSERVATIONS on EGYPT,* London: Printed for the Author, by W. BOWYER, 1743, p. 3

'There are two distances...'
  Ibid., p. 40

'This is, without doubt...'
  Ibid., p. 92

'a very fine gate...'
  Ibid., p. 73

'as Pliny calls it, the city of Mercury'
  Ibid., p. 74

'a grand portico...'
  Ibid., p. 74

Artists, Expeditions and Nationalist Competition (pp. 42–43)

'the English have got the Rosetta Stone...'
  Letter from Bernardino Drovetti to Linant de Bellefonds, quoted by G. B. Greenough in his unpublished 'Notes on the Trilingual stone at Grand Cairo: 1829', British Library Add MS 25659 f.2

Dominique Vivant Denon (pp. 44–53)

'huge masses of the ruins...'
  Denon, V., *Travels in Upper and Lower Egypt: During the Campaigns of General Bonaparte in That Country and Published Under His Immediate Patronage Volume 1,* New York, 1803, p. x

'There are some unlucky moments...'
  Ibid., p. 189

'We marched towards Thebes...'
  Ibid., p. xi

'TO BONAPARTE...'
  Denon, V., *Voyages dans la basse et la haute Égypte pendant les campagnes de Bonaparte,* London: C. Mercier for S. Bagster, 1809, p. v

'on my knee...'
  Denon, V., *Travels in Upper and Lower Egypt: During the Campaigns of General Bonaparte in That Country and Published Under His Immediate Patronage Volume 1,* New York, 1803, pp. ix–x

'demolished in order to build barracks...'
  Champollion, J.-F., from a letter dated 10 February 1829 and published in English translation in *Egyptian Diaries,* London: Gibson Square Books, 2001, p. 178

'I had seen a hundred things...'
  Denon, V., ibid., pp. x–xi

Pascal Xavier Coste (pp. 54–59)

'The 15th [of May]...'
  Alleaume, G. et al., *Pascal Coste. Toutes les Égypte,* Marseilles: Éditions Parenthèses, 1998, p. 42

Frédéric Cailliaud (pp. 60–67)

'A spectacle so unexpected...'
  Cailliaud, F., *Travels in the Oasis of Thebes, and in the Deserts Situated East and West of the Thebaid, In the Years 1815, 16, 17, and 18,* London: R. Phillips & Company, 1822, pp. 27–28

'After seven hours march...'
  Ibid., p. 28

'As I was sitting...'
  Ibid., pp. 30–31

'After traversing ... ten or twelve...'
  Ibid., p. 51

'I was almost out of my senses...'
  d'Athanasi, G., *A Brief Account of the Researches and Discoveries in Upper Egypt, Made under the Direction of Henry Salt Esq.,* London 1836, pp. 105–8; quoted in Manniche, *Lost Tombs,* Taylor and Francis, Kindle Edition

'the capital of all Ethiopia'
  Herodotus, translated by A. D. Godley, *The Persian Wars, Volume I: Books 1–2,* Loeb Classical Library 117, Cambridge, MA: Harvard University Press, 1920, p. 309

'Greeks and other Europeans...'
  Cailliaud, F., *Voyage à Méroé, au Fleuve Blanc, au-delà de Fazoql dans Le Midi du Royaume de Sennar, a Syouah et dans cinq autre oasis; fait dans les années 1819, 1820, 1821 et 1822,* Volume II, Paris: IMPRIME PAR AUTORISATION DU ROI, A l'imprimerie royale, 1826, pp. 48–49

'While the camels were being loaded...'
  Ibid., pp. 134–35

'Let's imagine the joy I experienced...'
  Ibid., pp. 141–43

William John Bankes (pp. 68–73)
'really vied with each other who should
produce the best sketches...'
    Quoted in James, T. G. H., *Egypt
    Revealed*, London: The Folio Society,
    1997, p. 88
'Mr Bankes said little...'
    Ibid., p. 92
'lighted with from twenty to fifty small
wax candles...'
    Ibid., p. 94

James Burton (pp. 74–81)
'He is a pleasant and well educated man...'
    Quoted in Thompson, J., *Sir Gardner
    Wilkinson and His Circle*, University
    of Texas Press, Kindle Edition,
    Location 1159
'I can refuse nothing to so dear a friend...'
    Quoted by G. B. Greenough in his
    unpublished 'Notes on the Trilingual
    stone at Grand Cairo: 1829', British
    Library Add ms 25659 f.2
'the English have got the Rosetta Stone...'
    Ibid.

Edward William Lane (pp. 82–87)
'As I approached the shore...'
    Lane, quoted by Thompson, J., 'An
    Account of the Journeys and Writings
    of the Indefatigable Mr Lane',
    Saudi Aramco World, vol. 59, no. 2,
    https://archive.aramcoworld.com/
    issue/200802/the.indefatigable.mr.lane.
    htm [last accessed 19 February 2020]
'was able, as scarcely one other...'
    Lane-Poole, S., *Life of Edward William
    Lane*, London: Williams and Norgate,
    1877, p. 27
'flying visit...'
    Ibid., p. 22
'a sight such as one hardly sees...'
    Ibid., pp. 22–23
'usual accumulation of bones...'
    Ibid., p. 23
'the contemplation of these details...'
    Ibid., pp. 23–24
'rather gloomy...'
    Ibid., p. 24
'Lane encountered one of these pillars...'
    Ibid., pp. 30–31
'Here we find a vast edifice...'
    Lane, E. W., edited and with an
    introduction by Jason Thompson,
    Description of Egypt, Cairo and New
    York: The American University in Cairo
    Press, 2000, pp. 274–75
'The epithet "El-Med'foo'neh"
(or "the buried")...'
    Ibid., p. 275
'Not a blade of grass...'
    Ibid., p. 370

Robert Hay (pp. 88–97)
'I should counsel all travellers...'
    Quoted in Tillett, S., *Egypt Itself.
    The Career of Robert Hay, Esquire
    of Linplum and Nunraw, 1799–1863*,
    London: SD Books, 1984, p. 34

'this piece of knowledge...'
    Hay diary, BL, Add MSS 31054:163;
    quoted in Thompson, J., *Sir Gardner
    Wilkinson and His Circle*, University
    of Texas Press: Kindle Edition,
    Location 2096
'now superseded the old school...'
    Ibid.

Nestor l'Hôte (pp. 104–9)
'Watercolour is the most expeditious...'
    Harlé, D. and Lefebvre, J., *Sur le Nil
    avec Champollion. Lettres, journaux et
    dessins inédits de Nestor l'Hôte*, Orléans:
    Editions Paradigme, 1993, p. 21
'These scenes are interesting...'
    Ibid., p. 152
'we hoped to find a temple...'
    Ibid., p. 155
'We returned, somewhat disappointed...'
    Ibid., p. 155
'Crocodiles are common...'
    Ibid., p. 154
'16 Dec 1828...'
    Ibid., p. 178
'During this time these gentlemen...'
    Ibid., p. 132

John Gardner Wilkinson (pp. 110–19)
'have ... the names of Dr Young's Mespheres
(Tuthmosis III) in the central lines.'
    Wilkinson MSS 'Journal 1821
    Egypt', 5, and Wilkinson MSS 'Letters
    to Sir William Gell', 5, quoted in
    Thompson, J., *Sir Gardner Wilkinson
    and His Circle*, University of Texas Press,
    Kindle Edition, Location 916
'all the English who had lately been in
Upper Egypt...'
    John Madox quoted in Thompson, J.,
    Sir Gardner Wilkinson and His Circle,
    University of Texas Press, Kindle
    Edition, Location 1502
'On Thursday evenings...'
    G. A. Hoskins quoted in Thompson, J.,
    Sir Gardner Wilkinson and His Circle,
    University of Texas Press, Kindle
    Edition, Location 2395
'the traveller, if unacquainted with Arabic...'
    Wilkinson, J. G., *Topography of Thebes,
    and general view of Egypt. Being a short
    account of the principal objects worthy
    of notice in the valley of the Nile [&c.]*,
    London: John Murray, 1835, p. 559
'a camp stool and drawing table'
    Ibid., pp. 559–60
'a lancet, diachylon and blistering plaster,
salts, rhubarb...'
    Ibid., p. 560
'The choice of his library will depend,
of course, on his occupations or taste...'
    Ibid., pp. 560
'He seldom hesitated but made a dash...'
    Wilkinson to Sir William Gell, Cairo,
    3 October 1832, Wilkinson MSS 'Letters
    &c.' Also see Wilkinson's comments
    in Jean Lacouture, *Champollion: Une
    Vie de Lumières*, pp. 471–72. Quoted
    in Thompson, J., *Sir Gardner Wilkinson

and His Circle*, University of Texas Press,
    Kindle Edition, Location 2884
'but he frequently made a happy hit...'
    Ibid., Location 2884

Hector Horeau (pp. 120–25)
'no nation on the Earth...'
    Horeau, H., translated by Naunton, C.,
    *Panorama d'Égypte et de Nubie, avec un
    portrait de Méhémet-Ali et un texte orné
    de Vignettes*, Paris, 1841–46
'Alas! the men, the rulers who successively
fell on Egypt...'
    Ibid.
'these young girls of nature...'
    Ibid.
'chanting in unison and clapping of hands'
    Ibid.

Karl Richard Lepsius (pp. 126–31)
'injurious climate'
    Lepsius, R., *Letters from Egypt,
    Ethiopia, and the Peninsula of Sinai.
    With Extracts from His Chronology of the
    Egyptians, with Reference to the Exodus
    of the Israelites. Revised by the Author*,
    Kindle Edition, Location 218
'The inexhaustible number of important
and instructive monuments and
representations'
    Ibid., Location 226
'the French-Tuscan expedition...'
    Ibid., Location 226
'A great many of these sepulchral
chambers...'
    Ibid., Location 226
'over rich, astonishing days'
    Quoted in Thompson, J., *Wonderful
    Things. A History of Egyptology. Vol. 1:
    From Antiquity to 1881*, Cairo and New
    York, The American University in Cairo
    Press, 2015, p. 203
'I should be afraid of being almost
oppressed...'
    Lepsius, R., *Letters from Egypt,
    Ethiopia, and the Peninsula of Sinai.
    With Extracts from His Chronology of the
    Egyptians, with Reference to the Exodus
    of the Israelites. Revised by the Author*,
    Kindle Edition, Location 3729

Archaeology Begins (pp. 134–35)
'My functions in Egypt are to see that no
one destroys the monuments of antiquity...'
    Letter from Auguste Mariette to
    Heinrich Brugsch, April 1859, quoted
    in Thompson, J., *Wonderful Things.
    A History of Egyptology. Vol. 1: From
    Antiquity to 1881*, Cairo and New York,
    The American University in Cairo Press,
    2015, p. 228

Giovanni Battista Belzoni (pp. 136–43)
'I cannot boast of having made a great
discovery in this tomb'
    Belzoni, G. B., *Narrative of the
    Operations and Recent Discoveries
    Within the Pyramids, Temples, Tombs
    and Excavations in Egypt and Nubia*

and of a Journey to the Coast of the Red Sea in Search of the Ancient Berenice and Another to the Oasis of Jupiter Ammon, vol 1., London: Murray, Kindle Edition, Location 2086
'From the moment these personages came to Thebes...'
Ibid., Location 2545
'Of some of these tombs many persons could not withstand the suffocating air...'
Ibid., Location 2571
'After getting through these passages...'
Ibid., Location 2571
'Once I was conducted ... through a passage of about twenty feet'
Ibid., Location 2595
'tolerably large and well painted'
Ibid., Location 3693
'The obelisk was now ready to be embarked...'
Belzoni, G. B., Narrative of the Operations and Recent Discoveries Within the Pyramids, Temples, Tombs and Excavations in Egypt and Nubia and of a Journey to the Coast of the Red Sea in Search of the Ancient Berenice and Another to the Oasis of Jupiter Ammon, vol. 2., London: Murray, Kindle Edition, Location 1088
'the greatest fall, or rather descent, of water'
Ibid., Location 1156

Jean-Jacques Rifaud (pp. 144–49)
'a character truly zealous in the search of antiquities'
Cailliaud, F., Travels in the Oasis of Thebes, and in the Deserts Situated East and West of the Thebaid: In the Years 1815, 16, 17, and 18, London: R. Phillips & Company, 1822, p. 52
'Though the pyramids were greater than words can tell...'
Herodotus, translated by A. D. Godley, The Persian Wars, Volume I: Books 1–2, Loeb Classical Library 117, Cambridge, MA: Harvard University Press, 1920, p. 457
'a country where ... people's morals collapsed'
Letter from Rifaud to Drovetti, quoted in Ridley, R., Napoleon's Proconsul in Egypt. The life and times of Bernardino Drovetti, London: The Rubicon Press, 1995, p. 145
'statues en granit'
Rifaud, J., Voyage en Égypte, en Nubie et lieux circonvoisins, depuis 1805 jusqu'en 1827 (1830), pl. 42

Joseph Hekekyan (pp. 150–63)
'If any fragments of human art are to be found...'
Letter Horner to Hekekyan, 27 April 1851, British Library Add. MS 37460.4 R°, quoted in Jeffreys, D., The Survey of Memphis VII. The Hekekyan Papers and other sources for the Survey of Memphis, London: Egypt Exploration Society, 2010, p. 92

'This colossus, which measured 15 cubits in height'
Hekekyan Papers British Library Add. MS 37452.256 R°, quoted in Jeffreys, D., The Survey of Memphis VII. The Hekekyan Papers and other sources for the Survey of Memphis, London: Egypt Exploration Society, 2010, p. 135

Amelia Edwards (pp. 172–77)
'stress of weather'
Edwards, A., A Thousand Miles Up the Nile, Boston: J. Knight Co., Kindle Edition, Location 326
'In order thoroughly to enjoy an overwhelming...'
Ibid., Location 348
'the effect is as sudden as it is overwhelming'
Ibid., Location 503
'our first business was to look at dahabeeyahs'
Ibid., Location 460
'Nor is this all...'
Ibid., Location 460
'here at Sakkarah the whole plateau is thickly strewn...'
Ibid., Location 1137
'We soon became quite hardened to such sights'
Ibid., Location 1137
'How pleasant it was, after being suffocated in the Serapeum'
Ibid., Location 1342
'Where, however, is the companion colossus...'
Ibid., Location 1407
'The temple has here formed the nucleus of the village...'
Ibid., Location 2586
'The ruins of the Great Temple of Luxor...'
Ibid., Location 2692
'Pray come immediately'
Ibid., Location 5987
'I am told that our names are partially effaced...'
Ibid., Location 6474
'sentimental archaeology'
Letter from Samuel Birch to Amelia Edwards, 19 May 1880 (EES III j. 19), quoted in Drower, M. S., Flinders Petrie. A Life in Archaeology, London: Victor Gollancz Ltd, 1985, p. 65

Sir William Flinders Petrie (pp. 178–83)
'no better lodgings are to be had anywhere for solidity and equable temperature'
The English Illustrated Magazine 1885–86, 440 ff., quoted in Drower, M. S. (ed.), Letters from the Desert. The Correspondence of Flinders and Hilda Petrie, Oxford: Aris & Phillips, 2004, p. 2
'When sunset comes near, it is time to go round to all the workings...'
Ibid., p. 7
'...there were sometimes sharp steeplechases after Arab dealers'
Ibid., p. 6

'It is a golden principle...'
Petrie, W. M. F., Naukratis. Part I. (1884–5), 2nd ed., London: Egypt Exploration Fund, 1888, p. v
'Beyond the civilized regions of modern Egypt...'
Petrie, W. M. F., Tanis Part I., 1884–5, 2nd ed., London: Egypt Exploration Fund, 1889, p. 1
'a Petrie dig is a thing with a flavour of its own...'
Letter from T. E. Lawrence to Mme Rieder 1912, quoted in Drower, M. S., Flinders Petrie. A Life in Archaeology, London: Victor Gollancz Ltd, 1985, p. 319
'from the right way to dig a temple...'
Ibid., p. 320

Marianne Brocklehurst (pp. 184–89)
'the two MBs'
Edwards, A., A Thousand Miles Up the Nile, Boston: J. Knight Co., Kindle Edition, Location 326
'one would have sworn that he and Egypt were friends of old...'
Ibid., Location 1136
'made the ascent'
Journey Up The Nile. The Egyptian Diary of Marianne Brocklehurst, Macclesfield: Macclesfield Museums, p. 21
'were content to visit the Tombs and ramble about the Sphinx...'
Ibid., p. 21
'We are unkindly bumped by the Philae and left on a sandbank'
Ibid., p. 30
'Still racing and chasing with the Philae and Fostat into Assouan...'
Ibid., p. 38
'Good wind to Keneh...'
Ibid., p. 34
'We spend the afternoon among Karnac's immense halls...'
Ibid., p. 35
'A. shoots a native instead of his quail – he quails!...'
Ibid., p. 66
'At night, an alarm of robbers...'
Ibid., p. 27
'a very old gentleman, very polite and pleasant for an old Turk'
Ibid., p. 35
'much secret conference over antiquities.'
Ibid., p. 35
'we stole off together on foot...'
Ibid., pp. 89–90
'We returned alone with our friendly Arabs...'
Ibid., pp. 90–91
'At last it was all arranged...'
Ibid., p. 91
'the features of his face were really pleasant and happy in expression...'
Ibid., p. 94
'The little Mummy was buried by night with great secrecy...'
Ibid., p. 94

'got everything bribed on board the steamer without difficulty'
    Ibid., p. 95

Percy Newberry (pp. 196–201)

'It is not difficult for one who has studied Egyptian archaeology...'
    Quoted in Naunton, C., 'The Archaeological Survey', in Spencer, P. (ed.), *The Egypt Exploration Society – the early years*, London: The Egypt Exploration Society, 2007, p. 68
'the harvest that hastens to ruin with every day that passes'
    Ibid., p. 68
'All these twelve thousand square feet have to be puzzled out...'
    Quoted in James, T. G. H., 'The Archaeological Survey', in James, T. G. H. (ed.), *Excavating in Egypt. The Egypt Exploration Society 1882–1982*, London: British Museum Publications Ltd, 1982, p. 146
'Dirty Dogs!'
    Quoted in James, T. G. H., *Howard Carter. The Path to Tutankhamun*, London and New York: Tauris Parke Paperbacks, 2001, p. 32

Howard Carter (pp. 202–11)

'I lay somewhat bewildered in my new surroundings...'
    Quoted in Reeves, N. and Taylor, J. H., *Howard Carter Before Tutankhamun*, London: British Museum Press, 1992, pp. 25–26
'The moment I first saw Egyptian art I was struck...'
    Ibid., p. 27
'To my horror I found the modus operandi in force...'
    Ibid., p. 30
'I felt that if I attempted to copy the scenes sculptured upon the walls...'
    Ibid., p. 49
'A few eroded steps led us down to the entrance doorway...'
    Ibid., pp. 49, 73
'It was midnight when we arrived on the scene...'
    Carter, H. and Mace, A., *The Tomb of Tut-Ankh-Amen vol. I.*, London, New York, Toronto and Melbourne, 1923, p. 80
'At first I could see nothing...'
    Ibid., p. 96

Norman & Nina de Garis Davies (pp. 212–19)

'Outline drawings, even the most accurate...'
    Davies, N. de G., *The Mastaba of Ptahhetep and Akhethepet at Saqqareh. Part I. The Chapel of Ptahhetep and the Hieroglyphs*, London: The Egypt Exploration Fund, 1900, p. 3
'lamentable injury was wrought to the texts of the tomb...'
    Davies, N. de G., *The Rock Tombs of El Amarna. Part I.- The Tomb of Meryra*, London: The Egypt Exploration Fund, 1903, p. 8
'Fortunately the whole can be restored from L'Hôte and Lepsius'
    Ibid., p. 8
'her coloured work is at least as good as mine...'
    Letter from Norman de Garis Davies to F. Ll. Griffith, 21 August 1908. Quoted in Thompson, J, *Wonderful Things. A History of Egyptology. Vol. 2: The Golden Age: 1881–1914* (Cairo and New York, The American University in Cairo Press, 2015), p. 237
'With this volume the Metropolitan Museum of Art commences an enterprise...'
    Davies, N. de G., *The Tomb of Nakht at Thebes*, New York: The Metropolitan Museum of Art, 1917, p. xxi
'Set in the midst of paintings threatened with disaster...'
    Davies, N. de G., *Five Theban Tombs (Being those of Mentuherkhepeshef, User, Daga, Nehemaway and Tati)*, London: Egypt Exploration Fund, 1913, p. vii
'whereas pure scholarship dates rapidly, faithful copies...'
    Gardiner, A. H., 'Norman de Garis Davies', in *JEA* 28, 1942, p. 60

Temples, Towns and Cities (pp. 222–23)

'All excavations destroy historical material...'
    Reisner, G. A., 'The Dead hand in Egypt', *The Independent*, Vol. 114, No. 3903 (March 21, 1925), p. 319

George Andrew Reisner (pp. 224–31)

'The foreign consuls began gathering antiquities...'
    Ibid., p. 318

'By the light of a candle he saw only dimly a chamber...'
    Reisner, G., 'The Tomb of Queen Hetepheres', *Bulletin of the Museum of Fine Arts*, Special Supplement to vol. XXV (Boston, May 1927), p. 8
'The native negroid [Nubian] race had never developed either its trade or any industry...'
    Reisner, G. A., 'Known and Unknown Kings of Ethiopia', *Museum of Fine Arts Bulletin*, vol. XVI, no. 97 (Boston, May 1927), p. 80
'It is the habit of most of us to condemn the public for its great interest in "mummies."'
    Reisner, G. A., 'The Dead hand in Egypt', *The Independent*, vol. 114, no. 3903 (March 21, 1925), p. 318

Ernesto Schiaparelli (pp. 232–37)

'The work was neither easy nor straightforward...'
    Quoted in Ferraris, E., 'The Tomb of Kha' in Greco, C., *Museo Egizio*, Modena, 2015, p. 134
'looked for all the world as though it had been set up but yesterday...'
    Quoted in Reeves, N., *Ancient Egypt. The Great Discoveries*, London: Thames & Hudson, 2000, p. 126

Hassan Effendi Hosni (pp. 238–41)

'lost generation'
    Reid, D., *Contesting Antiquity in Egypt: Archaeologies, Museums, and the Struggle for Identities from World War I to Nasser*, Cairo, 2015, p. 112

John Pendlebury (pp. 242–47)

'Hilary was our star turn...'
    Chubb, M., *Nefertiti Lived Here*, London: Libri Editions, 1998, p. 52
'Not on my dig, my lad'
    Ibid., p. 52

Walter Bryan Emery (pp. 246–53)

'The extent of this labyrinth is still unknown...'
    Emery, W. B., 'Preliminary Report on the Excavations at North Saqqâra 1964–5', *JEA* 51 (1965), p. 6
'search for Imhotep'
    Smith, H. S., 'Walter Bryan Emery', *JEA* 57 (1971), p. 199

Illustration Credits

a = above, b = below, l = left, r = right

Index

Page numbers in *italics* refer to illustrations

To Suzanna

Dr Chris Naunton is an Egyptologist, writer and broadcaster. He has published
a number of articles and books on the history of Egyptology, most recently *Searching for
the Lost Tombs of Egypt* (Thames & Hudson, 2018), and presented many related television
documentaries, including *Tut's Treasures – Hidden Secrets* (Channel 5, 2018, National
Geographic/Disney+), *Egypt's Lost Pyramid* (Channel 4, 2019) and *King Tut's Last Mission*
(Channel 5, 2020). He worked for many years at the Egypt Exploration Society, London,
acting as its director between 2012 and 2016. From 2015 to 2019 he was president of the
International Association of Egyptologists and in 2016 he became director of the Robert
Anderson Trust, a charity that provides support for young scholars visiting London to
further their studies and research.

First published in the United States of America by Getty Publications, Los Angeles
1200 Getty Center Drive, Suite 500
Los Angeles, California 90049-1682
getty.edu/publications

Distributed in the United States and Canada by the University of Chicago Press

Printed in China

ISBN 978-1-60606-676-8
Library of Congress Control Number: 2020935388

Published simultaneously in the United Kingdom by
Thames & Hudson Ltd
181A High Holborn
London WC1V 7QX

FRONT COVER
Top left: Hector Horeau, Temple at Philae. Griffith Institute, University of Oxford.
Photo: World History Archive/Alamy Stock Photo.
Top right: Joseph Hekekyan, South End of Horner's Excavation, Memphis. British Library
Add. Ms. 37452, f.261r. Photo: British Library/Bridgeman Images.
Bottom left: Giovanni Belzoni, Painting copied from the Egyptian tomb of Pharaoh Sety I.
© Bristol Culture (Bristol Museum & Art Gallery).
Bottom right: Sphinx with Dream stela, Giza, from the notebooks of the Prussian
Expedition to Egypt 1842–45. Berlin-Brandenburgische Akademie der Wissenschaften,
Archiv Altägyptisches Wörterbuch Inv.-Nr. Z.2429.

BACK COVER: Amarna excavation notebooks. Egyptian Exploration Society.

FRONT ENDPAPER: 'Remains of the Temple in the Afserseef. Gournou'. Robert Hay Papers.

TITLE PAGE: Album of sketches by Amelia Edwards.

FRONTISPIECE: The front cover of a notebook used to record inscriptions discovered
by the Egypt Exploration Society's expedition to Tell el-Amarna in 1931–32. Note the
clear instructions at the bottom: 'PLEASE RETURN THIS TO HOUSE EVERY EVENING'.

**Ancient
Worlds
Now**

Ancient Worlds Now: A Future for the Past is a
multifaceted Getty initiative to promote a greater
understanding of the world's cultural heritage
and its value to global society.

Sheikh Nasserallah.

Old Mosk, abandoned during the inundation

Sikket il Cantar'ah

Fragments of a colossal statue in red granite.

Well

THE VILLAGE OF METRAHENY.

(The site of the seat of active administration of the capital of the Egyptian Empire.

Sheikh Ilfakhry.

Mohammedan Tombs.

Fragments of a colossal statue in red-breccia, of columns and squared stones of the same material

THE RAS MOUKALID

Excavation 3.

Substruction in limestone breccia and quartz.

THE LONGITUDI

Pit dug for Saltpetre and for manure

Sheikh Youssouph.

THE ISLAND

TEL IL MOUKALID

OF

THE MELLAH OF THE BIRKEH

Trace of Wall in crude Bricks

METRAHENY.

Existing

traces

TEL REBIAH.

Lepsius's Excavation.

Trace of a wall in crude bricks

Excava A colossa Ramses

TEL REBIAH.